D0149317

30 Lessons
for Loving

Also by Karl Pillemer

30 Lessons for Living

30 Lessons for Loving

ADVICE FROM THE WISEST AMERICANS ON LOVE, RELATIONSHIPS, AND MARRIAGE

Karl Pillemer, PhD

HUDSON
STREET
PRESS

HUDSON STREET PRESS
Published by the Penguin Group
Penguin Group (USA) LLC
375 Hudson Street
New York, New York 10014

USA | Canada | UK | Ireland | Australia | New Zealand | India | South Africa | China
penguin.com
A Penguin Random House Company

First published by Hudson Street Press, a member of Penguin Group (USA) LLC, 2015

Copyright © 2015 by Karl Pillemer
Penguin supports copyright. Copyright fuels creativity, encourages diverse voices, promotes free speech, and creates a vibrant culture. Thank you for buying an authorized edition of this book and for complying with copyright laws by not reproducing, scanning, or distributing any part of it in any form without permission. You are supporting writers and allowing Penguin to continue to publish books for every reader.

REGISTERED TRADEMARK—MARCA REGISTRADA

HUDSON
STREET
PRESS

LIBRARY OF CONGRESS CATALOGING-IN-PUBLICATION DATA
Pillemer, Karl A.
  30 lessons for loving : advice from the wisest Americans on love, relationships, and marriage / Karl Pillemer.
    pages cm
  ISBN 978-1-59463-154-2
  1. Marriage—United States. 2. Love—United States. 3. Interpersonal relations—United States. I. Title. II. Title: Thirty lessons for loving.
  HQ536.P55 2015
  306.810973—dc23
                2014021221

Printed in the United States of America
10   9   8   7   6   5   4   3   2   1

Set in Adobe Garamond Pro

To Clare
May there always be a new path to explore

CONTENTS

A NOTE ON NAMES

All names in this book are pseudonyms, created by a random name generator. Any resemblance to those of actual persons, living or dead, is entirely coincidental. Indeed, finding your name in this book is the one way to be certain that you are *not* in it.

INTRODUCTION

Love and marriage in contemporary society create a world of questions. How do I know if the person I love is the right one for me? How can my partner and I communicate more effectively? How should we deal with conflicts that inevitably arise? What will get us through the predictable stresses of marriage, such as child-rearing, work problems, money issues, and in-laws? How do we keep our marriage vibrant and interesting? And the most fundamental question of all: How can two very different individuals come together and create a relationship that lasts a lifetime?

I wrote this book to provide answers to questions like these. But first I had to answer a question myself.

"Another marriage advice book?" When I set out on this project—which lasted years and involved interviews with hundreds of people—that's the question some of my friends and academic colleagues asked me. Do we really need another how-to volume for creating a happy marriage? Every bookstore has a whole section devoted to this topic. So, they asked, what can you hope to add to the overflowing shelves of marriage advice?

There's a compelling answer to that question—and it came from readers like you. Several years ago, I published a book called *30 Lessons for Living: Tried and True Advice from the Wisest Americans*. For that book, I surveyed over twelve hundred older people, asking them some of life's biggest questions: "What are the most important lessons you have learned over the course of your life? What are the values and principles you would like to pass on to future generations? How can young people get to the end of life without regrets?" I also asked them for their practical advice on specific topics: work, child-rearing, aging—and marriage.

It was the last topic that really captured readers' attention. Many people told me that after reading the marriage advice, they bought the book for friends and family members—just for that one chapter. I heard that the elders' lessons about love and marriage helped single people who were looking for love, as well as those in committed relationships who were trying to make them last a lifetime. The book became a wedding gift. Some couples were even inspired to create a "Leave Your Lessons" station at the wedding reception, where guests could record their advice for the newlyweds.

Over and over, readers of *30 Lessons for Living* told me, "That chapter wasn't enough—why don't you write a whole book about the elders' advice for love, relationships, and marriage?" I will be forever grateful for their persistence because it led me on a fascinating new journey. You hold in your hand the product of my quest: a guidebook from the wisest Americans on finding the right partner, establishing the groundwork for a lasting relationship, and keeping the spark alive for a lifetime.

In contemporary society, the search for love and lasting relationships has become complex and difficult. Shifting norms about marriage and the rise of social media have made finding a mate and deciding to commit more confusing. In our desire for relationship guidance, we turn to bookstores and go online. I've done so myself and come away disappointed. The available advice often comes in the form of pop psychology or books by celebrities on what, in their opinion, made their own glamorous marriages work so well.

The more I pored over these volumes, the more I felt that something was missing: the voice of lived experience. I wondered: Could we learn from people who have navigated the turbulent waters of marriage and reached the end of the voyage? Why not go to the source—the oldest Americans who have vast experience of love and committed relationships? I believed it was possible to collect that wisdom systematically and translate it into practical advice for people trying to get and stay happily married in an uncertain and difficult world.

When asked about what qualifies me to write a marriage advice book, my half-joking response has become: "I may not know that much about marriage myself—but I know a whole lot of very wise people who do." For this book, I conducted the largest in-depth interview study ever done of people in very long marriages—hundreds of individuals who have been in one relationship for thirty, forty, fifty years—and more. I wasn't interested in just a handful of stories; instead, I wanted to take advantage of the "wisdom of crowds," collecting the love and relationship advice of a large and varied cross section of long-married elders.

But I didn't stop there. Because one problem I've noticed about marriage advice books is that they tend to focus either on the very good or the very bad—but not both. Some authors have selected "successful" long-married couples and hypothesized what makes them so happy. Other writers (typically marital counselors) base their books on the problems brought to them by troubled couples. But to offer the best possible guidance, what's needed is the full range of marriage experience, from the blissful partners who have been happy

for a half century to someone who has wound up alone and unsatis-
fied after serial marriages and divorces.

To capture this range of experience, I created the Marriage Advice Project. Using social science research methods, I amassed a
group of over seven hundred older Americans who were interviewed
in-depth. (The methods are detailed in the appendix to this book.)
One sample consisted of individuals who were currently in long marriages. Because many very old people are widowed, I also included a
sample of elders who were once in long marriages but whose spouse
had died. The average length of the marriages was forty-three years;
the longest marriage was a one-hundred-year-old woman married to
her ninety-eight-year-old husband for seventy-six years. I tapped
these two groups of people to get answers to the questions, "How did
you do it? What helped you make the promise 'until death do us part'
a reality?"

But that's only part of the story—because some of the best advice
comes from people whose lives did *not* turn out as they expected. In
my own experience, I find that I have learned as much from my mistakes and failures as I did from my successes. For this reason, I also
included individuals whose marriages were unhappy and difficult.
Some of these people went through a divorce, whereas others stayed
for decades in an unfulfilling relationship. In this book, you will
learn from these elders who took wrong turns and made bad decisions. They were eager to share their stories, in hopes that other people might avoid mistakes they made.

Not only did I strive to include elders from both successful and
failed marriages, but I also worked to achieve a highly representative
sample in other ways. The seven hundred respondents include couples and individuals who are diverse by race, ethnic group, economic
status, sexual orientation, and religion. No study can perfectly reflect
all older Americans, but the Marriage Advice Project went a long way
in that direction. Instead of a book based on a small and select group

of people, the advice you will find here comes from a host of marriages good and bad, and from a group as varied as our country itself.

Why Consult the Oldest Americans for Advice on Love and Marriage?

After *30 Lessons for Living* was published, I appeared on the *PBS NewsHour* television program. A week or two later, I received a message from Edward, a college professor in New England. He wrote to me that my work "makes the assumption that the young have more to learn from the old than the other way around." He went on, "How do you know that the elderly are the truest experts on living well?" Like Edward, you may be asking: Why should I spend time listening to old people's advice about how to live my life?

As you are getting ready to learn from the oldest Americans about love and marriage, I think this is an important and valid question. Here are three reasons why the wisdom of older Americans is a uniquely important source of guidance.

The View from the End of Life Is Uniquely Valuable

Over the 1.5 million or so years of human existence, it is only for about the past one hundred years that most people have gone to anyone *other* than the oldest person they knew for solutions to life's problems. Anthropologists tell us that in prehistoric times, the accumulated wisdom of older people was a key to human survival. The old were the source of tried and tested experience, the true "elders" whom group members sought out in times of crisis.

So consulting older people is a natural thing for humans to do. In our society, we may not go to our elders for advice on the latest app or news about the teen celebrity of the moment. But for the big

questions of life—and especially ones involving love and marriage—
we, too, can profit from the time-honored tradition of seeking the
advice of our elders.

It's true that in our society, changes have taken place in the realm
of committed relationships and marriage. Most notably, many people
live together prior to marriage, and most do not wait until after the
wedding to have their first sexual experience. Previously, women were
much more likely to stay home and out of the paid workforce until
their children were grown. You might therefore ask: Is the elders'
advice really relevant to younger people struggling to create lasting
relationships in the world of Internet dating, hookups, "starter marriages," and dual-career couples?

The answer is a resounding *yes*. As in ages past, the oldest members of our society have one advantage over the rest of us: *They have
lived their lives.* Their experiences in and out of married life over
many years have led to a deep core of wisdom, to shared ways of
looking at the landscape of loving and interpreting its pathways and
contours. Most readers, I imagine, are in the process of creating or
working on a relationship in one way or another. You might be looking, starting out, committed, balancing work and family in the middle years, or an empty nester.

What the elders have that young people don't is something special: the view from the end. For them, it's no longer a mystery as to
how everything will turn out—it's already happened. They know
what became of youthful expectations and hopes, what barriers and
obstacles life threw up along the way, and in some cases what it's like
when the relationship ends. That vast reservoir of life experience leads
to a special way of thinking about love and marriage—and one that
can enrich your life and your relationship.

America's Elders Are a Unique and Extraordinary Generation

People in their seventies and beyond have lived through experiences many of us in the United States today can only imagine. Their lives have often included what psychologists call "ultimate limit situations." These are situations that must be faced consciously with courage and resolution, and that push us to the limits of our endurance—situations like illness, failure, oppression, loss, crushing poverty, and risking death in war. It is precisely these life experiences that lead to wisdom. America's elders have this kind of wisdom more than the rest of us because on average they have been through many more ultimate limit situations. This perspective offers a unique lens through which younger people can view their own lives.

Therefore, the elders are incomparable sources of lessons for love, relationships, and marriage. And their advice is especially relevant now. Many couples today are still suffering from the effects of the recent economic downturn. Who better to give advice than people whose lives were decimated by the Great Depression? Our country has been engaged in wars abroad for more than a decade; shouldn't we learn how to cope from our World War II and Korean War veterans and their spouses? If we fail to do so, we are missing some of the best sources of practical advice for love and marriage available to us.

The Elders Have Experienced Every Joy and Problem That Occurs in Love and Marriage

The elders have gone through all the marital problems and traumas that keep younger people awake at night. All of them have dealt with health issues—their own or their partner's. They have suffered through children's problems with school, sex, alcohol and substance abuse, and sometimes with the law. Some couples have gone through every parent's worst nightmare—the illness and death of one of their offspring. Growing up in tough economic times, many have known job loss and poverty that is almost unimaginable in the United States today. Women confronted sexism, and minority elders sometimes suffered brutal racism. In addition, they know firsthand this reality: The vow "as long as you both shall live" really applies to only one person in the couple. Some of the elders lost a beloved husband or wife—and learned how to go on living.

Thus, they bring deep, personal knowledge of every marital problem a couple can go through. Readers from their teens to the Baby Boomers and beyond will find that the elders offer a fresh and often surprising perspective—and one you can begin using today, whether you are searching for a partner or wondering how to keep the spark alive after decades.

That's why (as I did in *30 Lessons for Living*) I refer to my respondents with a special term. Rather than struggle with what to call older people (from the boring "senior citizen" to the odious "golden-ager"), throughout the book I call them "the experts." Why I do so should be clear by now: I consider them to be genuine *experts on living*. We may have forgotten this in our ageist and age-segregated society, but when it comes to love and marriage, our elders are indeed experts: not scientific or professional experts, but storehouses of invaluable lived experience. It was there for the asking—and I asked for it.

What's in This Book—and What Isn't

In this book, I rely on information gathered using standard social science methods. The core of the Marriage Advice Project is a large-scale survey of approximately seven hundred older people (age sixty-five and over) in the United States. In this national survey, detailed interviews using open-ended questions were conducted, audio-recorded, transcribed, coded, and analyzed using qualitative sociological methods (see the appendix for more information). Other sources augmented these data, including focus groups and self-report questionnaires.

All interviews began with the questions, "Thinking back over your life, what are some of the most important lessons you feel you have learned about marriage? One way to think about this is: If a young person came to you and asked for your advice about having a happy marriage, what would that be?" For the rest of the interview, specific questions were asked about a range of issues, including advice for choosing a mate; suggestions for how to deal with stressors that affect a couple; ideas to help a young couple considering splitting up; the role of intimacy in a relationship (and how it changes); and their core values and principles for marriage.

The richness and depth of the interviews astonished me. Although many respondents were contacted at random by a stranger, they opened their hearts and minds, offering profound advice and wisdom. They talked about love, they talked about frustrations, they talked about rewards, and, yes, they even talked freely about sex. The herculean challenge for me was fitting their advice into a single volume—I shudder to think how much wisdom was sacrificed to the "cutting-room floor" because a book just can't weigh three pounds.

The result is an advice book that I believe is like no other one available. From hundreds of hours of interviews and thousands of pages of transcripts, a set of thirty lessons for loving emerged. The book is organized in four chapters that follow key stages in the development of a committed relationship—finding the right partner; learning to communicate and handle conflict; dealing with stressors; keeping the "spark" alive over many years—and a final chapter that presents the elders' core principles for long and fulfilling relationships.

Each chapter contains six lessons that convey the elders' advice. The chapters do not focus on generalizations and platitudes. Instead, they cut to the core of elder wisdom by offering specific recommendations, creative ideas, warning signs, and strategies. Throughout, I have focused on practical advice that readers can *use*, and not just ponder. In fact, the first four chapters end with a lesson on the "trade secrets" of the elders—concrete tips you can experiment with right away. All the chapters are richly illustrated with examples of fascinating experts and their lessons for loving.

Here's what this book is *not*. I am a great admirer of "evidence-based approaches" to improving marital and family life. There are programs, treatments, and methods that are based in research and have been tested through rigorous, randomized, controlled research designs. The work of prominent social scientists like John Gottman and Howard Markman is an excellent example of this approach—and it is one I heartily endorse. Other books rely on the results of research studies and experiments in various fields, offering advice based on such empirical evidence. Again, that approach is to be highly commended.

In *30 Lessons for Loving*, you have something different. The advice here comes directly from older people who have lived their lives and reflected on the themes of love, romance, and long-term committed relationships. Consider the material you are about to read as if you had posed questions to a wise and trusted older person. A reviewer of *30 Lessons for Living* suggested that it was like having a thousand grandparents in a room all offering you their advice. The premise of this volume is the same: that actual living, breathing people with significant experience—the "experts"—are extraordinary sources of relationship advice. Of course, no information in this book should be confused with professional psychological or medical opinion—for that you need to seek out a professional for individual consultation.

A Note on Terminology

You will see that I use the terms "marriage," "spouse," "husband," and "wife" throughout this book. That is something about which I thought long and hard, because there are five million cohabiting couples in the United States. For some of those individuals, moving in together represented a powerful commitment, akin to marriage in their eyes. Further, although an increasing number of states permit same-sex couples to marry, under many state laws they are denied the benefits of legal marriage. This book includes interviews with long-term, same-sex couples (whose advice, I will note, is virtually indistinguishable from heterosexual couples), for whom marriage was only recently, or still is not, an option.

I use the term "marriage," however, for two straightforward reasons. First, the wording reflects the advice of most of the experts, because very few were in long-term cohabiting relationships. The elders primarily talked about marriage, and this is a book based on what they told me. The other reason has to do with style rather than substance. By the twentieth time you were forced to read "in marriage and other committed relationships" and "husbands, wives, or domestic partners," I fear that you would be ready to put the book down.

However, with the few exceptions in which the experts' advice specifically refers to the formal and legal aspects of marriage, the lessons apply to cohabiting couples who view themselves in a committed union. Depending on your situation, you should take the recommendations for "marriage" as advice for "entering a committed relationship," and feel free to mentally substitute "partner" for "spouse." Most of the cohabiting couples in the Marriage Advice Project affirmed that they viewed their relationships as analogous to legal marriage. The world of committed relationships has expanded over the past decades, but the fundamentals still apply. As we turn to the "lessons for loving," I think you will agree.

30 Lessons
for Loving

CHAPTER 1

Evening the Odds:
Lessons for Finding a Mate

My advice? Be extremely careful about who you marry. The most important thing is to pick someone who is a good candidate for marriage. You can't make something out of nothing. When you're young, it's easy to be bowled over by how someone looks. But that isn't enough.

You need to look for things like fidelity, honesty, caring, and humor. Find out what their long-term goals are; what their feelings are about success, achievement, money, raising children. Outlook on religion is important, and another one is how they feel about their own family—their mother, father, siblings.

You have to think carefully about who you can actually live with. If you think things are funny and the other person doesn't, you have a built-in problem. If you are tidy and the other person is a slob, you have a problem right from the beginning. If you hate the other person's parents or family, you have a big problem. Add them up and some of these are big enough where you should look at them fairly and squarely and not marry the person. That's how lots of people kid themselves—they say: "But I love him or I love her!" Sorry, but that's not enough.

—Jennifer, 82, married 59 years

I sat in an upscale bistro in midtown Manhattan with five women in their midtwenties. My dinner companions included up-and-coming professionals in advertising, medical research, psychology, and the human services. They represented a range of relationship statuses: unattached, beginning a relationship, involved but experiencing doubts, and "nearly engaged." In exchange for the best artisanal cheeses in New York City, I sought their answers to the question that launched this book: What do younger people want to know from the longest-married Americans about getting and staying married? I planned to interview hundreds of people, some of whom had been married twice as long as my guests had been alive. And I needed to know: What should I ask the elders?

A different place, a different time, another dinner. I'm in the basement of one of the liveliest student bars in my town, named after an infamous nineteenth-century serial killer. Joining me are eight fraternity brothers; we gorge on mounds of cheesy garlic bread, burgers, and fries. One intrepid member of my fraternity focus group takes on the "Monster Burger Challenge," consuming a twenty-ounce bacon cheeseburger and a huge order of "loaded fries" in under a half hour (and winning a T-shirt in the bargain).

My query to both groups was, "What questions do you desperately want answered about relationships, love, and marriage?" I had expected the men and women to have markedly different ideas, but to my surprise there was one burning question for both groups. (I learned from other discussions that it also obsesses singles in their thirties, forties, and beyond.) And so it was among the first questions I asked hundreds of the oldest Americans:

"How do I know for certain that a person is the right one for me?"

In interviews, I pushed the elders on this topic. I asked for as much detail as they could provide on how someone in love can be certain that this particular man or woman is the one with whom to spend a lifetime. Are there special signs, a foolproof formula, a magic bullet to know that we've found Ms. or Mr. Right? After all that effort and countless hours of interview time, what was the definitive answer to that question? Umm, well, you see, actually, it's . . .

You never know.

That's right. Close to 100 percent of the experts are in agreement on this one point: You can never be absolutely sure that you have found the right person. In fact, the most common responses to that question—how do you know that you have found the right person to marry?—went like this:

You never know.

You can't be 100 percent sure.

You've got to just take your chance.

I don't think you can actually tell.

Do you ever know?

So where does that leave us on the topic of mate selection? Do we throw up our hands in despair? Fortunately, as you will see in this chapter, the elders actually have a treasure trove of advice about finding the right partner. Further, they believe that the best way to have a lifelong, fulfilling marriage is to make a very careful choice. So if there is no certainty about choosing your spouse, how should you go about it?

I found a mentor in Roxanne Colon, eighty-six, whom I interviewed at a neighborhood center in the South Bronx. While we were chatting before the interview began, I learned that Roxanne likes to gamble occasionally—she needed to end our interview on time because she was on her way to bingo ("It's just twenty dollars," she assured me). She was the first of the experts to give me the solution to the "you never know for sure" dilemma. Roxanne, like other elders, agreed it's impossible to be certain you have made the right choice. But then she told me something very enlightening:

> You know, to me, marriage is like a gamble. You get married and when it comes out good, you win. When it's no good, you lose and you divorce. So that's the way I looked at it. Sometimes the beginning is beautiful and then, you know, you're playing roulette and if you win, you win—or then all of a sudden, you lose.

That sounded rather negative, and I told Roxanne so. She laughed and asked me if I was a gambler. I confessed that I enjoy going to a casino a few times a year. She raised her eyebrows and asked me: "Well, don't you try to even the odds?" She went on:

> So, okay, you accept that marriage is a gamble; you can't ensure that things are perfect. But you can up the odds in your favor by how you choose somebody. You know, the values that you have, how you respect each other. Study the person before you get married and ask the tough questions. Like I said, marriage is a gamble. So what you do with the gamble is you try to make the odds in your favor.

Everything suddenly became clear. I thought back to an evening spent at a casino with my friend Peter. He used the opportunity to explain the arcane betting rules and strategies of the game of craps. It turns out that there is a wager in craps called the "free odd bet" that allows you to even the odds—at least on that one bet. I learned that you should always take that bet, but many people don't because they aren't aware of the benefits. The conclusion was clear: There is never any certainty in a game of chance like craps, but every sensible player does his or her best to even the odds by choosing bets carefully. That's exactly what the elders urge you to do in choosing a mate.

Have you ever had the experience of learning a new word, and then it seems like you see or hear it everywhere? After Roxanne Colon opened my eyes, I realized that many of the experts were making the same point. Like Karen Hopkins, sixty-seven, who told me: "It's just like throwing the dice. You really don't know. But you can feel it out by learning about the person, whether they're right for you. By communicating with them and courting them you should learn that information." Or Arthur Fields, seventy-two, who pointed out: "You don't really know for sure; that's the gamble. But if you date for some months and get along and are compatible and have similar interests, your chances are pretty good."

So here's what it comes down to, and what this chapter is about: *evening the odds.* There are many things you can do to push the odds of a good marriage in your favor. But the only time you get the chance is *before* you say "I do." The experts, as we will see in Chapter 5, believe that trying to change your partner after marriage is a very bad bet. The more time and effort that you expend in making the right choice, the greater the chance of evening your odds of a happy marriage. Take the advice of Patricia Rannoch, eighty-three, on this one:

> To be honest, right to the day you walk down the aisle, you're still not sure. I have one unmarried son now and he's asking me these questions. I said, "You really don't have one hundred percent certainty that this is the right person." Sometimes you just have to take a chance, you know? So you take a chance. But—

make an educated guess! You have to really try to get to know each other.

In this chapter, the experts offer their advice on how to make your "guess" more educated—that is, to even the odds. They begin with lessons that help you understand what it means to "trust your heart" and "listen to your head"—and they insist you need to do both. They point out three key warning signs that a person may be definitely "wrong," and they highlight the critical importance of making sure your core values align. To cap things off, we will learn five "trade secrets" of the oldest and wisest Americans for picking the right person for a lifetime.

LESSON ONE
Follow Your Heart

When I was a child, exchanging valentines on February 14 was a big deal. We would march down to the Benjamin Franklin 5 & 10 store and purchase a package of the little messages, addressing them to each member of the class (no exclusions allowed for kids you didn't like!). The motif on each valentine was the symbolic red heart (bearing no obvious relation to the actual organ). Often we accompanied our card with a few of those nearly inedible heart-shaped candies, imprinted with "Be Mine" and "Secret Admirer." From kindergarten on, we understood that the heart was the seat of love. No one quite knows the origins of this symbolism, but we still discuss love as a "matter of the heart," talk about broken hearts, and describe someone as a "heartthrob."

In choosing a mate, the experts use precisely this kind of language. When asked the question, "How do you know that a person is the right one for you?" I heard again and again ideas and expressions reflecting this answer:

Follow your heart.

The experts believe in love. Although one might think that some of the oldest respondents married because of family pressure, religious obligation, or social expectations, there were no differences among the age groups in the endorsement of love as the sine qua non of marriage. When I sorted through responses to the question, "What advice would you give to a younger person about choosing a mate?" a top answer was: "Be in love."

Thus, Andy Brewer, ninety-four, gave this vigorous endorsement:

"Love. And love means working every day to keep the fires of love burning." Bob May, at sixty-five one of the youngest experts, echoed that sentiment: "I'm marrying you because I love you and only on that basis. That's the reason I will stay with you—because I love you." Whether you are looking back over thirty years or seventy years, the experts view profound love as the secret to choosing a mate. As Sean Cooper, sixty-nine, put it:

> The thing of it is, don't love each other for wealth or money. You have to love each other because you love them. You feel that in your heart. You don't care if they get old or if they get sick or if they get wrinkles. You don't care about anything else, but just for them. You love them. And you don't pretend to love them because of what they give you; you don't pretend to love them because they've got money. You just have to love them because it's somebody that you'd like to spend the rest of your life with.

So love is at the core of selecting a mate. But is this really a useful insight? As I expect you are doing right now, I asked myself: How does that observation help someone trying to sort out complicated feelings for another person? I have to admit that recommending love as a basis for marriage in our culture is analogous to making a strong argument that the sky is blue. I needed more from the elders if they were going to help me answer the question posed to me by young working women, fraternity brothers, and singles of all ages: *"How do I know that this person is right for me?"*

I'm glad to report that with the help of the experts, I learned the secret to "following your heart." And it's not just an amorphous idea of being in love. Instead, when you are making the decision whether to go forward in a serious way, the experts told me there's one specific thing to look for: *the in-love feeling*. Its presence or absence is the diagnostic tool you need to decide "should I stay or should I go?"

Pay Attention to the "In Love" Feeling

In the search for a partner, nearly all of the experts described a powerful "sense of rightness," an intuitive and almost indescribable conviction that you have made the right choice. Call it what you will—a spark, an intuition, a gut feeling—but they agree that you shouldn't commit to a relationship without it. That's what following your heart means.

I admit that this profound sense that the person is right for you sounds intangible and even a bit mystical. And the elders often struggled to put this all-important criterion for choosing a mate into words. But for the experts, this particular ineffable feeling is highly predictive of a successful marriage. And in even stronger terms that warn you about the flip side of the in-love feeling: *Never get married without it.*

My mentor on this issue was Delores Neal. Delores and her husband, Dave, both ninety-three, were married on February 14, 1940. That's right—they recently celebrated their seventy-fourth wedding anniversary on Valentine's Day. Both are still in fine health and are active in their community, and their long life together is, they told me, their greatest treasure. Delores was the one who first alerted me to the essential nature of the in-love feeling.

I asked her the question my young advisers placed front and center: How did she know that Dave was the right one for her? For a minute, she sat lost in thought, and I sensed that she had traveled back in time, savoring a recollection of the early days of their courtship. Snapping back to attention, she told me:

> I can remember that when I was dating Dave and I would look
> at him and I would feel something. I wouldn't know really how
> to explain it. But when I looked, I felt it. And then another

thing: When he and I would be in a room together with a lot of people, he would be looking at me and I would be looking and there was just a connection. There was just something . . . Now, Dave was a good-looking young man, but that wasn't it. There was just something deep that I felt—that I had never felt with any of the other people that I had dated. So trusting your instincts has a lot to do with it.

Over and over, the experts described this same "in-love feeling." Most remarkable was the nearly identical wording they employed; it varied little from person to person. When asked how they knew their partner was "the one," they would often hunt for words, and then wind up referring to this special feeling This sensation involves a conviction of overwhelming rightness that builds on, but ultimately defies, a solely rational explanation. According to Lan Tung, eighty-eight:

> I think that if you really get the right person, you have to feel it. When you get the right person, then I believe that you will have the feeling that he is the one, she is the one. Of course sometimes as you get closer and get to know the other person more you may find, "Oh, my feeling is a little off base." But you have to get that original initial feeling, then you can pursue things further.

The experts were able to shed additional light on what "the feeling" means. An important component of the feeling is a clear sense that this is a person with whom you would like to spend a lifetime. As Dave Nelson, sixty-four, described it:

> Then you get to the question, "Well then, how do I know when to get married?" I don't know that you really do. But you *can*

rely on your intuition about your relationship to say: "Can you see yourself being with this person the rest of your life?" And at some point the bulb is going to go off and you'll say, "Well yeah, I can see that." You may not know why, but you somehow can see that. How do I know they're the right person? If you have that feeling, that you can see yourself being with them the rest of your life, then that's maybe as good as you're going to get at knowing.

Bryant Walker, sixty-five, added to this idea, noting that even if "a lifetime" may seem beyond your conception, "the feeling" involves a sense of there being no endpoint to the relationship:

My previous relationships were all good, but in all of them I sensed an endpoint to it. You know, a finite point. So it made sense to me to end it eventually. But then I began a relationship with a woman and simply realized after three months that I didn't sense the endpoint. To make sure I wasn't mistaken we continued the relationship for two more years and lived together the final year, and there was still no sense of an endpoint somewhere in the future. It's a feeling I had. So we married in 1979 and are still together and enjoy each other's company, and I love her as much today as in 1979.

Perhaps even more important than the in-love feeling is the opposite; let's call it the "this is wrong" feeling. Many experts also described this feeling in remarkably similar terms: as a visceral, intuitive, nagging sense that the relationship is just not right. It may be so faint that you have to search your feelings carefully for it. But the experts tell you from their own—sometimes tragic—experience that you ignore the warning of that feeling at your great peril.

A vivid and poignant example of this hard lesson came from

Kathy Andrews, seventy-eight. Kathy was married to Ben for twenty years until she finally got up the courage and resolve to divorce him. Following thirteen years of single life, she met and married her second husband—a very fulfilling marriage resulted that has lasted twenty-five years.

Kathy has led a well-examined life. Determined to understand the fiasco of her first marriage, she underwent extensive counseling. So impressed with the positive results, she studied for a master's degree in social work and became a counselor for the remainder of her career. Having stumbled through the relationship with Ben, she brought an insightful awareness to her second marriage, directly taking on problems and working with her husband to resolve them. Both personally and professionally, Kathy qualifies as a true expert on the ins and outs of marriage.

When I asked for her advice on how people can avoid the problems she encountered in her first marriage, she told me that it all came down to the this-is-wrong feeling. She recounted her story eagerly, hoping that younger people might learn from it:

> It was not a good marriage. Although he worked in a helping profession, he was emotionally and verbally extremely abusive. He got kicked out of different jobs because of the way he was. And after our divorce, he went through several more marriages. I'm just saying that I didn't do a real good job of picking my first husband.
>
> After I was married to him I could look back and see some red flags that I was too immature—I was nineteen when I married him—to recognize at the time. But I just assumed he'd be a lot better than he turned out to be. When we were dating, we of course had some good times together or I wouldn't have married him. There were things I liked about him. He was looked up to by a lot of people.

But there was one warning I should have paid attention to, and I hope younger people will listen to this carefully. Here's the thing—I sort of had a sick feeling somewhere down there. A gut feeling that at some level, I knew that I wasn't really in love with him and that this was a mistake. It was a warning sign. But I wasn't wise enough to realize it at the time. I just kind of shut my mind to it.

Kathy paused, and we sat in companionable silence for a moment. I felt that she was appreciating the chance to review her married life on a deep level. She looked off in the distance, as if forgetting I was there, and told me a story that was almost cinematic—I could vividly imagine the scene.

There was a ritual in our college. It was well intentioned and supposed to be how your fellow students would share your joy. When a guy got engaged, a bunch of other men would dump them in the school fountain outdoors. For girls it was different; they dragged them into the bathtub and doused them in there.

It was my turn, and of course many girls looked forward to this; they were proud of having a future husband and I suppose they liked the fact that others might envy them. And for me, well, I was getting engaged to someone everyone looked up to. I knew I should be happy and excited. But when they came to me for the dousing, I noticed a sinking feeling in my stomach.

Kathy then did something that I can't adequately portray in print. She told me, "I was—this wasn't quite right." Where I have put a dash, she made a sound, half sigh, half moan, that conveyed a sense of wrongness I have never forgotten. It was a strangled premonition that a horrible mistake was being made. She went on: "It's a feeling that's hard to describe. It was a feeling like: 'I don't think so . . .' "

But Kathy felt there was no way out. "Everybody's expecting it, you have the plans made, and what else do you do? I mean, I thought it would go away. I thought I could make it work." The marriage was disastrous and ended in divorce. Kathy's message is that you may know on some level if the relationship is just wrong, but it requires listening carefully to the inner voice. You need to follow the warning of the "this is wrong" feeling, even if there is social pressure to stay the course.

In the Rodgers and Hammerstein musical *South Pacific*, we are offered this advice about love: "Who can explain it, who can tell you why? Fools give you reasons, wise men never try." The experts do a remarkable job of telling you how to look for love concretely, while admitting they can't really explain it. In their long experience, being "in love" will be a different experience for each individual, and one—despite thousands of years of poetic attempts—that ultimately defies description.

However, the experts pointed to a single, specific feeling of the rightness of the relationship as the key to a decision to commit. They exhort you to look for it, to pay attention to it, and especially to heed the warning of the "this is wrong" feeling. When in doubt, they suggest you talk with others. Elders in your own network can be excellent sources for feedback on whether you've got the feeling. (Many of them have been through this experience a few times.)

I'd like to give the last word to Dave Nelson. He has a scientific background and understands the importance of a rational approach. But he is also a spiritual person who places great value on introspection, reflection, and insight.

How do you know he or she is the right one? The question your young people were asking may have been one of "Can you trust your intuition?" How do you know? Listen to yourself. If you're not used to doing that, do the best you can. But that's where the answer is; it's in your intuition.

I think if you try to rationalize it, you'll go through the books and read all the things you can about what you should do and shouldn't do and you'll check off your checklist and have all those things right. But at the end of the day if you don't have that intuitive feeling, you can't go on.

Fall in love. What does that mean? Something that you don't understand. I interpret that as something deeper within us that comes out of intuition. Something we're born with. Falling in love means that intuition tells you this is the right thing to do, without knowing for sure. You can't know it for sure, but when you see it you understand it.

LESSON TWO
Follow Your Head

Love means a lot to the experts, as we saw in Lesson 1. But their view is in fact much more complex. Yes, they tell us, the in-love feeling must be present or you should not commit to a relationship. But they also warn that following *only* your intuitive feeling of love is a prescription for disaster. The lesson we will look at now complements and balances the first one: The in-love feeling has to be there—but it's not enough.

I can't put it any clearer than Stanley Moody, sixty-six, did. He told me: "The glow of love shouldn't wipe out all the logic and the rational common sense that you need to make the decision of who you're going to marry." Because marriage is much more than just the feeling of being in love—you can fall in love over and over and never find your way to the altar. Instead, marriage is a formal economic and legal arrangement, which nearly everyone hopes will last forever. It makes couples' financial lives inextricably entwined. It paves the way for children, a commitment that entails both moral and legal pressures to stay together. The experts therefore offer this lesson: Once you've assessed your heart, you need to logically and rationally assess the potential for a satisfying, lifelong relationship.

As I was puzzling out this issue, one of my mentors stepped in to help me understand the balancing act between heart and head. Eunice Schneider, seventy-three, described how she settled on her husband, Ray. Eunice went on her first date with Ray when she was fifteen and he was sixteen. They "went steady" in high school, but were separated when she entered nursing school and he served in the army.

When Ray came out of the service, the couple married and have been happily together for fifty-three years. For Eunice, the first step was clearly the in-love feeling:

> You know, we were from an era where we didn't live together first, so we went back to our own houses every night. Well, I think what happened for me personally was it became harder and harder to say good night, to see him leave. That started to show me that I felt like I didn't want to live without him. It's like there were not enough hours in the day to be with him, and when we were apart, we couldn't wait to be back together again. And that was my first clue.

But once love was established, Eunice took immediate steps that involved following her head. She wasn't afraid to closely assess what the practical aspects of life with Ray would be like:

> And then I started to look at some of the things in a very practical sense. Is this guy going to be a good person? Are we going to be able to live reasonably well? Is he the kind of guy that's going to be a slug and make me do all the work or is he going to be able to earn a good living? Does he have a good work ethic? The first thing that a couple needs to do is to get to know each other—I mean *really* get to know each other, deciding if you have the same goals for life and for marriage. Because if one member of the couple has an entirely different idea of what they're looking for in life from the other person, it's never going to work.

Her careful assessment of Ray perfectly exemplifies the balancing act between head and heart that the experts describe. She laughed at herself as she noticed her attempt to emphasize both sides:

Yes, I think it's important to talk about goals. The other thing is to get past the physical, you know, how a person looks. Naturally, I'd be lying if I didn't say that there is a certain amount of attraction, of physical attraction that draws you to a person. But he also had a real good sense of responsibility, and that drew me to him. But he was kind of cute, too!

Attractive *and* not being a slug. Responsible *and* cute. It's precisely this attitude that the experts endorse, and it's what they mean by following your head as well as your heart.

Due Diligence

As I sifted through the experts' advice on how to use your head, it became clear that what's needed is a systematic process for evaluating one's partner. Fortunately, several of the elders provided ideas for just such a process, based on a business metaphor. Lest this seem unromantic, recall that's *exactly* how they want you to evaluate your relationship. Bracket romantic love in one compartment of your brain, then take a good look at whether your partner has objective characteristics that make him or her a good lifelong mate.

What you need to do before committing to a relationship, the experts advise, is to conduct "due diligence." This dry legal and financial term distances you from what experts variously refer to as "passion," "rainbows and butterflies," "rose-colored glasses," "hormones," and similar terms for the way love blinds us to practicalities.

Due diligence in the business world is often used when companies are considering a potential merger. One major concern in the due diligence process is the financial well-being of the prospective partner. Equally important, however, is what is known as a "compatibility audit"—do the styles and principles of the two companies fit together? Also examined is the stability of the prospective partner—is it healthy and poised for future growth? What is the organizational culture like? That is, will the two partners be able to get along if they become one?

Applying this approach to the "merger" that is marriage is what the experts mean by "following your head." Love, according to the elders, does not mean parking your reason at the door. And if your love won't withstand this kind of close scrutiny, they question how deep that love was in the first place. Now that you're serious, the questions should move to the forefront of consideration: "Is he or she good marriage material? Is he or she likely to be a responsible and committed partner?" To come back to our basic rule, answering those questions objectively is a major step toward evening the odds in selecting a mate.

In earlier times (and in some cultures today), the due diligence process would have been carried out by parents or other family members. In fact, some of the experts from countries such as India and China experienced this process. For example, Lai Lian, seventy-nine, came of age in a Chinese American community sixty years ago. Her aunts learned that a young Chinese immigrant was looking for a wife. They approached Lai Lian's parents and a meeting was arranged.

They fell in love, and the marriage worked out perfectly over the next fifty years. Why did it succeed? She explained:

> The two older women did a search of his background, but it's up to us afterwards. They do the matching, you know, the meeting and the matching. That's a lot of work done, and then you can decide. Looking for somebody is not easy. Finding him, it was a blessing from heaven. Here's the right person.

My guess is that with few exceptions, readers will not rely on family members to carry out the due diligence process—so you're on your own. But the experts say there is a set of important and practical issues you should carefully assess before you commit to a relationship. You need this kind of due diligence, they argue, not just before marrying. In contemporary society, it's worth exploring these issues even before making a serious commitment.

Ready to get practical about choosing a partner? If so, the experts suggest you look for answers to three major questions for your due diligence process. Remember, you've established that the in-love feeling is already there. These questions can help you determine whether to act on that feeling.

Question 1: Will Your Partner Be a Good Provider?

"A good provider." Although this phrase may seem a bit old-fashioned, as I listened to the experts, I came to respect it as an invaluable guide to evaluating a prospective partner. The ability to make a living is highly relevant today. Most couples in our society need two incomes to achieve their financial goals. Therefore, men and women alike need to ask the question: Will the person I'm in love with be economically viable? As it has been forever, marriage is an economic institution in which most people pool their finances. Your economic success and standard of living will be connected inextricably to that of another person. Therefore, you need to ascertain: *Will my partner be a good provider?*

For this reason, the experts exhort you to look for a "hard worker." They believe it's key for you to marry someone with a strong work ethic, who takes his or her career seriously, and is committed to career success (as he or she defines it). Conversely, the experts pointed out the lifelong difficulties you might encounter with a partner who has weak (or no) career goals, is uninterested in getting ahead, or simply has a distaste for hard work. Cecilia Fowler, seventy-six, observed this lack of ambition in her first marriage:

It's hard to think about material things when you're physically attracted to someone; it's hard to put that aside. But one thing to look at is both of your attitudes toward work. If you're a hard worker and you want to push, push, push, and the other person doesn't, it's hard. It's awfully hard to be working all the time and someone else is sitting there watching you. Imagine what two people could accomplish if both were filled with the same fire and drive. But if one has to be carried all the time, that's hard. So you should look at the personality of the person. Do they want to succeed in school, or succeed in their work, or succeed period? It's something you need to take into consideration.

A key step in the due diligence process is therefore a careful observation of your prospective partner's work habits. Does he bounce from job to job? Is she unable to make career plans and plugs away in a dead-end job, without looking toward the future? Even worse, does he or she not even look for work, instead depending on you for support or asking for loans? The experts argue that such behavior is unlikely to change. Even someone not looking for a lucrative career must be able to hold up his or her end of the marriage bargain: that both individuals will contribute economically to the union. If that evidence isn't there, the experts say, carefully consider whether this is the relationship for you.

Question 2: Is He or She Financially Responsible?

Although important, being a good provider and earning a decent income isn't everything. Another item to examine is your partner's ability to handle money. And this is something you can observe closely while dating. The experts believe that conscientious money management is highly diagnostic for the relationship's future. In addition to a willingness to work hard and get ahead, they recommend that you assess your partner's sense of financial responsibility.

Money may not be the root of all evil, but it certainly is the root cause of a lot of marital dissatisfaction. The experts remind us that marriage means that you will be financially dependent on each other. If you are like most couples, you will merge your bank accounts and make major financial decisions jointly. Further, in marriage you will become responsible for each other's debts. In a nutshell, you will be truly wedded to your partner's financial attitudes and behaviors, which will affect your life as much as his or hers. If the behaviors are risky or reckless, the experts want you to think carefully about committing.

Eric Goodman, sixty-nine, offers this caution:

> One of the most frequent reasons for marriage breakups has to do with financial problems. It may be the ultimate cause for uneasiness about continuing a marriage. And those are things that people can generally tell in advance. If you're talking about somebody that's totally profligate in their spending habits, it's a warning sign.

What's the best way to tell if your partner's financial attitudes and behaviors are a potential problem? The experts offer a straightforward diagnostic tool: Is he or she deeply in debt? They do not mean the "good" kind of debt, such as a student loan. Instead, do they rack up credit card bills, burdening themselves with exorbitant payments? As Eric put it, "Overloading yourself with debts—that's clearly a problem area."

You can't entirely predict your future spouse's approach to finances. But the experts assert that past behavior is a good predictor of the future. If you decide to ignore this warning sign and marry the free-spender, they suggest that you be prepared to keep your finances separate and maintain a watchful eye on your financial situation. As part of your due diligence, follow the advice of Herbert Montgomery, sixty-six, and ask yourself: Do I trust him or her enough to merge our finances?

> One of the roughest things that young married people face is financial differences. You start out before marriage and he has a checking account and she has a checking account; she has her bills and he has his bills. But when you're married—it's *our* bills and *our* checking account. They need to have enough trust in the person they married to be able to trust when things are not separate anymore. And if they trust and love that person enough to marry them, then they should trust them enough to share their bank account with them.

Question 3: Will He or She Be a Good Parent?

When people are in the early stages of a relationship, parenthood seems remote and is not likely to come up for intensive discussion. Raising that topic can be threatening; it implies a level of seriousness that can make one or both partners say, "Don't go there." However, before you make a serious commitment to another person, the experts argue that you should do your best to evaluate your partner not only as a lover and companion, but as a future parent.

The place to start may seem obvious: Does your partner actually want to have children? The experts say that this issue is far from obvious. It needs to be carefully discussed, because it is one on which partners make assumptions like this: "Of course, he/she wants to have a family, who doesn't?" But as Nadine Perkins, sixty-five, points out:

> In fact, a couple may disagree substantially on this issue. In my job, I sometimes counsel young people and a lot of times they

say: "Oh well, we'll just bracket that question for now." But sometimes people actually have pretty strong feelings about whether they will or won't have children. And one person can say, "I really want children." The other one says, "Well, I'm not sure," and they let it go. But sometimes that really means no. And I have seen heartache there as a result. So I try to push them on this. They should ask: "Well, what can you imagine your life might be like in ten years? Does it involve children?"

Karla Burnett, seventy-six, suggests discussing the number of children you would like to have:

It's important to have the same general philosophies about wanting children or not wanting children. You need to know about details: you know, if you want a big family, if you want a small family. "I'd like to have three, how about you?" And he says, "Well, maybe two or whatever." This can help you decide.

The next step is to go beyond the simple question of whether you want children. A good way to get to the heart of your prospective partner's views, according to the experts, is to add even more details to the discussion. Because you not only should assess whether you and your partner agree about becoming parents; you also want to get a sense of what kind of parent he or she will be. Spending time thinking about the specifics of what your family would be like can help you in that assessment. As Gertrude Bennett, seventy-one, suggests:

Before a marriage happens, you need to agree on whether or whether not to have children. But then, talk about specifics. Of course I realize that circumstances can change, but what I'm saying is you need to agree together before all these little ones arrive on things like discipline. What would you do about this

and what would I do about that? Let's agree before we get into
it and don't know what to do.

The experts suggest that you also try a discussion of your own
family backgrounds. Were they permissive? Controlling? Based on
that experience, how do you feel about discipline? Talk about how
both of you were raised. In addition, they suggest you observe firsthand how your partner relates to children. Look for an opportunity
to babysit for a friend or relative's child—and take a close look at how
your partner behaves. Are kids a source of pleasure—or of boredom
or irritation? Spending time with a youngster can be a valuable spring-
board for a conversation about child-rearing attitudes and values.

Have these discussions as early in the relationship as it is comfortable. Because the experts encourage you to take a look at your
partner and ask: Is he likely to be a good father, or is she likely to be
a good mother? If not (and you plan to have children), it's time to
think twice about the relationship. The elders also remind you that
the question of children is closely related to their earlier point that
your mate be a good provider. It will cost the average couple around
$250,000 to raise a child born today. So a realistic part of due dili-
gence is to consider these two issues in tandem.

Taken together, these three topics embody the idea of using your
head—the perfect complement to feeling in love. Of course, these
questions aren't the only important ones. You should add to your list
the other areas of concern that are important to you, creating your
own due diligence process. If you don't, your marriage may suffer the
effects of unmet expectations and serious disappointments—which
the experts tell you can be avoided by asking the right questions as
early as possible.

LESSON THREE
Values Come First

Americans love the idea that "opposites attract," when two radically different people overcome their differences and live happily ever after. Movies replay this theme again and again, from *My Fair Lady* to *Pretty Woman* to *You've Got Mail*. It even shows up in programming for kids—witness the enduring popularity of Disney's *Lady and the Tramp* and *The Little Mermaid*. We hope and believe that even if love can't conquer all, it can bridge the gap between opposites—because isn't love all that matters?

In answer to that question, the experts say: *Nope.*

Among all of the advice about choosing a partner, one particular lesson stands out. Many of the elders view this recommendation as the most important component of selecting a compatible mate:

You and your partner must share the same core values.

They maintain that much of what is good in a long-term marriage comes from having similar values and worldviews, and conversely much of what goes wrong results from incompatible value systems. For this reason, the experts say that the most important task a couple must accomplish before making a firm commitment is to answer the question, "Do we share the same values regarding the most important things in life?"

There is, however, a significant barrier to finding answers to that question. When I conducted focus groups with younger people in preparation for my interviews, it became clear that deep discussions about fundamental worldviews don't fit in well with modern courtship. Formerly taboo subjects like sex now feel more amenable to discussion than "heavy" existential conversations early in a relationship.

I have heard many twenty-somethings list criteria for a partner along these lines: is good-looking, has a good job, is funny, has a nice personality, and shares similar interests. Such factors, however, are not what you most need to identify before making a commitment, according to the experts. These characteristics are the easy ones, and you need to tackle a harder challenge: finding out if your fundamental values about life align.

What do the experts mean by core values? Values are the basic principles we use to make decisions, and the standards by which we judge what's important in life. Our values help us decide our top priorities, and we use them to select our jobs, our friends—and yes, our spouses. Research shows that our values remain fairly stable after we reach adulthood, so getting to know what he or she values is critical information about a prospective partner. The experts agree and offer this advice: You will do much better over the life course with someone who supports your core values.

Warren Barris, eighty-six, put the issue very clearly:

> Most important is understanding the other person's values to see
> if they reasonably relate to your own. What do they care about?
> How do they think about the world? *What matters to them?*

"What matters to them?" This is the question that must be answered when it comes to values—and the experts urge you to do it as early in the relationship as possible. Bob May compares the exploration of values as a form of a "background check":

> Have similar values. Hang around them enough so you know
> who they really are. I guess, in a way, do a background check. I
> don't mean a police background check. I'm talking about find-

ing out who the person is, where they came from. Don't base your decisions about somebody on physical attraction because as the years go by, that fades. You've got to find something richer and deeper—your beliefs, your values, the importance of rearing children—those kinds of things, to really make a rich marriage.

The experts who identified themselves as sharing the same core values with their partners reported a powerful benefit: having few serious arguments. Ron Mason, eighty, will tell you that he's not the most analytical guy in the world. He was a career navy officer, including a tour of duty in Vietnam, and admits his communication style can sometimes revert to the way he would talk to sailors who had to follow his orders. He wanted to avoid working out lots of problems in the course of a long married life. So what he did—and for which he has been grateful for over fifty years—was optimize his chances by finding a mate with the same values:

> You can prevent a lot of problems this way. You should go about it at the beginning. Before you make your choice, you have to find out that their background and their way of looking at things are along your view on the ways things should go. But if you have divergent personalities and ideas of what's right and wrong, and what you want to do and what you don't want to do right at the very beginning, well, it's not going to get better. It's going to go downhill. That's why we get along! Because our values aligned, we were compatible right off the bat. We've been married fifty-three years now. And we're still kicking on down the road.

In contrast, the experts say that value incompatibility is a profound threat to a long-term marriage. Darren Freeman, seventy-three, used a turn of phrase that highlights the basic problem:

It's not just about having differences in your focus or view-points. It's more than that. Some people have polar souls, so different that all they are doing is fighting and arguing all the time because they constantly want to go in different directions.

"Polar souls"—it's a highly evocative phrase that sums up the experience of those experts who found themselves in a marriage where core values weren't shared. That's the level where opposites just don't work well together.

The experts are both serious and unanimous about this lesson, and they are willing to state it strongly: Think twice (or many more times) before committing to a relationship with someone who does not share your core values. They believe that the chances of success in such a union are minuscule. Personalities can be complementary. Different interests can spice up a relationship, exposing both of you to knowledge and activities you might never have otherwise tried. But a clash in basic values, they warn, is something a marriage cannot easily survive.

The Values Discussion

How do you determine if your basic values align? The experts say there's only one way to do it. It may seem awkward or uncomfortable, but you need to set a time, or several times, and have a very explicit values talk. This is something you need to do both before you commit as well as throughout your marriage—a lesson I learned from Derek Gavin, seventy-one.

Derek is no stranger to tragedy in marriage. He was happily married with a young daughter when his first wife was diagnosed with a terminal illness. After a two-year struggle, he was left a widower at age forty. He married again when his daughter was nine years old and has been in a second satisfying union for fifteen years. He told me that the loss of his first love made him treasure the second even more, as he realizes how fragile life can be. Reflecting over two successful marriages, the issue of coming to a clear understanding of values was the cornerstone of his advice. The early thrill of being in love, he points out, keeps people from exploring one another's values—and that's a mistake.

Compatibility of value systems is the thing that I think is really important. This is one of the mistakes people make when getting married. They need to make sure that they understand the values and expectations of the person they are contemplating marrying. I see young people who don't have successful marriages bemoan the fact, "Gee, if I only knew this before I got married . . ." But there's no reason why they can't know those things! Serious preparation in terms of seeking out the value system of a prospective partner is often lost on the young, because it feels too good just to be in love. They don't want to jeopardize that feeling of infatuation by delving too deeply into value systems.

Derek, who has thought so much about aligning values in a successful marriage, learned this lesson through child-rearing. He saw firsthand how values can clash:

Let me tell you how I've learned that. When I married my second wife, we were both widowed and we both had nine-year-old daughters. So we came to this marriage when the kids were just getting ready to go through that lovely period of adolescence.

And it was all hands on deck for the first five years of our marriage. Both kids were spoiled only children—especially my daughter, whose mother was very sick for the last two years before she died. Of course, she suffered the difficulties of "Poor me; my mother's sick." Everyone spoiled her rotten—including her old man. And then to follow that almost immediately by trying to rein in the rebelliousness of adolescence—well, we had our hands full for the first couple of years.

My response to that transition period in young women was a heck of a lot different than my wife's. And that caused some major issues in terms of discipline, limitations, guidelines, and things like that. I had a lot to learn. And it took a while to learn what I needed to learn. We approached the whole going-through-adolescence thing completely differently. We laugh about it now, but when we were going through it—wow!

The solution, according to Derek, was a serious look at their values:

Once we discussed our values, I learned to appreciate the parenting skills my wife brings to our relationship with our daughters and what I bring with my parenting skills. It's true with any issue: When you understand and appreciate the values of a spouse, and your values are perhaps changed or come more in communion with your spouse, that's a real healthy thing, you know? Then you wind up with a blended set of values. But you simply have to talk about what your values are, and the earlier the better.

When you are assessing values to decide whether a person is right for you, how should you approach the task? Values can widely range from how to spend free time to how to raise children, so you and your partner must decide together what core values need to be discussed. To get you started, here are some suggestions from the experts for three topics, and how to open the conversation:

- *Values about children.* What kinds of goals do you have for your children? Is what they achieve most important, or is just raising a happy kid your goal? In terms of upbringing, is it more important to you that children be well behaved and respectful, or that they be given freedom and room to make their own mistakes?

- *Values about money.* How much money is necessary to live a good life? Are you looking for a comfortable, middle-class lifestyle, or something more? Is having time more important than having money, such that you would be willing to have less in order to work less?

- *Values about religion.* How important is religion to you? If you are of different faiths (or one of you is religious and the other is not), in what religion will your children be raised? How will you deal with opposition from relatives if you are marrying outside your religion?

You can, and should, address other areas that are important to both of you. Sit down, look each other in the eye, and delve into what you really value in life. If you need help, some experts suggested writing down your values and comparing them. One couple chose what they considered to be the most important domains in marriage—for them, these included money, children, career, religion, friends, and sex—and each wrote down one value for each domain. This exercise led to a powerful discussion about value differences. If you are stuck, a search on the Internet for "values clarification" will lead you to exercises you can use and lists of values you can discuss. At a minimum, you will have an interesting discussion. But it may also lead you to a better decision of whether the relationship has a future.

There is unanimity among the experts: *You will have a better chance at marriage if your partner values the same things in life that you do.* In fact, core similarity makes marriage so much easier that you may not notice it. When you and your partner see the world in essentially the same way, marriage often seems to move along in a harmonious and untroubled flow.

Grant Hamlin, sixty-seven, helped me understand this message. Grant is an accomplished jazz musician who emanates "cool." He talks like a jazz musician, too, and he used an expression that captures the experts' message:

> To avoid serious conflicts, the first thing you certainly need is just being in the same groove. Being in a similar place, in that sense. I know of a lot of folks who have different interests and they're able to remain together. But I come back to certain values and principles where there has to be a commonality. In the same groove means somebody who really shares your view of life, you know, and your long-term objectives. You might get there differently, but you have that shared commonality of where you want to be and how you want to plan your life course together.

As Grant says, being in "the same groove" doesn't mean you are exactly alike. But just as a smooth jazz line seamlessly incorporates various instruments, you are oriented toward the same goal— composing a tuneful and harmonious life together. Many of the elders told me that if your values are aligned, you and your partner are in tune with each other—in the same groove. But if that harmony isn't there, they say, you are likely to be in serious trouble.

LESSON FOUR
You're Marrying a Family

It's a common belief that when couples marry, they create an independent unit, unfettered by the ties of extended family. We believe we're different from past times and traditional cultures, where relatives placed extensive demands on the married couple (think about the Jane Austen novels and then fast-forward to movies like *My Big Fat Greek Wedding*). Much has been written about the isolated nuclear family that was freed from the burden of obligations to kin by geographic mobility and weakened norms of family responsibility.

Not so fast—the ties remain. Studies show that most people are enmeshed in close relationships with their extended family throughout life. Mothers, fathers, siblings, and other kin form the core of what sociologists call our social convoy that surrounds us throughout our lives. Here's the best evidence: When times get tough, most people head straight to their families for the emotional and material support that friends and acquaintances can't or won't provide. In sum, research shows that we remain tied to our families of origin long after marriage.

The experts concur. Many expressed this lesson in almost identical wording:

You don't just marry a person; you marry his or her family.

By this they mean that your partner's relatives will be a lifelong ingredient in the recipe of your married life. Therefore, an essential part of evening the odds is to take your prospective partner's family into consideration before committing. That's the best way to avoid serious in-law problems that can cripple a marriage.

Most people, however, don't think about in-laws much while

dating. We spend our time analyzing interactions with each other and focusing on our personal feelings, desires, and conflicts. But once you are married, each partner brings a cast of diverse—and sometimes quirky or difficult—family members to the marriage. Unlike your spouse—whom (I assume) you freely chose—in-law relationships are involuntary. And that's the crux of the issue: We're stuck with our in-laws. If we like them, it's a bonus. If we don't, we can be locked in a lifelong struggle to minimize conflicts and accommodate to disappointments.

In Chapter 3, I'm going to share with you the experts' advice for how to create the best relationships possible with your in-laws after you are married. But careful mate selection can help prevent these problems from occurring—or at least prepare you for them. They told me that choosing your in-laws wisely greatly enhances the chances of the success of your marriage. Those who did so reported warm relationships that strengthened the spousal bond. Ann Price, eighty-six, was typical of these elders:

> I was fortunate to marry into my husband's family, and he had a wonderful mother. I mean, she was more like a mother than a mother-in-law. She treated her daughters-in-law like her daughters. If you can have that kind of relationship with your parents-in-law, you're very, very fortunate.

If you are not in that lucky situation, however, it's important to know it early. The experts caution that if there are serious negatives, *don't ignore them.* Because merging two families can be even more difficult than merging two individuals in marriage. Cindy Barber, seventy-two, put the fundamental issue succinctly:

> There are big differences between two families that cause you to have to work at it. But everybody's got them. You know, I fig-

ured out a long time ago that the only trouble with in-laws is that *they are not you*. They don't have the history you have. That's what makes your family easier to deal with, because you know what to expect. But your in-laws' biggest sin is they're not you and they're not your family.

Darren Freeman has been married twice, and in both cases he has managed complicated relationships with in-laws. He shed light on the challenge we all face in negotiating this potential minefield:

You can't escape dealing with your in-laws. You have to make the call about things like whose house do you go to for Thanksgiving, how do you handle the grandchildren and grandparent relationship, and so forth. There is no handbook about how to blend together two people's family experiences, to come up with a solution about how not to be overshadowed by one spouse's parents. I don't think Windows has come up with a program yet about how to live your life with your in-laws!

Scientists agree. Studies of newlyweds find that satisfaction with in-law relationships is strongly correlated with overall marital happiness—and it's especially positive when the partner feels he or she has been given "in-group status" in his or her spouse's family. There is a tangible payoff as well; couples in good relationships with in-laws receive more financial support and help with child care. On the flip side, marriages in which there are discordant in-law relationships have lower chances of succeeding over the long term. There's no question: In-law relationships really matter.

Laura Klein, seventy-three, didn't realize the difficulty she was getting into with her husband's family. She stuck it out and made the best of the relationship, but she wishes she had paid more attention prior to marriage:

I think after you get married you just have to be bound and determined that you're going to make things work. Because there were a lot of things I found I didn't know, and a lot of things about my family that he found out that he didn't know. I hear people saying all the time, "Well I'm marrying him, I'm not marrying his family." But how untrue that is. You do marry the family. You have to interact with his family, but you're protective of your own family. There's no way that we could successfully be married and not get along with our extended family. Even after three years of going together, I did not realize this until I got married.

Some of the experts take a firm stand on this issue, recommending that if your relationship with your partner's family is extremely difficult, you should not go further with the relationship. This view may sound extreme, but my job is to convey to you their advice—your job is to decide whether to follow it. Some experts made precisely this decision and backed away from a partner in the face of family opposition and dysfunction. Others who had marriages dissolve linked the breakup in large part to the in-laws' failure to accept them.

William Schultz, sixty-eight, is one of those who hung in there, but he advises couples starting out to carefully examine the family situation and consider whether it's worth it. His advice may seem powerfully worded, but it was echoed by many of the experts in the same—or even stronger—terms. Your in-laws can make or break your marriage. As William described it:

Here's the situation. If you and your partner-to-be go see each of the families and one of the families is definitely against their child's choice of a mate, you can marry that child, no problem. But if the in-laws-to-be don't like the prospective mate, they're going to be continually sniping at the person and eventually, unless the person you marry is awfully strong, the family is going to win.

It can lead to divorce, it can lead to isolation of your marital unit, it can just cause an untold amount of grief. I was basically told by my wife's family: "Hey, we don't like you." I know I used to love it when my father-in-law told me I was a bum—sorry, I'm being sarcastic, but that's the way it was. It was not a good situation. In fact, a week before the wedding, they tried to get my wife to call it off.

Both parties need to realize they're not just marrying each other. They're taking on the whole family tree. Pay close attention, during those early meetings, to family and their interaction and how they behave. The knowledgeable spouse-to-be can decide whether it's a deal-breaker or not. I'm inclined to say that if these things are bad enough, it's better to break the deal than to get into it and hope it'll get better. It's like climbing Pikes Peak, a long uphill battle, and I'm not sure it's worthwhile.

The key phrase here is "bad enough." Because many of the experts (as we will see in Chapter 3) had less than optimal in-law relationships, but through hard work and patience rendered them tolerable. Other elders, with their spouse's support, resolved the unpleasant family relationships by fleeing from them; geographical distance proved the safety valve that reduced the unpleasantness. What you should beware of, according to the experts, is a combination of a highly toxic set of future in-laws and a partner who is enmeshed with or inseparable from them. The experts won't make your decision for you. But they say failure to take your future in-laws into account when selecting your mate is a critical mistake.

LESSON FIVE
Three Warning Signs

Choosing a life partner feels like an immensely complex task. We struggle against uncertainty, trying to anticipate a potentially life-long outcome based on what are inevitably insufficient data. We cannot accurately predict how we will feel about someone a year from now, let alone fifty years hence. And we certainly cannot foresee every event that will occur to challenge the bond between us and our partners. The experts have already spoken: When it comes to settling on a life partner, you never know for sure if you have made the right choice.

These facts might make you throw up your hands in despair at finding guidance to make your choice. But fortunately, sometimes things are actually *less* complex than they seem. Take the example of health behaviors. The dizzying array of studies—sometimes contradicting one another—that appear in the press make good health decisions seem impossible. But actually, scientists *can* tell you that there are some things—such as smoking, being obese, or using heroin—that are obviously terrible choices. You can become bewildered by supplements, fad diets, and new fitness programs, but certain health behaviors are so unambiguously bad that engaging in them is clearly a wrong choice. You may choose to do them, but you can't fool yourself into believing you are making a good decision.

The same is true of marriage, according to the experts. They convinced me that an enormous amount of marital suffering can be avoided if people would take into account three warning signs. The experts believe these three signs are so clear that moving ahead with the relationship if any are present is a huge mistake. They have seen enough wrongheaded decisions to believe that few people enter marriage entirely ignorant of these warning signs. Jeanette Newman, sixty-six, put it plainly:

> When you see the red flags, you better pay attention. Save yourself a lot of trouble. Sooner or later, he's gonna show himself up, or she's gonna show herself up. A lot of people make that mistake, saying: "Well I didn't know." Oh yeah, you knew! You better believe you saw the signs. You just thought that you were in love and you thought that you could take the risk. But listen, this is the person who you took into your life and you told yourself that you could trust. So be smart about it before you get into a marriage with a person like that, because some part of you knows it's a mistake. Yes, you do.

My daughters are fans of horror movies involving ghosts and poltergeists. One thing always amazes me when I watch with them. The first time the disembodied voice rasped in my ear, "Get oooouuuut!" I would get out so fast that it would make your head spin. But the hapless teens or bewildered family members decide to stick it out as ghostly vengeance is wrought upon them. That's what the experts mean—some behaviors tell you to *get out* of the relationship. However, all too many people ignore the clear signs, get married, and live through a horrendous period (or even an entire married life), suffering the consequences of that disastrous decision.

As you read this lesson, you might ask, "Are the experts stating the obvious?" To that I say: These points can't be all that obvious, because thousands of people every year make a poor choice about whom to marry. My hope is that hearing these often-ignored warning signs from seven hundred people with enormous experience in and out of marriage may convince at least some readers to avoid a huge mistake. And those of you already in committed relationships, take note: These warning signs still apply. They are a good diagnostic tool for deciding whether your marriage needs a fix or an exit strategy. You might still be making a wrong choice, even after years of marriage.

Warning Sign 1: No One Likes Your Partner

It's a common scenario. Someone—let's call her Beth—meets a man, Jim, and is strongly attracted. They begin to date and soon she is spending all of her free time with him. She introduces Jim to her friends, he watches TV with Beth and her roommates, and after several months, she takes the step of inviting him to her family's home for Thanksgiving. Beth (who has been through several relationships and would very much like to settle down) feels she finally has found the one for her. She's in her late twenties—isn't it about time?

There's only one cloud on the otherwise bright horizon: Beth is aware of a certain wariness on the part of friends and family. No one comes out and says anything directly, of course, because that's not what people do. But when she went home again at Christmas, there was an oblique conversation with her father, in which he asked in an offhand way if Jim was upset about something during the Thanksgiving visit, or was he always that moody? Her mother, with a lapse of her usual tact, wondered aloud if Jim has any interests other than fantasy football and the stock market.

It becomes clearer when Beth and her girlfriends meet at a bar to unwind on a Friday evening. After a drink or two, Beth gushes about Jim, but no one seems to take up the theme and she winds up confused and hurt. As they are walking to the subway afterward, her closest friend (having steeled up her nerve), hazards this observation:

"Beth, I'm apologizing in advance for saying this, and you have to promise not to hate me. But when we've hung out together, Jim seems kind of mean to you. I guess it's supposed to be funny, but he gets sarcastic. And last time, when you were a few minutes late meeting us, he got mad and couldn't let it go even after you apologized. It's not just me—everyone else feels this way."

Beth is dumbstruck. But what does she do? One response would be defensive anger. Friends don't understand; they are jealous of her relationship; they just need to get to know Jim better. This is the best chance she has at happiness, so why can't they all be happy for her? As these feelings accumulate, Beth might shift more of her attention and free time to Jim, pushing her toward a commitment.

Or she could listen to them. Listen deeply and receptively to their questions, assuming that they come from love and concern for her. She could engage in a thought exercise, asking herself, What if they're right? Because this is exactly what the experts advise: Listen carefully to warnings from friends and family about your prospective partner. You may ultimately reject their negative assessments, but it is worth taking them very seriously. Because according to the experts, *if no one else likes your partner, that's a very serious warning sign.*

Marian Lawson, sixty-eight, cautions you to avoid the temptation to ignore the feedback you get from others about a relationship:

> My sister told me I was making a mistake. My best friend told me I should wait. But I just didn't listen. There was a warning there that should've been acknowledged and wasn't. It's hard to read those signs when you're falling in love with someone, you know? You can look for things, but I'm not sure if you're really going to see them when you're in that state. So check out how your friends and family feel; it could have saved me years of grief. Go to a second person who is sympathetic to both of you and see if they can help you see what's fundamentally happening.

In the United States, we have long departed from formal family approval of a mate (although certain ethnic groups sometimes still engage in this practice). Most of us are left to solve the equation of what makes the right partner by ourselves, often using our limited experience and popular culture as a guide. In the absence of match-makers and arranged marriages, you can protect yourself by actively soliciting the opinions of your family and friends. One person may not get along with the partner, but if the evidence mounts, the experts say: Take the negative feedback seriously. If others disapprove because of prejudice (based on race, for example), such concerns can be dismissed. But the experts say it is a mistake to ignore persistent concerns from people you trust, who tell you that your partner does not treat you well, is making you unhappy, or isn't right for you. Listen carefully, and if you continue with the relationship, at least you do so forewarned.

Warning Sign 2: Explosive and Disproportionate Anger

In the Marriage Advice Project, I had the pleasure of sitting with couples who have been happily married for six decades or more. Sometimes I didn't want to leave the conversation, because being with them was like relaxing in a comfortable armchair by a sunny window. But I also had the experience of sitting nervously on the edge of my chair as someone told me about his or her harrowing experiences in a marriage that either suddenly or slowly went terribly wrong. Some of these survivors found fulfillment (and safety) in a second marriage, whereas others never acquired the ability to trust enough to enter into a relationship again.

When I asked them for their advice about marriage, I noticed a common thread in their recommendations to younger people. Many individuals for whom marriage had turned out to be a fiasco offered the same warning sign, and one they exhort younger people to take with the utmost seriousness: *explosive and disproportionate anger while you are dating.*

Of course, everyone gets angry once in a while, whether it be from hitting your thumb with a hammer or having someone cut in front of you in line. What the experts are talking about is different. They tell you to beware of a person who has a bad temper, who seems to "get angry over nothing," and in particular whose anger is out of proportion to the situation. Further, they warn you that these outbursts often won't be directed toward you while you are dating. During courtship, the experts say, people strive to keep their anger toward the person they are trying to impress under control. Therefore, you need to look carefully at how he or she responds to frustrating situations and toward other people.

Charlene Carlson, seventy-six, dodged a bullet with a man with whom she was becoming seriously involved. She told me:

> I dated someone and I was in the subway with him in the city, and we missed the train because we were on the wrong side of the platform. We were walking up the stairs and he took a whole bunch of change out of his pocket and he said some terrible things and threw all of his money down the stairs because he was very angry that we had missed the train. And when that happened, I looked at that person and I said, "This is not a person I want to spend my life with." It only was a minute, but you know, it was very telling. You can tell what kind of a person he or she is if you miss your plane, if you lose your luggage, if you are caught outside on a rainy day, or something like that. In those stressful situations if they're going to just stand there and curse up a storm or throw something, ask yourself if you want to spend your life with a person with those coping skills.

The experts pointed out that you should look carefully at anger directed toward other people, because similar feelings are likely to be directed toward you later (even if this is not apparent early in the relationship). Beverly Elliot, sixty-nine, had an unhappy first marriage that lasted three years. She would have avoided this mistake if she had taken the evidence of anger in the workplace more seriously:

> I think you need to pay attention to behavioral signs, you know? Somebody who never likes a job, can't get along with their employer—that should have been a warning sign to me that I was dealing with somebody who couldn't function very well in the world and would go to extremes. He was always getting angry with someone at work, so he kept on losing jobs. Because of the anger, he was never able to be happy in a work group. That should have warned me off.

It was not just women who wished they had seen the danger of explosive anger and run in the opposite direction. Derek Cross, seventy-seven, experienced that situation with his wife, Sally. Although the couple has remained married for fifty years, in part because of their strong religious beliefs, he still has doubts as to whether the marriage was the right decision. He told me:

> Don't get married in a rush. We were engaged for six months. If I had known her longer, I think I might have called off the marriage, because Sally would get angry too easily. That bothered me. If there is no anger, you can resolve anything. I should have seen that her anger was irrational and uncontrollable.

His voice broke as he told me:

Sometimes the only thing I could do was to leave. Get in the car and drive. The first year we were married, I remember in the cold of winter, getting out on the road and weeping so hard I couldn't even drive. I would tell myself, how can we be so happy much of the time and then every few weeks we get into a fight like that? It spoils everything. I can't stand arguments, not with my wife or anybody else. An argument to me is violence, and I am a peaceful type of guy.

My wife didn't have that quality. She explodes like a bomb. She didn't have any patience with the kids or with me. I should have paid attention to it early, because I'm sure there were signs. But unfortunately, I didn't.

Committing to marriage with a person who has a bad temper puts long odds against the relationship. In fiction and film, such a person can seem attractive in a dangerous way (think Heathcliff in *Wuthering Heights*). But in the experts' long experience, anger that can't be explained or controlled—even if directed toward others or toward inanimate objects—is a warning sign that must not be ignored.

Warning Sign 3: Your Partner Lacks Control over Alcohol

This may seem like another obvious point: Who, you might ask, enters into marriage with someone who has an obvious drinking problem? I'm sure you already know the answer. Plenty of people do just that, and according to the experts, they regret it. People like Glenda Wright, eighty-one:

I met William when he got out of the service, and he was a good-looking man. And I loved that he was a little on the wild side. Well, his drinking was part of that wild side. He came to the house once to see me, and I could tell he was drinking, and I sent him away. He went, but it was clear he didn't understand why. There were even clearer signs than that. We were out with friends and he had a lot to drink. He walked me home and it was clear he couldn't walk any further. I certainly wasn't letting him come in, and he actually stumbled, fell down, and slept for a few hours on my lawn. That's what I should have noticed. If he couldn't control his drinking enough to make a good impression while we were dating, what would happen after we were married?

The experts noted that there are inherent difficulties in determining whether alcohol is a true warning sign, especially for younger people. We typically begin serious relationships in our late teens and early twenties; a significant proportion of individuals find their future marriage partner in college. And college is proverbially a time of excess. (I live in a student neighborhood in a college town, and believe me, I know what excess at that age looks like.) This pattern persists into the early twenties, especially in urban areas where much meeting and dating takes place in bars. So is arguing that alcohol use is a key warning sign for marriage not very useful, or even absurd?

Actually, as often happens, the experts' advice on this topic is more nuanced than the simplistic "Don't marry a drinker" attitude you might expect. When it comes to this warning sign, the experts offer three critically important messages.

The first is the most obvious one: If someone has a true alcohol addiction—that is, he or she is an active alcoholic—walk away from the relationship. A number of the elders had experience with alcohol abuse in their marriages. Remember that we are talking about the generation who came of age in the era of *Mad Men*, where two-martini lunches and cocktail parties were the norm. In addition, many men came back from World War II or Korea with drinking habits picked up during military service. Without exception, those elders who ignored a serious alcohol problem profoundly regretted it. According to the experts, you place the chances of a happy marriage in jeopardy if you marry someone who is clearly alcohol dependent.

The second point relates to the question, "What about a person whose drinking behavior is closer to the normal range?" When does alcohol use become a warning sign? For the experts, it's all about *self-control*. They place a very high value on conscientiousness—living with a sense of proportion and caution regarding risky behaviors. It is in this domain, they tell us, where a lack of self-control is especially problematic. And that is what you need to determine whether it's a warning sign. Is your partner able to control drinking behaviors, or is he or she controlled by them?

Sophia Spencer, seventy-seven, summed up elder wisdom on this issue:

> I believe that if you watch your guy or gal carefully, you will know when it comes to drinking. Does their behavior go over the line? Do they tell you they aren't going to drink too much on a given evening, and then go ahead and do it anyway? Are they in a social setting where moderate drinking is called for, and they drink too much? When we were dating, my future husband came to a Christmas reception at my parents' house. The only alcohol was a punch with brandy in it, and he couldn't keep away from it, and wound up embarrassing me in front of my family.

The experts' third point is this: Lack of self-control over drinking is highly unlikely to change, despite your partner's promises to do so. It's one of those areas where people do not change as much as we hope they will. Of course, we've all seen a seemingly wayward young person who straightens up (with maybe just the occasional lapse) after getting married. But remember that the experts are talking about *evening the odds*. If you want to increase the chances of a happy marriage, you must choose someone who—even if he or she enjoys drinking—doesn't lose self-control. Although the experts focused on alcohol because drug abuse was rare in their relationships, times have changed. The same rule applies for abuse of drugs—view it as an obvious warning sign not to be ignored.

LESSON SIX

Five Secrets for Choosing Your Partner

We have now traveled through much of the territory of finding a life partner. The experts have told us how to even the odds of success by choosing the right person. They've advised in general about what qualities to look for in a mate and which ones to avoid.

But one of the beauties of getting advice from our elders is that they aren't afraid to be highly specific. I now want to share with you the experts' insider tips for avoiding a bad marriage decision. I love Cajun cooking, and my favorite cookbook author, Paul Prudhomme, calls this kind of advice a "lagniappe"—a little something extra added for good measure (like the thirteenth beignet thrown in for free). Think of these lagniappes as trade secrets of the experts. All of them can be applied to help you come to answer the age-old relationship question: Should I stay or should I go?

1. Spend Time in Challenging and Unusual Situations

You've met someone, you've dated for a while, and now you are thinking of taking things a step further. The experts propose a key diagnostic test to use early on for whether the relationship has a real future. Dating and "hanging out" typically involve going out to clubs and movies, watching TV at home, and maybe a weekend away in a bed-and-breakfast. And that's not enough, according to the experts. To decide to move forward in a relationship or to back off and keep looking, you should have experiences together that are outside your normal routine.

Before the relationship has gone on too long, they want you to see your partner at his or her worst—or if not the worst, at least in a stressful and challenging situation. They have plenty of ideas for how you can put your relationship to the test. One common suggestion was an outdoor adventure of some kind where you are forced to step out of your comfort zone.

Ralph Perkins, sixty-seven, met his wife in college, where they had the opportunity to engage in service activities together. The deep knowledge gained from that experience contributed to their successful forty-two-year marriage.

> If at all possible, go on a work camp together or something like that, where you see each other all muddy and dirty doing stuff, and see how that goes. Do some things that are out of your normal routine and put it to the test. See how you deal with it. We did things like volunteering where you see how people live who are living in poverty. You could do that kind of thing, working for Habitat for Humanity, working in groups of people, and being in different situations.

Other experts strongly endorsed a camping trip—and the more rugged, the better. Gene Roy, seventy-five, learned an invaluable lesson from just such an experience:

> It's nice to start off with conversation and that starts building a base, but actions reinforce or undermine the words. So you have to really live it. I went on a difficult hiking trip in a national park with someone and we had known each other for quite a while. But then we got into the woods where there was no water and there were bears. We ran out of food and all that stuff—then, all of a sudden, we found out we really didn't know each other at all.

Not a camper? Some experts proposed that you can test your commitment by taking a long car trip with just the two of you. The idea is that if you can travel well together on your own and under a bit of duress—not just, say, a weekend at a beach house with friends—you've passed an important compatibility test. Doris Steele, seventy-one, says:

> Take an extended driving trip with the person you want to marry for eight hours a day. See if you can keep each other interested and not fight about where to get off the highway, where to get food. That will give you lots of good information!

Two other suggestions don't involve going anywhere, but they can still help you test the limits. Pay careful attention, the elders propose, to how your love interest responds when you are sick. Are they supportive? Or do they run in the other direction until the fever, chills, and vomiting are over? (Of course, sickness isn't a test you can plan, but it's sure to come up if you date long enough.) The other suggestion for deciding if you are compatible? Try painting a room together (or some other complex household chore that requires cooperation). The point is this: To come to a decision on whether to move forward in the early stages, get out of your dating routine and do something difficult and different.

2. Make a List

It may sound calculating or unromantic, but the experts suggest that you write down a list of the things you want out of the relationship. Perhaps even more important is to note what you *need* in the relationship—the characteristics of the person that must be present to make the marriage work. The experts noted that not only is this a good exercise when you are deciding whether to commit, but it's also useful while you are still looking for a relationship. Thinking out what you need in a partner and what is a deal-breaker can help you avoid relationship dead ends.

This tip brought success for Rowena McCabe, sixty-nine, who had an extremely difficult marital history. Her first marriage ended when her husband abruptly left her, without any warning. Her second marriage was also very difficult: Her husband became mentally ill and violent. Worried about her child, she ended the marriage. These experiences led her to make a list. She met a man who became her third husband—and to whom she has been very happily married for eighteen years. Here's what she did:

> When I met Graham and decided to get involved with him, I
> sat down with a piece of paper and I wrote pros and cons. I was
> in my thirties at that point and I said, "Hmm, you know, this
> is what I want." And this guy had those qualities—many more
> good ones than bad ones. By that time in my life, I was awake
> to what I needed. And really sitting there with a piece of paper
> did it. It may sound cold-blooded, but I made a list of what I
> and what he could bring to the situation. At this point I had a
> little boy and what he needed was very important to me. And it
> turned out very well.

Making a list can also help you weigh the pros and cons of a potential partner. When Kristin Beck, eighty-three, got fed up with her fiancé, she carried out this exercise:

> I would sometimes think, "Why would I marry this person? He is
> so obnoxious and I can't stand him anymore." Then I'd say to
> myself: "Okay, there are just all of these things that are wrong with
> him." So I'd get out a piece of paper and I'd write down whatever

was wrong with him. And then I'd think, "Well, then, to be fair I'd better write the positive things." And the positive list was always my longer and stronger one! So we got married after all.

No one can tell you what should be on your list—that's up to you. But the experts say that when you are deciding whether to commit, a list can be very helpful.

3. Do a Sense-of-Humor Check

The experts believe that some future marital problems can be diagnosed based on the question, "Do we think the same things are funny?" Sense of humor is important, the elders say, for two reasons.

First, it is a strong indicator of compatibility. If you laugh at the same things, you are likely to be "in the same groove," seeing the world in similar ways. As Al Davidson, seventy, put it, when looking for a partner you should ask:

Does she laugh at my jokes? Does she get it? Or is she just laughing because she's being polite? How real is this? Because you're looking for a similar outlook and approach to life and that's hard to define, but sense of humor can tell you a lot about that.

There's a second reason to take a careful look at your partner's sense of humor: You will be stuck with it for many, many years. If his idea of high humor involves practical jokes and yours doesn't, rest assured that you will not find the whoopee cushion more hilarious fifty years from now. Angela Briggs, seventy-four, told me:

I think it's really important, humor. It's a problem for us in that as time has gone on, we've realized that our senses of humor aren't always on the same track, and that can create a kind of vacuum. The kinds of things he thinks are funny don't appeal to me, and that just becomes more and more grating over time. It's pretty difficult in a relationship.

If you find the same things funny, however, it enhances the relationship over the decades. Jordan Sherman, ninety-four, demonstrates the rewards of laughing together for a lifetime:

I have a kind of unusual sense of humor that she finds extremely funny, which I find good. And we do an awful lot of laughing. It's a good relationship. I come up with stuff every day. She laughs an awful lot. I think our attitude is what gave us sixty-six years of marriage. I think that's what kept this together. And we're still joking together; we still have fun together.

4. Watch How Your Partner Plays Games

I must admit that this particular test of a potential mate had never occurred to me. A number of elders, however, suggested that watching how someone plays games can tell you a lot about their eventual suitability as a marriage partner.

I interviewed Chen Xiu, seventy-four, in a senior center that primarily serves a Chinese American community. I didn't realize its significance at the time, but on my way to the interview, I passed a large room where Chinese elders were seated around card tables, playing a game with determined intensity over the clicking of tiles. The center director informed me that the game was mahjong and that it was a favorite activity in the center. I therefore wasn't entirely unprepared when I sat down to talk with Chen Xiu, accompanied by coffee and sweet custard pastries from a local Chinese bakery.

Chen Xiu has been married for fifty years, having met her husband during some of the most turbulent years in China's history. After several years, the couple immigrated to the United States and had two children. Although she adapted well to American culture, Chen Xiu remains proud of her traditional Chinese worldview. From elders in her family, she learned an invaluable lesson that she passed on to her own children:

> In Chinese culture, we listen to the older generations. And they told us, if we want to see a person—how the personality is, how the manner is—watch him play mahjong. So you can see, win and lose, how he deals with this kind of pressure. You can know that person, how he deals with stress, with loss, or with success. And failure—like in life—how he deals with that. From these little things, you can just see the person.

My first reaction was, Hey, I need to know more about mahjong! I learned that mahjong involves considerable skill, calculation, and strategy, as well as the ability to handle stress. So I now understood her reasoning behind this recommendation. She went on to add: "Because when you are just talking, in some ways you can pretend. You can hold something in front of yourself. But sometimes, when it comes to the real things that people do, that shows you the real personality. That is what mahjong does."

And not just mahjong. Jessica Cruz, sixty-eight, feels the same way about her culture's game: dominoes. Like almost all of the elders I met from Puerto Rico—and indeed from throughout the Caribbean—Jessica played dominoes. "We used to go to a club to play dominoes there. I love to play dominoes and he liked it, too. It's nice; it's fun. And it keeps your mind sharp, you know? Even in somebody's house, when you come in, the first thing you see is a table with dominoes." And the game helped her choose her husband:

Here's how I knew he was the right person. I met him and we started playing dominoes, and then I knew. Young people today seem to look for people in bars. But if you watch somebody play a game like dominoes, you get a good sense of their personality that way.

So whether it's mahjong, dominoes, soccer, softball, or a friendly game of Scrabble or Monopoly—observing our partner's actions in a game, the elders tell us, can speak louder than words.

5. Talk to Trusted Elders Before You Get Married

So you're about to take the leap into marriage (or a serious, committed relationship). There is one more thing to do: Find an older couple who have been together for decades. Sit with them. Talk to them. Observe them. I can guarantee that it is a unique experience. In the course of an afternoon or evening, you will see how much you really want this outcome for yourself. And it may become clearer whether your partner is the one with whom you can achieve what this couple has.

Pepper them with questions. Tell them about your relationship and the decision you are facing, and ask them, "How do we know for sure?" Find out what problems to anticipate and how they overcame them. By talking with a long-married couple, you will gain a sense of the long view of what you are getting into. It allows you to envision your own relationship for the coming half century or so, and to consider whether your partner is really the one with whom you can make it to the marital finish line. There's no better source for advice than long-married elders, so why not take advantage of them?

CHAPTER 2

Communication Is the Key

You must be open to talking about and discussing things. Never let that stop. You need to communicate with each other about everything that's of any importance at all. Don't just settle down and say, "Well, I'm married now. He's mine or she's mine, so I don't have to worry about talking." Communication is a central part of any type of relationship, but it's most important in marriage, because you become so dependent on each other and you've been through so much together.

You can pretty much say the way you really feel; that's the best thing about marriage. Your husband or your wife knows you so well that there's a freedom of expression that's absent in most every other relationship. And the intimacy of knowledge between you can make just the act of talking a wonderful thing. Don't ever let communication dry up, because it truly keeps your marriage alive.

—Federico, 83, married 60 years

When it comes to marital communication, you may not think immediately of the oldest Americans as your guides. They were raised before the open atmosphere of the 1960s with its emphasis on honesty and "telling it like it is." They grew up without the overwhelming influence of today's psychotherapeutic culture. Gender roles were more rigid, and men often conformed to the strong, silent type. So when it comes to the oldest generation, we have a mental image of Grandma knitting and Grandpa reading without a word passing between them, as the clock in the parlor loudly ticks the passing minutes.

But nothing could be further from the truth. When asked, "What's the secret to a long marriage?" the experts' overwhelming response was *learn to communicate*. In fact, if we add up every mention of communication in all of our interviews, it is by far the most frequently mentioned topic in the entire study. When asked about a particular problem in marriage, the experts were very likely to mention communication: lack of it as the source of the difficulty, and getting better at it as the solution.

Particularly surprising to me was a prime source of this lesson. After many years as a gerontologist, I shouldn't hold any stereotypes—but hey, I'm human. So I have to admit that I was often surprised when I interviewed one kind of person—one type of man, actually. I can't think of another way to describe them other than as "tough old guys." You've seen them, I'm sure. Your mechanic might be one, or a farmer who lives down the road, or one of those men having a beer at the veteran's club. Maybe you have one in your family.

These guys look tough—they might be eighty, but you wouldn't enjoy being in a fistfight with one of them. They're lean and leathery, they've spent their lives working hard at physically demanding jobs, and they don't say a lot more than needs to be said. Almost all of the tough old guys have been in the military and in one war or another—World War II, Korea, Vietnam. They've lost jobs, made it back from having nothing, been shot at, been in fights, and worked twelve-hour days to keep food on the table. For all of our navel-gazing about masculinity these days, the tough old guys feel like what people mean when they say "real men."

So as I began interviewing the oldest Americans about marriage, the tough old guys made me nervous. They'd sit across the table from me with a "let's get on with it" look while I fumbled with my tape recorder. No, they didn't want the refreshments, and how long would this take? But they had agreed to talk about marriage (with wifely prodding in some cases) and they were going to do their duty.

And then, to my surprise, most of them opened up. They talked about their wives, their children, and what married life meant to them. They told me about leaving for a war a few weeks after their wedding day and keeping in touch with a new bride through letters. They shared that having a stable and secure marriage and being a good provider were sources of intense pride—part of what it means to be a man. And yes, some of them choked up talking about the love they feel for their wives.

But by far the biggest surprise was how strongly the tough old guys made one recommendation: *Learn to communicate.* For many of them, lack of experience in expressing their feelings was exacerbated by several years of yelling at others, and being yelled at, in the military. They cited the difficulty in communication as the biggest challenge in the early years of marriage (as did their wives).

But even they learned how to do it. I've never forgotten the story of one man who mastered communication, even though it took him half his life. If you think you can't learn how, Jack Simon, seventy-one, is why I don't believe you. Jack is a tough guy, and few people have had as tough a life. You wouldn't realize it immediately because Jack is polite, in the way that Southerners are. But in a grim voice, he summed up his experience:

> I was raised in a dysfunctional family. All my family drank. I drank. I was in jail a lot—for nearly eight years if you add it all up. I was in reform school as a kid. I'm not that big myself—I'm only about five foot seven and I only weigh about one hundred and forty pounds. But I don't let people mess with me. I've been shot, stabbed, beat, fell off a building, and I lived through it all.

His marital history showed the same impulsive pattern until age forty. He then decided to change his life—and his relationship to women:

> I was married a few short times before I met my current wife. Pretty soon, it'll be thirty-one years with her. For years with women, I would just go for looks, you know? I had a lot of trouble and the marriages didn't last very long. You've got to meet somebody; you've got to talk to them; and you've got to go for what they got in their heart, and if that person more or less wants the same thing in life that you do.

Then came the turning point in his life:

> See, I was forty years old and had come to a place in my life at that time where I said, "You've got to quit living for yourself." In forty years of my life, the only thing that mattered to me was everything had to be my way. And that's when I finally grew up, because when you're serious and say "I do" for the rest of your

life, you've got to give a little bit, too. You can't have everything your way. I met my wife and I wanted to give her a good life. Because she'd had it even harder than I did. I finally realized that I wasn't the only one that had a tough life.

What made the difference for Jack, so that after forty years of family unhappiness, broken relationships, and personal pain he could create a happy marriage lasting for more than three decades? He says it's simple: He learned how to communicate.

Well, the main thing is I've learned how to sit down and talk. Like when a decision comes up, like going to buy a new car or do some work on the house, my attitude used to be: "Hey, it's my way or the highway." Well, I finally met somebody I cared enough about that what she thinks matters to me. You know, everything is not my way. We sit down and discuss it and if she has the better idea, we go with her idea. So that's the biggest thing I've learned.

I've given a tough old guy the floor, and in this chapter you'll meet a few more of them. But as you will see, all of the elders—men and women, rich and poor, PhDs and those with a sixth-grade education—believe that communication is the indispensable key to a long and happy marriage. In the six lessons you're about to read, they offer specific and practical advice for breaking down communication barriers and opening up pathways for a lifetime of talking to each other.

LESSON ONE
Talk, Talk, Talk

When you meet a couple for the first time, one of the things you quickly register is their communication style. During your post-dinner analysis on the car ride home, you may point out: "Boy, Bob seems quiet," to which your partner says, "Yeah, but Carol never lets him get a word in edgewise!" Or you may have been struck by their sparkling conversation and the way their cheerful banter showed mutual interest and affection. How a couple talks to each other makes a strong impression on us—perhaps because routine interaction styles seem so diagnostic of what's going on in the relationship.

Married people communicate in many diverse ways and in different amounts. There are those couples who talk all the time, whereas others reserve conversation for occasions when something absolutely has to be communicated. There is also great variation among individuals; some of us are compulsively chatty (guilty as charged!) while others are reserved, introverted, or just claim they are comfortable being silent for long periods of time. It might appear that the best advice for communication style is whatever works for a couple. Given the level of diversity, can the experts provide us with an unbreakable rule when it comes to communication?

Indeed they can. There is one lesson for communication that is so critical and so universally agreed upon that the elders would like to hit you over the head with it. Regardless of your own level of reserve and conversational style, once you are in a marriage, you need to mentally add one more marital vow: Have and hold, care for each other in sickness and health—*and talk*.

Yes, you have to talk. Not all the time, if you don't feel like it. And not at the risk of driving your partner insane (again, guilty as charged!). But when there are important issues in the relationship, decisions to be made, disappointment or dissatisfaction that is festering—then things are different. At such times, you simply *must* be able to talk rationally, constructively, and freely about important issues, or the marriage is not likely to be happy or even to last. How important is this lesson?

Imagine a roomful of elders willing to yell at you (and believe me, some of them are).

"I'm just not much of a talker," you say.

"You have to talk to your partner," they respond.

"I find it awkward to discuss personal issues," you say.

"You *have* to talk with your partner!" they respond more loudly.

"We're so busy, we hardly have time to talk," you say.

"You *have to talk with your partner*," they respond.

"Hey, I'm a guy! We're just not that good at expressing our feelings," you say.

"You have to talk with your partner! Now stop making these idiotic excuses!" (They're irritated now, so we'd better stop.)

There is no way around it. From ninety-five-year-old Midwestern farmers whose conversations focus on tractors and the weather to sixty-five-year-old New Yorkers talking daily to their psychoanalysts, they agree: There's no way to last happily for three or more decades unless you can both be, or become, talkers. It's easiest if you marry someone who can comfortably share ideas and feelings. But even if you didn't make that kind of match, this is one area where you can put your foot down. The elders tell us that if your partner simply clams up when you need an open discussion, you must demand a change.

My immersion in the lives of hundreds of long-married couples has convinced me of one thing: The happiest marriages involve a lifetime of talking—and talking, and talking.

Typical of the enthusiasm for open and continual talking was Clifton Griffith, seventy-one, who made the point in a colorful way:

Well, it's just important to keep yapping at each other constantly. I think the only time I've ever seen my wife really worried about me and us is when I "wouldn't talk about it." And I worked pretty hard on it, to make sure that we dealt with issues as soon as possible and ironed things out. I don't think there's any big recipe for that; I just think it's constant attention. There has to be some work at taking things in a good direction, and it's not something you kind of get around to once a month. You know, to me it just never stops.

For Clifton, there's just no other way to make a marriage last:

It's amazing: If you step back and look at marriage clinically there's no reason that it should work. Okay, there is no God-given reason why something like that ought to work for thirty years, forty years, fifty years. But it does. And the reason is that the parties are attentive to it twenty-four/seven. Keep yapping at each other constantly, ongoing dialogue, that's right. The technology has helped a little bit. I have an office on one floor of our house, she has an office on another, and I e-mail her and vice versa all the time. It's another communication outlet and it helps reduce some potential friction.

No one put it as bluntly as Joshua Gibbs, eighty-one: "If you can't communicate, then there's no intimacy. You're just two dead ducks." That's how bad it gets. And in fact, the experts reported that communication failures were the most frequent reasons why their marriages ended. They became "two dead ducks" with no way to invigorate the relationship.

In reflecting on her first failed marriage, Bethany Dunn, seventy-four, pointed toward the avoidance of simple talking as the rift that eventually ended the marriage:

> Well, there were touchy points and I simply avoided them, which might not have been good. It got so approaching the problem head-on caused arguments. I suppose I didn't want to do anything that would cause an argument. Probably what was wrong with our marriage was that I never learned any ways to communicate, and he never learned any either. And resentment built up, and that's a bad thing. I think that was one of my faults, that I didn't talk about it, and that's where communication comes in.

Sometimes a marriage begins with strong communication, and then a change—slow or sudden—occurs. The experts make it clear: When people stop talking, it's a major warning sign that something is wrong. Jan Dennis, ninety, provides a typical example:

> Let's say that you do have a good relationship with your husband, and all of the sudden things sort of dry up as far as conversation is concerned. Well, I think that's a danger sign happening there. Have him tell you what's on his mind, and can you work it out? Is there something that you have done or not done? Are you different from how you used to be when you were first married? Changes in how you communicate show danger signs within a marriage.

The experts' lesson is to continually monitor the quality of communication and take action if it begins to deteriorate. If you let problems go on too long, they say, it can quickly become too late.

It would be a mistake, however, to focus only on the role of communication in solving problems. Equally important, frequent and vibrant conversation enhances the relationship and keeps it alive, vigorous, and interesting. Cora Chambers, seventy-two, put it bluntly: If you aren't going to talk with your spouse in an open and enjoyable way, she asked, "What's the point?"

> Always, always talk to one another. That is very important because you lose sight of your marriage if you don't talk. What's the sense of two people living together if they're not going to communicate about things that are happening to the family or in the world, you know? Talk about politics, talk about health, talk about anything. Just keep the dialogue going and open. We get along; we talk and keep things together. It's the best thing. If you don't communicate, then you're not going to get along.

Many of the experts suggested the following as a diagnostic test: When you go out to dinner, can you maintain a mutually interesting conversation throughout the course of a two-hour meal? They acknowledge that couples can at times relax into a mutually comfortable silence. Nevertheless, the elders believe that no matter how long you have been married, a meal out should include friendly conversation and not stony silence broken only by "pass me the salt."

Jan Dennis put it this way:

> I really believe that a couple needs to be able to talk to one another. I remember a time that Bill and I were having lunch at a fancy hotel. We went in and they seated us at a table, and we were having our lunch, and we were talking away. Then, all of the sudden, I said to Bill, "Look around you, honey," I said. "There is practically nobody talking to one another while they're having lunch with each other." But you can always find something to talk about. You can! I mean, you may have to dig

around to find something that both of you are interested in, but keep talking to one another always.

I can almost hear the skepticism on the part of some readers. Okay, men—*I'm talking to you*. At the risk of a potentially sexist generalization, it seems fair to say that more men than women indulge in the "I'm just not a talky person" excuse. So if you are a man reading this and already in a defensive posture, listen closely: Our large sample of experts is populated with many men who started out in marriage more reserved and taciturn than you are. And guess what? They found ways to open up.

To sum up: It's fine to accept differences in communication style, understanding that some people are bigger talkers than others. But there's probably no greater danger for a marriage than when talking dries up. When this happens, be worried—be very, very worried. The good news, however, is that it's never too late to open up the lines of communication. Don't believe me? Let's end with a dramatic story to prove that point.

In my interviews, I heard many unusual and interesting marriage stories. As time went on, though, I became a bit jaded, believing that nothing more could surprise me. But I learned I was wrong when I listened to the remarkable love story of Christy and Sean Wilkins (now ninety and ninety-two). They are inspiring proof that second chances do exist and that it's never too late to make positive changes in a relationship.

Most important, their lesson is that communication is at the core of a happy marriage and, as you will see, this couple had a chance to experience two different modes of communication—with dramatically different results. Christy began the story of her marriage:

My husband and I started dating young and got married young. I guess we were not much more than children. It was okay at the start. We were married in 1941, and in 1944 we had our little baby girl. But then these were the war years. I had a baby of four months, and Uncle Sam wanted my husband and he had to disappear for two years. I believe in that time we grew from children to adults. And we became independent of each other.

As we got back together again after the war, we survived for some years, but our communication broke down. It just broke down. He was busy doing his thing and I was busy being a homemaker and a mother and all the things that are involved. As time went on, things were lacking in the family, and I guess I needed more attention than I was getting. And as we both saw that we were not communicating or connecting, we did divorce.

Well, he had a fifty-year marriage with somebody else and I had a thirty-five-year marriage in that span. And both of us were content in our marriages. We closed the door on each other. But I believe we left the window open! Because as time went on, years and years later, we had both lost our spouses. I lost my husband in the late 1980s. He lost his wife just about ten years ago.

After his wife died, I called him to wish him belated sympathy and try to give him a little bit of advice on widowhood. We talked one day in 2005, and he called me the next day and asked me out to dinner. We started dating again, and it was almost like the clock turned back to 1952, like we had never been apart. And we saw each other almost on a daily basis and within six months we got married again—in June, exactly sixty-four years between our first marriage and our second marriage. We decided to give this one more try. We put the past behind us and we're just living a good life now.

How does a marriage end in failure and heartbreak, but then become extraordinarily fulfilling more than a half century later?

Given her unusual before and after experience, I was eager to learn what made the difference. Christy didn't hesitate to tell me that it comes down to one word: communication.

> Well, I will say you have to communicate. That's what broke down. You need to communicate. You need to be on the same level and you have to be there for each other all the time. If you don't, one or the other will look for greener pastures. And I think that's what happened to both of us. And we realize now that this should've never happened. We should've stayed together. If it were today, we certainly would've gone to marriage counseling and we would've straightened out our communication problems. I would say go for marriage counseling before you take the step we did. Don't ever forget to communicate!

Christy's parting thoughts reflected her belief that one thing distinguishes her first marriage to Sean from her second: their ability to talk to each other. And you don't have to wait sixty years to learn how to communicate. The payoff can be tremendous.

> I don't have anything more to say except this: If there are misunderstandings and there are mistakes being made, confide in each other, talk it over, communicate. I'd certainly say we're happy with each other. We wouldn't have it any other way. We often said we're glad we're back together again. We had these twelve years in our life before when we were young, and when we got together again we said to each other, "God willing, let's hope we have another twelve years to see whether we can do it right this time!" And so far, we have.

LESSON TWO
No One Is a Mind Reader

In the obstacle course that constitutes marital communication, the experts point out a major hurdle: assuming you know what your partner is thinking and feeling. One of the great things about marriage, of course, is how deeply and intimately one gets to know another person. Through years of talking and observation, we come to feel that we understand our partners as well as we do ourselves. We believe we know their preferences, habits, attitudes toward the relationship, and overall worldview. More important, we expect *them* to intuitively understand what's going on in our heads *without our communicating about it.* According to the experts, this familiarity leads to an expectation that if left unchecked can destroy a relationship.

The elders used a concise phrase: *No one is a mind reader.* Mavis Griswold, seventy-six, underscored the point: "I say that to my husband all the time. I'm not a mind reader. Even though we've lived together all these years, if there's something you really need me to know, please tell me. I'm constantly saying that." However, the temptation to believe your partner can read your mind is almost irresistible. We assume that our partners, if they really loved and paid attention to us, would "just know" what we want and need. And that common belief, the experts tell us, is a total myth. They point to the "mind reader assumption" as one of the major sources of arguments and disagreements in a marriage—and even of divorce.

Nina Hogan, seventy-eight, admits that she married too young and without enough knowledge of her first husband's interests and character. Although she is glad she eventually got up the nerve to leave him after fifteen years of marriage, Nina acknowledges that she was partly to blame for falling into the mind reader assumption trap:

> The most important lesson in a marriage is that you've got to talk to your mate and you've got to express what you feel. When my first husband and I were ready to get a divorce, I started telling him: "You never did this and you never did that." You know what he said to me? "Well, why didn't you say something?" The first thing I thought was, "He's trying to get out of trouble." But then I realized that it's true: You've got to say something.
>
> Part of that problem was my upbringing. My family were poor African Americans living in Georgia, and I was raised in the 1930s and '40s. In those days, you just had limited expectations for yourself. You mostly wanted your children to have a better life. If I had been the kind of woman that I am now, I could have said to my first husband, "Stop this foolishness. I won't put up with it anymore. If you're going to act that way, I don't need to be with you." But I wasn't smart enough in those days to say that, you know? So my advice is, you've got to say something! You can't just assume another person knows what's going on in your head.

The experts pointed out a fascinating—and damaging—assumption that couples laboring under the mind reader assumption often make: that they view the same event or situation in the same way. It's easy to do. After all, both partners are going through a common experience, so why wouldn't they interpret it in an identical fashion? The elders tell you that there's a simple reason: *You are two different people.* Unless you examine factors that make you react to the same thing very differently, you may be doomed to unresolvable arguments.

For example, Beverly Elliot and her husband, Reuben, seventy-two, see eye to eye on most issues. While in college, their son experienced difficulties and eventually left the school. Beverly told me that she and Reuben saw this event very differently:

> When Charlie dropped out of college, it was not happy for either one of us. But we had to do a lot of talking about what it meant to each one of us individually. It meant something different to Reuben than it did to me. Reuben's father was a successful businessman; Reuben went to an elite school. But my parents were offspring of immigrants and I was one of the first to go to college. Well, having my son drop out hurt me at a level that it just didn't hurt Reuben; he didn't care at that level, okay? We felt differently because of our different biographies. And so the same thing meant something different to each of us. But by talking we developed an action plan, and it worked.

Reuben, in his turn, summed up the larger issue beautifully:

> You have to be able to try—and sometimes this is very, very difficult—you have to try to understand what the other person is thinking in any given situation. The main thing is that everybody—including your partner—has their own ideas about their world. Even though you're in a very intimate relationship, the other person is still another person.

Many of the experts reported that this understanding that "we're different people" came as a burst of revelation well into the marriage. It can take years to really comprehend the challenges of uniting two worldviews—but the earlier you begin, the better. Cheryl Sims, sixty-six, summed it up perfectly: "When you're young, you have false conceptions, but as you get older, you learn that if you want to stay married you have to learn to compromise. *Because you're two separate individuals trying to live one life.*" Understanding this core difference—and that neither of you is clairvoyant—will resolve a remarkable amount of conflict.

Overcoming the Mind Reader Assumption

How can we break away from the assumption that our partners know what we feel, think, and need without actually telling them? It takes work, but the experts have some very concrete advice for how to overcome the mind reader assumption. Sometimes married life is complicated, so let's breathe a sigh of relief when the experts tell us that things are *simpler* than they seem. The antidote to the mind reader assumption is this:

Ask until you're sure you understand.

According to the experts, every couple needs to institute a comfortable process of asking each other for their thoughts, checking things out, and making certain that they understand each other's motivations and desires. Let me share with you the approach of one couple I came to deeply admire.

In this project, I met some true marriage sages. These individuals were in very long marriages in which they had negotiated financial, health, and child-rearing problems. They had learned and grown from each of these experiences while paying close attention to the quality of the marriage. Most important, they are the kinds of couples people go to for advice, so they had practice in sharing lessons for a happy marriage.

Lucia and Stanley Waters, both seventy-five, are one such couple. What's created a vibrant (and still romantic) relationship over fifty-five years is their constant attention to communication. They are keenly aware that regardless of how close they may be, no one is a mind reader. Lucia told me:

I think sometimes we're not always clear about what we want to happen. So don't be afraid to say what you really want to happen. One thing that I do that I think is very helpful is I clarify what Stanley says. I want to make sure that I understand what he is really saying. I repeat back and I don't assume I really understand, because nine out of ten times I might be wrong about what he is trying to say. So you need to ask questions, reframe your answers, try not to take offense.

We realized early on that disagreements often came about when we weren't really understanding where the other person was coming from. So I will say, "Are you saying . . . ?" or "Do you mean . . . ?" Because sometimes we really are in the moment and we say things that we really don't believe. So I always repeat back to him what I think he's saying and then he'll either say yes or he'll say, "No, where'd you get that idea?" That happens a lot—that I'd totally misunderstood where he's coming from. Or I'll say, "You thought this," and he'll say, "Why would you say that? I would never think a thing like that."

Even after a half century together, Lucia uses this approach almost daily:

We found it has saved us so much trouble if we clarify back and reframe our answer and really think about, what did he really say? In fact, I just did that the other day on some silly thing where I said what he felt and it made him angry. He hadn't expressed his feelings that way, but I heard it in my head and it wasn't true. And it's always enlightening when that happens, kind of makes you go, "Whoa!"

Try this technique of repeating back what you believe you heard your partner say; many people are often bowled over by how differently their meaning was interpreted.

Would you like to go beyond the introductory level and try an advanced technique for getting over the belief that you "just know" what your partner thinks? Several experts made this suggestion: Actually argue your partner's point of view. Gilbert and Jennie Ballard, both seventy-two, are a fascinating and unusual couple whose professions involved issues of communication, negotiation, and reaching consensus. They recommend that when you are having a disagreement, one of the most effective things you can do is take your partner's point of view and energetically argue it. Jennie told me:

> In my experience, the hardest thing in the world for people to do is to understand the point of view of people that they disagree with. And I often give this advice: Identify some subject where you have strong feelings, and construct the strongest, most intelligent argument you can for the opposite point of view. Working on that skill, it seems to me, is particularly important in creating the conditions for a long-term relationship. Otherwise you end up being nastier, less understanding, less sympathetic, and feeling victimized because you don't understand how anybody could believe that or say that or do that unless they were just trying to harm you.

Other elders agreed. Debra Duncan, eighty-seven, put it so clearly that it could be pasted on your refrigerator to remind you: "Try to visualize their side of the story. Suppose you were them and you felt the way they do. Then how would you feel about *you*?" It's not easy to take on the role and ideas of your partner. But if you succeed at this technique, you will have moved from the false notion of being a mind reader to a genuine understanding of what's going on in your partner's mind.

Finally, the experts say that if you get confused, *keep asking questions*. When in doubt (and even when you are pretty sure) ask your partner what he or she is thinking, feeling, or wants to do. Their part of the deal is to be honest about what's going on in their heads. Andy Johnston, seventy-five, is a very straightforward person. He made it a point to encourage not making assumptions right from the start of his relationship:

> Well, I'll tell you what we did in the beginning. I said early on in the marriage, "Don't assume anything. If you want to know, ask me. And don't assume I think this or I think that—just ask. I will tell you the truth!" And that's worked great. My wife never assumes I want to do anything—if she wants to know, she asks. And vice versa. I don't assume she wants to go somewhere or whatnot; I just ask her. But it's got to be completely honest.

Perhaps most important of all is staying aware that you are two separate people who see the world in different ways. No, he really may not know intuitively what you wanted for your birthday. Yes, she's telling the truth when she says she thought you wouldn't care about missing Monday night football to attend the PTA meeting. The experts propose that you drop your assumptions, ask your partner to describe his or her feelings, and understand your mate well enough to be able to summarize his or her point of view. Until neuroscience provides us with a mind reading app, this effort is the best any of us can do.

LESSON THREE
Mind Your Manners

A man and a woman come together in the office conference room to discuss the purchase of a new copier.

The woman begins: "I think we really need this new copier; it's very critical for our business to run smoothly."

The man says: "Honestly, I disagree. I don't think we can afford such a large purchase at this time. In my opinion, it isn't a worthwhile expense."

The woman says: "Well actually, my staff are the ones who do all the copying. So I believe that this decision should really be up to us. And I do think we can fit this in our budget."

So far, a typical business conversation, the kind we've all had countless times. You can imagine a civil back-and-forth, leading to a mutually satisfying decision. At worst, there may be a disagreement that a higher authority must resolve.

Now imagine that at this point in the discussion, the man slaps his hand on the table and yells, "I can't believe you are so selfish! You always think only of your own needs and never about anyone else's. It's so stupid and self-centered, the way you act."

The woman responds, "Just shut up! Just shut up right now! I can't stand how you always bring up my personality characteristics. It's like you're trying to destroy what little self-esteem I have left!"

And so the conversation escalates.

Or imagine yourself in your cubicle at work, and a coworker comes by. This person is good-hearted but both talkative and dull, and you know you are in for a boring few minutes. She smiles and says to you, "Boy, let me tell you about the crazy weekend I had!"

To which you say, "Can't you see I'm really busy now? It drives me crazy the way you just interrupt me in the middle of what I'm doing. With you, it's always blah, blah, blah!"

The point of these anecdotes is that they don't happen at work, or at least not very often. Further, we almost never relate this way to coworkers, casual acquaintances, retail clerks, or service providers. And why is that? Because unless we're pushed to a breaking point, in all of these interactions *we're polite*. We follow the rules our parents drummed into our heads: Be courteous and use good manners or people won't like you.

Ah, but in the family, with our wife or husband? Therein lies a key paradox of married life. We feel comfortable and accepted at home. We see our spouse as the one person in the world who has to accept us as we are and no matter how we behave. It's precisely that atmosphere of trust and comfort that causes us to drop the array of social lubricants we use to smooth difficult interactions in every other context: politeness, tact, consideration, a pleasant tone of voice, watching our words. Marriage thus offers a double-edged sword: Where we feel most comfortable is also where we feel the most comfortable to be impolite, discourteous, ill-mannered, and even nasty. We believe that "for better or for worse" gives us the privilege to tell our spouse exactly what we are thinking, in its uncensored form.

What a mistake, according to the experts. The failure to observe the same rules of polite behavior we use everywhere else in life sabotages marital communication and leads to countless unnecessary fights. And it does so needlessly because we know how to behave politely in other situations (with a few exceptions, like those soccer parents heaping abuse on the referee from the sidelines—you know who you are!).

The experts recommend that you take a step back and observe

your conversations with your spouse. After watching how you oper-
ate in a day or two's worth of interactions, ask yourself: Is this how
I would talk with a coworker, someone in church, or a casual friend?
Or am I using a rawer and rougher standard? Hope Weaver, seventy,
pointed out that following the same norms for communication with
people in other contexts can help you avoid one of the most negative
aspects of marital communication: lashing out in ways you later
regret.

> Often it's easy to be impolite. You have a lot of pressures at the
> moment and have to get off to work or whatever you're doing
> and you push being pleasant aside. You get caught in daily life
> or momentary frustrations or anger and strike out and do dam-
> age, and usually it's not over any important issues. It's simply
> peevishness or dissatisfaction. You can do an awful lot of dam-
> age and cause an awful lot of hurt in a few moments. And you
> may not feel the same way in another hour or so, but you do at
> that moment. So just watch what you say and do. Think about
> communicating in a courteous way. That's what I would say.

The damage that can be done by a single unkind or impolite
comment is striking; one unpleasant remark is not easily forgotten
and can undo many positive interactions. Marcia Massey, sixty-eight,
provided an example from her generally positive relationship with her
husband:

> My husband said to me one day, when he must have thought I
> was babbling about something, "I don't think you have any-
> thing important to say." And I was so wounded by that, and it
> took a long time for me to get out of him how that happened.
> Then he learned to say I'm sorry. Saying "I have made a mistake
> and I'm sorry"—that's very important, too.

We should be grateful to the experts, because in this lesson they give us one of the easiest ways to improve marital communication—and one you can start doing immediately. We all have long experience in being tactful and using good manners, which we employ many times a day to avoid anger and hurt feelings. Taking my earlier example, when your boring coworker launches into a tedious story, you would engage with the person, look interested (even if for the shortest time possible), and politely extricate yourself from the situation. You would not sigh loudly, pointedly ignore them, look at your phone, and finally tell them off for bothering you. But we do, unfortunately, feel free to behave this way in our marriages.

Therefore, you should make a daily practice of politeness. Janet Greene, sixty-five, and Robyn Palou, sixty-seven, have been together for twenty-one years in a very happy and deeply committed relationship. As Janet told me:

> I think it's really important that you respect each other. And that means that you not say things that you wouldn't say to somebody else. I mean, it's not as though because you're married or partners that you don't have to be sensitive to the other person's feelings. It's about having good manners and being polite. You can't treat your partner any worse than you would treat a friend if you're upset about something. I know that sounds ridiculously obvious to say, but many couples are not able to do that; they forget, and act and speak inconsiderately.

Politeness and courtesy, the experts told me, are an invaluable help in getting over difficult periods in a marriage. Tracy Gibson, eighty-six, is an introspective and analytical woman who had a complex relationship with her husband over forty-three years until his sudden death. The marriage included the stress of conducting two highly charged professional careers. Under pressure from her husband, she suspended her work for a number of years, but keenly felt the negative impact it had on her career chances. The couple also struggled with sexual incompatibility and an episode of infidelity. Given this complicated and ambivalent history, I was surprised at the simplicity of Tracy's main lesson for a happy marriage: the importance of simply being *nice*.

> I think that the golden rule, to be nice, pays off in the long run. To be polite and pleasant to your spouse, instead of saying, "I've got to nip his bad behavior in the bud," or "I want to change things." Try to always be the nicest person you can be. I know that doesn't sound very earthshaking, but it's a good life lesson, no matter what you do. My husband was better at this than I was. He was such a nice guy. That is important in all of your relationships, but particularly the person you share the most with.

My assumption is that you are pretty much aware of what the experts mean by polite behavior, and you know deep down how it contrasts with what many of us do in marriage. According to the elders, you can immediately improve your marriage by following a very simple politeness rule. If you are of a certain age, you were taught this rhyme:

> Hearts, like doors,
> Will open with ease
> To very, very little keys.
> And don't forget
> That two of these
> Are "I thank you,"
> And "If you please."

And yes, that really is what the experts want you to do in your relationship: Use simple good manners. If your wife hands you a cup of coffee, say thank you. If you bump into your husband or knock something over, say, "Excuse me" or "I'm sorry." Demands are out; not "Change the channel!" but "Could you please change the channel? Or "Do you mind if we change the channel?" The comfortable informality of married life leads us to drop simple polite speech— and that's a mistake.

Tony Mathews, seventy-five, put it this way:

> It's all about demonstrating love and having mutual respect. I think as people are around the same person for a long time, they forget to be polite and just say please and thank you, or offer one another a hand—simple things that can mean a lot. I know of so many couples where one person becomes grouchy because things aren't exactly right. I think it's a matter of not forgetting those simple things that make up politeness.

As they say in the infomercials: Try it for a week and see if it has an impact on your day-to-day communication. During that time, pretend that your spouse is someone you want to impress. Simple politeness may just transform your disagreements into respectful conversations.

LESSON FOUR
All in Good Time

I sometimes wonder why we so quickly forget childhood's most important lessons. I've regretted, for example, not attending to the cardinal rule of elementary school: Never sit in the front row if you can help it. On those (few!) times I've dozed off during a long lecture merely three feet from the speaker, I've wished I'd remembered that principle.

There's another unwritten rule of childhood that is highly applicable to the topic of marital communication and conflict. Remember when you really wanted something badly? To sleep over at a friend's house, to stay up late to watch a special program on television, or to bring home a puppy from the litter next door? With manipulative savvy, you would carefully plan the exact time for the request. Certainly not just after Mom had reprimanded you for forgetting to do the dishes, and not the minute Dad arrived home from a bad day at work. No—you would wait for precisely the right moment to communicate. And if it looked like the conversation was going badly, you would withdraw and make a new attempt at a more auspicious time.

According to the experts, if we want smooth marital communication, we need to become attuned once more to the crucial issue of timing. In their view, many conversations would not become disagreements, and many disagreements would not become all-out battles, if people asked the simple question, "Is this the right time?" For excellent communication and reduced conflict, a key is reading cues from your partner, understanding when the best time is to raise an issue, and—particularly important—when to step back from a difficult conversation when necessary.

The experts note that the issue of timing comes into play in several different ways, from choosing the right time to talk to taking time out. Let's look at how you can use attention to timing to improve communication in your relationship.

Choose the Right Time to Talk

All too often, the experts tell us, we decide that the right time to talk about an issue is the moment *we want to talk about it*. In so doing, however, we can waylay our spouses with a concern at precisely the wrong time for him or her. Pay close attention to your partner's mood, level of energy, and degree of distraction before you initiate the discussion of a potentially contentious problem. You don't need to prepare an elegant dinner or bring home flowers and candy to soften up a spouse for discussion. But picking a time when your partner is receptive is a powerful tool in limiting conflict.

In their long relationship, Marianne Dunn, sixty-eight, and Rhoda Newman, sixty-four, have learned to communicate in a warm and understanding way. Rhoda told me that what's needed when an issue comes up is patience—the ability to wait until another time if a discussion isn't working.

> I think it's sort of a balance. It's important, if something's bothering you, to bring it up. But at the same time, you certainly don't want to say anything that's permanently hurtful. We don't tend to argue a lot, but when we do and it seems like things are heating up a little, we just let go of it and then come back to it. We circle back another time and say, "Okay, let's go back to this conversation we were attempting to have about this issue." It's a balance. "I love you, so I don't want to hurt you." But on the

other hand, it's important that we both say things that are bothering us. Picking the right time really helps.

Leona Stevenson, sixty-five, suggests that couples become sensitive to when their partners are most amenable to a potentially difficult discussion. She and her husband made this discovery, and their serious arguments were greatly reduced.

> I am an evening person. He is a morning person. When I first get up and come downstairs, don't hit me with "This isn't working, what should we do about this?" when I've been awake for five minutes. And after ten o'clock at night, he's very tired and I can't have a meaningful interchange with him then.
>
> So we said: "What time of day is a good time for us to have a disagreement about something that we need to discuss?" And we discovered that was early evening, after we'd had time to regroup after work, but before it gets too late. We had to negotiate that because he would attack me in the morning when I first got up, and I wasn't ready to discuss anything except to fight. And at night he's too tired and we can't have a meaningful discussion about some disagreement. So we actually negotiated when we can have a discussion and found a time that we could do that.

Take a Break from Each Other

It sounds so simple: When things aren't going well in a discussion, *back off*. And yet many of the elders admit that this was a difficult lesson to learn. Is there a couple who hasn't experienced this dialogue?

"I don't want to talk about this anymore. I need a break."

"Oh no you don't! We're going to hash this out now, so you stay right here!"

Often, according to the experts, this strategy exacerbates the situation when what you may actually need is a strategic retreat.

Jack Simon, whom we met earlier, overcame a difficult family and marital history to find happiness in a thirty-one-year marriage. But he knows that when conflicts occur in the relationship, maintaining control over his anger can be a serious problem. His solution is stepping back from the situation before it escalates:

> Well, here's the way I do it. You see, I've got a terrible temper. And I've learned that I need to keep my mouth shut. Because when I get mad, I say things that hurt people's feelings; things I shouldn't say. So I just go outside and start piddling around in the garage and mess around with my lawn mower or some of my tools and stuff and let everything cool down. Then I come back and try and discuss it, when nobody's mad anymore. Walk off and cool down and then try and discuss it later; that's my advice.

I was fascinated by how many of the couples I interviewed had developed their own special method to put a stop to an escalating but unproductive argument. May Powers, seventy-one, bases her insights on her career as a psychotherapist as well as her experience in a fifty-three-year marriage. May and her husband use this strategy:

> We do something very explicitly and my husband and I make jokes about it all the time. That is, being willing to start again. That's one where we actually say, "Okay, let's start again." I used to be a person who had to process things to death. My husband is definitely not that kind of person, so it was like he was being

beaten over the head with a two-by-four of processing. Then I would be frustrated because it wasn't getting anywhere. So one of the things that we both had to learn is that there comes a time when you just have to stop, shut up, and start again later.

The "step back" phrase can take many forms, and the experts showed their creativity in creating "it's time to stop" signals. Vera Patel, sixty-seven, and her husband, Suresh, seventy-two, told me, "When we get in a bind, we say: 'Let's zoom out. Let's zoom out, you know?'" The idea this couple has is zooming out to the big picture and letting a specific argument lie for a while. Kathleen Hunter, seventy-six, and her husband use a phrase that's less polite, but it works for them: "We have this thing now where we say, 'Zip it.' If one of us is not listening and just wants to go on and on, blah, blah, either one of us can say 'zip it,' and we take a break and come back to it."

Give it a try in your relationship. Come up with a code word or phrase that means "I can't talk about this anymore, but I will be willing to do so later on. Let's drop it for now." Feel free to borrow "let's start again," "zoom out," or even "zip it"! Even better, find your own "time out" phrase; it helps to make it something you can laugh about. Don't forget the experts' advice, however: Your phrase does not mean "it's over"—instead, it's an agreement to come back when the time is right.

One of the true sages I interviewed was Chen Xiu, whose philosophy of life is steeped in Chinese culture. She endorses taking a break when things heat up:

If conflict occurs, well, there is the Chinese saying, "Take a step back, and you can see the whole sky." Just step away, a little bit. Just step back and then you see other things.

Try a Distraction

When your home becomes a battlefield, the experts suggest, it's worth creating a distraction to help you work your way out of the conflict. First, try a change of scene. Simply moving to a new environment—rather than the one in which you have been fighting all day—worked for many of them. Gertrude Bennett underscored this strategy:

> I only know that my instinct tells me to say, "Okay, I know something isn't right here, what can we do about it? What would you like to do to make it right? What do you say we go for a little walk, or let's go out and have a snack somewhere and talk about this." Where there are no other people around to interfere and the phone doesn't ring, and you can say, "Okay, I know something's been wrong today, what is it? What can we do?"

I heard many suggestions from the elders based on this idea: If a disagreement avoids resolution, find something enjoyable to do (even if that seems like the last thing you want to engage in at the moment). It can be a change of venue, as Gertrude suggests, or any other activity that gets you away from an unproductive argument. Be creative. If you need inspiration, here's the kind of thinking the experts propose, courtesy of Anna Ostrogny, eighty-one:

> After my husband and I were married, we moved to Europe, and therefore we had nobody to give us advice. It's very difficult when you first get married. Maybe he does things or I do things that are not pleasing. But we had no one to turn to; we just had each other. And we worked it out. Here's how. We both loved to play cribbage. So we made a deal that whenever we got into a

spat, he would grab the cribbage board and I would grab the cards, and we would play cribbage. And the cribbage board was our savior a lot of times.

And the Final "Trade Secret" About Timing . . .

I wanted to keep you in suspense for the final piece of advice. It was one I hadn't expected, but the minute I heard it from the experts, my first thought was: Why didn't I ever think of that? It now seems obvious to me, but when looking for communication helpers, few of us turn first to . . . *food*.

When asked how to prevent a major blowup, a surprising number of experts recommended offering your partner something to eat. One of the worst times to have an intense discussion is when you are hungry. Some speculated that it might have to do with blood sugar levels or being tired, but whatever the reason, they suggest that when a big fight is looming, the immediate solution might be—a sandwich.

Gloria Hernandez, seventy-three, learned this trick from observing her son's marriage:

> My son and his wife's first year of marriage was very difficult. I remember sitting at their wedding and thinking, "Oh, they love each other so much. They'll be married forever." Well, within the first six months I was like, "Oh my gosh. I don't know." But it's so interesting, because they learned that often when they start to go at it, my daughter-in-law will make him a sandwich. Nothing pleases him more.
>
> He had to say that to her. "I need a sandwich when I'm really tired because I act like this when I'm hungry." And for her when she gets out of control, he has to offer her a cup of tea. So

whenever they're with us, if I hear her offering him a sandwich or him offering her a cup of tea, I know that's their code for each other to say I need some help from you.

I will admit that I have seen this in my own marriage. In particular, when my wife and I are traveling, we will become so absorbed in the new environment and in sightseeing that we forget to eat. Just like clockwork, around seven p.m. or so we begin to argue about something—who got us lost, why it's my fault or hers that we got to the museum after it closed, or some other trivial issue. One or the other of us then suddenly remembers and asks, "Hey, when did we last eat?" Our mood change after dinner is simply astonishing.

Okay, this suggestion isn't a cure-all. But why not give it a try? A pastrami sandwich or a piece of pie not only costs less than marriage counseling, it is also probably more fun! Pay attention to timing—even being aware of when it's time to eat. According to elder wisdom, *what* you say may not necessarily be as important as *when* you say it.

LESSON FIVE
Three Danger Signs

Throughout the lessons in this chapter, our discussion has been based on an assumption. In offering the experts' tips and ideas for improving communication and reducing conflict, we've assumed that both members of the couple are generally well-meaning individuals who care about each other and have a basic desire to make the relationship work. Their best efforts may not succeed, but their hearts are in the right place. If their communication attempts fail, it may reflect unawareness, immaturity, or lack of relationship skills— but not malice. Unfortunately, not all marital conflict and communication is so benign.

For this book, I deliberately sought out people whose lessons emerged not only from the joys of marriage, but also from problems they had experienced. And as we've seen already, some very powerful advice comes from those experts who experienced disastrous relationships. My interviews uncovered at times the dark side of marriage— situations where a partner was abandoned, threatened, or emotionally or physically mistreated. These stories were painful to hear, but in some cases it was precisely these individuals who had the most useful lessons to share.

I learned from these elders about communication breakdowns that are unlikely to be solved by "home remedies." The experts— based on their own experience and witnessing that of others—want you to know about three potential problems in a marriage that are so serious they should set off a warning siren. These behaviors go far beyond the kinds of spats, tiffs, and disagreements we've discussed so far. The presence of one or more of these issues points to a relationship in serious trouble—and one for which you should seek help from outside sources.

Danger Sign 1: Violence—Once Is More Than Enough

The perils of domestic violence are so well-known that I will not dwell too long on this danger sign. But the experts put it first and foremost. And it's critically important for this reason: Entering marriage after experiencing dating violence is shockingly common, despite decades of warnings from counselors, physicians, and researchers. In fact, as many as 40 percent of dating couples report that violence has occurred in their relationship, and a significant number wind up getting married anyway. So it's clear that many people do not pay attention to violence, hoping it will just go away.

Not so, say the experts. On this issue they are unequivocal: *If your partner hits you or tries to physically hurt you in any way, even once, get out.* There may be extremely rare exceptions where a single slap or push occurs impulsively and is later profoundly regretted and forgiven. But the experts don't see it that way. If it happens while you are dating, they firmly state, it will happen in your marriage; and if it happens once in marriage, it will happen again. The experts believe that second chances for some offenses are possible (even in the case of infidelity, where depending upon the circumstances, many say that another try is possible). However, *not a single one* of the elders believed anyone should stay in a relationship where violence has occurred.

Let the voices of people who made the mistake of not heeding this warning sign and lived to regret it sink in:

Violet Marsh, seventy:

If someone is abusive to you early in a relationship, it's not going to get any better as time goes by. It will get worse. If there's an abusive situation, get out.

Leah Stone, seventy-one:

I got into an argument before we got married and he hit me. I just turned around and that was it for me! That should wake you up—wait a minute, this is not what I want.

Jeanette Newman:

If he hits you one time, you'll know he's going to hit you again. No woman should put herself through that. Never. We never should let nobody lay their hands on us.

I could spend a long time offering you detailed—and sometimes terrifying—accounts from experts who made the mistake of marrying someone who was violent during courtship, only to have the physical abuse escalate after marriage. These victims were mostly women, but also included several men. My guess, however, is that readers are aware of the dangers of marital violence, the degree to which women in particular feel trapped and unable to escape, and the devastating consequences for both the victim and the couple's children.

Given that a significant number of people do ignore the warning signs of dating violence, I will let Devona Patton, sixty-eight, do the talking. She chose to ignore violence while dating and lived for over a decade in terror of her husband. Finally, in desperation, she fought back, knocking him unconscious with a frying pan while protecting her son. She found the strength to leave and begin a new life, but she and her children still bear the scars decades later. For any reader involved in a relationship where violence has occurred, I hope you will listen to the urgency of her words:

> If you see flaws at the beginning that are killer flaws, recognize them from day one. There are certain clues that you get that you must pay attention to. If the person acts violent—*what are you doing there?* Run, run, run! Run, you know? Learn to spot the freaking clues and run!

Danger Sign 2: Your Partner Is Controlling

In any marriage, couples try to influence each other's behavior. If we dislike one of our spouse's actions or choices, we may cajole or even demand a change. Much of the negotiation that goes on within couples has to do with making our desires known and trying to influence our partner to move toward our way of doing things. A cardinal warning sign, however, is not an attempt to influence, but rather to *control*.

If your partner engages in aggressive and persistent attempts to control you, your other relationships, and your behaviors, you should take a very serious look at the relationship. In the experts' view, the underlying causes of such controlling behavior—insecurity, suspiciousness, jealousy—constitute a very poor basis for a marriage. Such attempts at control can be subtle at first, but later expand to the minute aspects of a person's life.

For Vicki Morrison, sixty-seven, control was demonstrated insidiously until it destroyed her marriage:

> Watch out if he's controlling—if he expects you to sit and wait for hours, if he takes you away from your family, and he tries to isolate you early—because it's going to be his way, if he is very

controlling. One thing was the way he held my hand. And people may ask, "Well, what's wrong with that?" But he never let go. Every time we were in public he had to hold my hand. That's control. He had to control me the entire time. He didn't want me to say anything out of place. He always let me know he was right there.

We don't see it sometimes because we are wearing rose-colored glasses, which is what happened to me. Well, I divorced him. That was tough, because a single mom with two kids, that was a very rough beginning. But I had to do it.

Controlling behavior exhibits itself in some predictable areas. One common theme has to do with money. Mary Morton, seventy-one, told me:

My first husband was very controlling. We had a joint checking account, but he kept the checkbook. He would give me so much a month for groceries, but if I needed anything, I had to save my grocery money and sneak a purchase because he was unhappy if I asked him for money even though I was working and earning a salary.

Eleanor Bailey, sixty-nine, identified excessive jealousy as another dangerous controlling behavior:

In my first marriage, I was very young, just nineteen, and as it turned out, the young, handsome man I married was extremely jealous. And I'm a very truthful person, but he would not believe what I would say about situations regarding other people. Just after a short while I knew that wasn't something I wanted to go through all my life, so that ended that. So definitely make sure they're not a jealous person, because that can just really ruin things. Watch out if they have to always have you by their side and don't trust you very much with the opposite sex. That kind of control, that's terrible.

Controlling behavior can be subtle, and you may not notice it at the outset. By the time it becomes apparent, it may be difficult to extricate yourself from the relationship. The experts offer a very useful tip if you are worried about this problem: Ask other people. Your suspicions are more than enough to go on, and you should check them out with people you trust. Ask your family and friends whether they notice potentially dangerous controlling behaviors. This "reality check" can save you from future heartache.

Danger Sign 3: Your Partner Demeans You

Like excessive control from a spouse, demeaning behaviors can be insidiously slow in developing. But there is no question, in the eyes of the experts, that demeaning and denigrating you—in private or in public—is a clear danger sign. It is your partner's job to build up your self-image and to promote you in positive ways to others. When the reverse happens, they say, you and the relationship are in trouble.

In marital research, these negative behaviors have been given a strong term: contempt. The psychologist John Gottman describes contempt as one of the "horsemen of the apocalypse" for a marriage; that is, one of the most damaging behaviors in which a partner can engage. Demeaning and contemptuous behaviors go beyond criticism, because they contain an element of cruelty. Contempt involves hostility and devalues the person as an individual worthy of respect.

A hallmark of demeaning behavior is insults. It may sound like a high standard, because arguments do get out of hand and name-calling can be hard to resist. But the experts are clear on this point:

Be very careful of a partner who insults you during an argument—it usually is a profound sign of disrespect. As Susan White, sixty-nine, pointed out:

> You should not tolerate insulting behavior. Once those words come out of your mouth you can never put them back. My second marriage is to a man who understands that. My first marriage was to a man who didn't. And that's why you have to know the difference between someone having a good sense of humor or being insulting. You have to not let a disagreement escalate and get out of hand. Especially avoid all name-calling of any kind, even if it's simple words like "stupid" or "dummy" or "idiot." Those are minor names, but even those should be avoided because they have an insulting effect.

Direct insults are straightforward. But in some cases, demeaning behavior can be a tricky warning sign to detect. That's because degrading remarks are often masked as attempts at humor, where the insult can be shrugged off and the recipient told that he or she "can't take a joke." According to the experts, sarcasm and teasing are the two most dangerous forms of "hidden" demeaning behavior.

Sadie Singleton, seventy, talked with me over tea and biscuits in her comfortable living room. Witty and intellectual, she is very pleased with life with her second husband, Walter, seventy-three. Married for forty years, both Sadie and Walter learned from their troubled first marriages how to succeed the second time around. For Sadie, respectful communication is key to her second marriage's success. She learned its importance the hard way, through her first marriage to Harry, which lasted three years.

> In my first relationship, I didn't understand concepts like understanding and listening. What you need to do is pay attention

to behavioral signs, you know? Somebody who is persistently, consistently always sarcastic and critical, that should have been a warning sign to me that I was dealing with a person who couldn't function very well in the world and would carry things to extremes.

Sarcasm should always be a warning sign. It's mean-spirited but is always done in the light of joking. It's bitter. He could get away with it because he was very funny. He could make fun of everybody. Except himself, you know? And in the beginning I thought that was hilarious! What a quality, you know when you're an adolescent? It was cool, but it doesn't work as a life skill, or in a marriage.

It's true that demeaning language can sometimes be changed. But you must address this issue early in the relationship before it gets out of hand. Some people excuse insults, sarcasm, or contemptuous criticism because they are, after all, "only words." The elders could not disagree more. As Ruby Burgess, sixty-nine, emphasizes, building up your partner is one of the relationship essentials:

> When a person tears down another and tells them they're no good or that they're a lousy person, they will start thinking they are a really bad person. So you've got to be sure that the other person makes you feel good about yourself. It can be the most damaging thing in the world if they make you feel bad. The most essential thing I've learned is treating my husband in a way that makes him feel good about himself. Tearing a person down damages that person. It's the worst thing you can do.

Here is a test for your marriage: Does your husband or wife make you feel better about yourself? If not, the experts say, it is a serious warning sign.

When you encounter these three problems in your relationship, the message of the experts is straightforward: *Tell someone and get help.* The experts who suffered in silence universally wished they had told someone about these problems. They suggest beginning by opening up to family members and friends, and they also endorse professional counseling. (We look at the experts' views on getting help in Chapter 4.) Here's what *not* to do when you encounter one of these three danger signs: Wait and hope that things will just get better. Violence and controlling or degrading behaviors mean you need to consider your own safety and seek help.

LESSON SIX

Five Secrets for Great Communication

The experts have told us that effective communication involves creating an atmosphere of openness, avoiding harsh judgment, and being polite to our partners. However, establishing this kind of communication environment can require substantial effort over the course of years. Most of us need some direct, concrete steps we can take to achieve such a lofty ideal. Given their practical natures, the experts are happy to oblige.

Here are five of their "trade secrets" for communicating when the lines aren't as open as they should be. In the first lesson in this chapter, you were told, "You have to talk." But it can be tough to do that, so the elders offer tips to get the conversation going that you can start using today. And if one doesn't work, try another!

Tip 1: Set Ground Rules for a Discussion

The experts acknowledged that having a discussion about a contentious issue is rarely easy. At times it can be a minefield, with both partners carefully negotiating uneven ground, leery of a potential explosion (and not being sure what will set it off). In such situations, they recommend developing a structure for the conversation. Creating a set of rules for how you will speak to each other and ensure both of you have your say helps avoid the invisible trip wires in the conversational field. For example, many couples learned to set a time limit for a difficult discussion. They may agree to go at a difficult topic for a half hour; if there's no resolution they come back to it at a later time.

Some of the experts employed a rule to ensure that one partner has the chance to "have the floor" for a time. Alison Roarke, sixty-three, and her husband encountered difficulties after one of them had been away on a business trip; when reunited, both put their need to talk first. They came up with a wonderful solution I've put into practice myself:

The place that I found that my husband and I were having problems is when one of us would go away for work. We'd go to a conference or something, we'd be stimulated, we'd be away for a week. Then you come home and the other person's been at home being the drudge. So we figured out a system. We said, "Okay, when you come home, whichever of us that is, you get to talk. Tell me all. You have the floor. Tell me all about your trip. Everything you loved about it. You talk until you're done. I'll ask questions to show that I'm interested. When you're all done, then I can talk about what my week was like." But really give them the floor and give them that chance to kind of shine.

And that's really worked for us. It's even better if you say: "We're going out to eat that night!" We go out to eat and the person who has been away gets to talk.

The rules individual couples developed for important conversations were so varied that they can't quickly be summed up. The important task for you and your partner is to find rules that work for you. Is it a time limit? When you can have a serious discussion? How much time each of you gets to talk? Even discussing the ground rules can help you develop a healthier communication style.

Tip 2: Avoid the Temptation to "Fix Things"

The experts pointed out a behavior that they view as a "communication killer." And the problem with this behavior is that it stems from the best intentions: love and concern for the other person. Sometimes one partner simply wishes to be listened to while expressing sadness, stress, or upset. However, in an effort to help, his or her mate jumps in immediately to try to solve the problem. What your partner wants most, according to the elders, is to be heard and helped to come to his or her own solution. In such cases, a spouse's desire to "fix things" is unwelcome and shuts down the conversation.

I do not wish in any way to endorse stereotypes, but I am only stating the facts when I note that both male and female experts pointed to men as the major culprits. Men were usually named as the "white knights" riding in to solve their wives' problems.

Patsy Schultz, seventy-two, was typical in her description of the problem:

> Oh gosh, there have been some very stressful times. My mother died within two weeks of our being married and my husband just didn't have a clue how to deal with that. We were both very young. Men try too much to fix things instead of just listening and hearing what a woman has to say. It took my husband a long time to learn how to not just jump in with a "this is what we should do" plan and just listen to what I was saying.

Fortunately, the men I interviewed often became aware of this problem and were able to tamp down the urge to be the white knight. Clark Hughes, seventy-seven, eloquently described his learning process:

> I would say that one of the things that I've learned is that as a man, I tend to be a fixer. If my wife is complaining, I want to do something about it and make it right. The problem is, first of all, there's tons of things in life you can't fix. And the second thing is that often the other person just needs to be heard and

validated. So control that fixer impulse and really be there for the other person, and be able to endure the suffering when you can't make something go away.

Of course, lots of times when there's something painful, there's a desire to go do something, whatever you can. There's nothing wrong with that; that's absolutely right. But often, for the really big ones, it isn't that easy. It's more a matter of being with the other person and suffering with them, even though it's really hard to watch somebody you love suffer.

Tip 3: Pay Attention to Actions as Well as Words

It's true that the experts highlight verbal communication—they want you to keep talking. But in addition to conversation, they suggest that actions can speak as loudly as words. If your partner sometimes is less than attentive with compliments and praise, take a look as his or her behaviors as a sign of hard work to convey deep feelings of concern and affection.

As I listened to the elders' advice on this topic, a classic example popped into my mind from the musical *Fiddler on the Roof*. After decades in a very traditional marriage, Tevye badgers Golde to declare whether she loves him. Golde reflects on the twenty-five years she's lived with him, fought with him, starved with him, shared his bed, and admits, "If that's not love what is?"

Actions alone cannot substitute for an open conversation on important issues. But they can communicate warmth, affection, and caring—if we look carefully for them. Research shows us that we are sometimes not consciously aware of supportive actions performed by our spouses, but our mood improves anyway as a result of such support. If you feel your mate doesn't say all the things you want to hear, it can help to notice how he or she demonstrates love and concern in other ways.

According to Lucia Waters:

> One of the strategies that I did was I loved to cook. I show my
> family my love through my chocolate chip cookies and they
> have great medicinal value! For Stanley, I made sure that some-
> how I always had food for him and when he'd come home, the
> house was as calm as you could get it with a pack of kids in it.
> Sometimes you have to do more than talk. You have to have
> some action along with that.

Shane Kingston, seventy-three, admits that his wife is the communicative one and that he is harder to draw out. Nevertheless, he
says, people can sometimes communicate without words—especially
when it comes to expressing affection:

> There may be a way of—you know, you touch somebody or you
> stroke their hair or bring them flowers or whatever. There are a
> lot of different ways to communicate.

According to the other experts, talking is very necessary for a healthy
relationship. But when it comes to expressions of love, care, and support, watch carefully what your partner *does* as well as listen to what
he or she *says*.

Tip 4: Be Honest (Most of the Time)

It will probably come as no surprise to you that a top communication
tip from the experts is "Be honest." What was striking to me, however, was how strongly they emphasized this point. For example,
when asked, "What should someone look for in a marriage partner?"
honesty was often the first trait mentioned. For good communication, partners need to establish an atmosphere of honesty in the relationship from the very beginning.

Trevor Garfield, eighty-one, has been married for fifty-seven years. The issue of honesty was the dominant theme in our interview. He told me:

> Be open and honest and have confidence in your partner. You've got to be honest with them; you can't hide anything. Make sure you're not afraid to talk about money, about work, about the marriage itself. If you start off on the right foot and you have nothing to hide, honesty becomes just routine. I mean, that's what a marriage is—two people who are honest with one another.

According to the experts, an honest partner allows for the independence and freedom from jealousy that characterize fulfilling lifelong relationships. Clarice Galloway, seventy-three, has been in a committed relationship with Meghan for forty-four years. Her advice is to be trustworthy:

> For me, the thread that goes through all of it is trust. That's the key because it can really get you over a lot of things. If you don't feel secure, if you don't trust your partner to be honest, you're not going to want them to go see friends separately perhaps, or you will worry when they develop other interests that don't involve you. To keep a relationship really fresh and interesting, you just can't be together twenty-four hours a day. Honesty makes you comfortable with not being together twenty-four hours a day.

But there's one important nuance to this tip, according to the experts. They distinguish between honesty and trustworthiness on the one hand, and *tact* on the other. Many highlighted the value of selectively softening an honest response when it might be hurtful if expressed precisely as we feel. The now-proverbial example of a question that does not need a completely candid answer was given by a number of experts: "Do these pants make me look fat?" The key point, the elders say, is that honesty is required on any matter of deep importance to a relationship. On matters of taste and opinion, however, a judicious evasiveness is just fine.

Tip 5: Write to Each Other

Many of the experts found a very helpful technique to address communication problems: writing to each other. Somehow, the act of writing—carefully, clearly, and in detail—about how one feels about an issue often helps solve thorny communication problems. Sabrina Burke, ninety, discovered this early in her relationship with her husband:

> If we had something that we disagreed on, we would sit down. He'd write why and I'd write why. And then we exchanged letters; he read mine and I would read his. And then we'd decide that we have to do something about whatever it was. So I'd recommend that people just sit down and write a letter to one another. Tell why they are angry or what's wrong. And then pass it on. She'll read it or he'll read it and maybe decide, "Well, gee, maybe I *am* being mean about it," and decide to change.

The experts offer one caveat, however. When they say "write to each other," they do *not* mean texting, G-chatting, or other instant messaging. To assist when communication is blocked, the writing needs to be thoughtful and reflective, taking enough time to avoid miscommunication. You can use e-mail—but it still needs to follow the format of a letter, and not a hastily dashed-off message. The experts view such instant communication as a prescription for *miscommunication*. Here's a time when being old-fashioned can help your relationship.

CHAPTER 3

Getting Through the Hard Parts

I would say that marriage is much harder than you think it's going to be. It's much tougher to live with somebody twenty-four hours a day, seven days a week, than you anticipated. There are times when you just want to throw up your hands and give up and think that it's just not worth it. It takes an awful lot of stick-to-it-ness, with the basic feeling of: yes, this is valuable; yes, I want to do it; yes, I love him. There are other moments, of course, shining moments of real connection that you don't have with other people—intellectual, emotional, and physical experiences that you would never give up. It seems to me that marriage is a process. You never get there; you're always in process. It's always more work than you can possibly imagine. In my case, it was worth it.

—Samantha Jones, 80, married for 47 years

I have been through a wedding. Well, I have been through several, including my own. But not too long ago, I experienced (intensely) my oldest daughter's wedding. Objectively, and with no influence of paternal pride whatsoever, it was *absolutely lovely* and probably *the best wedding ever.*

With that out of the way, I know I'm not alone in feeling that there's something special about a wedding—something that spells hope, romance, and a bright future. I have never forgotten the words of the proud mother in the classic film *Father of the Bride*. Ellie Banks is trying to convince her husband, Stanley (the wonderfully grumpy Spencer Tracy), why weddings are important:

> Oh, Stanley, I don't know how to explain. A wedding. A church wedding. Well it's, it's what every girl dreams of. A bridal dress, the orange blossoms, the music. It's something lovely to remember all the rest of her life.

It's a rare person who attends a wedding and doesn't leave with a sense of excitement for the new couple who are beginning their future together. Embodied in the ceremony are glowing hopes and dreams for a lifelong relationship. And many people who are madly in love and pondering marriage have this same sense of optimism. They say to themselves, We've made it this far together (be it one or a few years); how hard can it be once we're married?

Not to rain on anyone's parade, but I can only tell you what the experts told me, from people who say their relationship is the best thing that ever happened to those who struggle daily to stay together. According to the oldest Americans:

Marriage is hard.

Many couples now live together before marriage, and one might expect that this type of "test drive" would make people aware of the challenges marriage can bring. However, the period of cohabitation is often relatively short and the partners are still young when they marry. In the afterglow of the decision to make such a major commitment and the excitement of the wedding, the view of marriage can take on a rosy hue. Thus, there is a positivity bias when a marriage begins, with lofty expectations for the melding of two minds and hearts. It's likely that very few people enter into marriage with this thought foremost on their mind: *Marriage is hard.*

But it is, according to the experts. Cindy Barber encapsulates how joy, fulfillment, and great difficulties all come together in a long and satisfying marriage. She told me:

Okay, marriage is for adults. It is not for children. Both my husband and I were married to other people very young, unsuccessfully. So it is a second marriage for both of us. They were just both wrong. And that's how they ended.

Be sure, when you do get married, to think beyond the wedding. Think to what life will be. What everyday life will be. Not your date nights, not wonderful vacations, but think about: Are you going to be able to reasonably and rationally and pleasantly deal with one another through the dirty laundry, the stack of dishes, the house that needs cleaning, the—whatever? Are you going to be able to deal with the minutiae that make up everyday life? Because everyday life isn't, in and of itself, exciting. A wedding is a terribly exciting thing, but that's not real life. That's one day. Does that make any sense?

It certainly did to me.

In the interviews, I asked a question that sometimes brought our respondents up short: "All things considered, which of the following statements best describes your degree of happiness in your relationship with your spouse? Would you say extremely unhappy, very unhappy, a little unhappy, happy, very happy, or extremely happy?" After an hour or more describing the ups and downs of a long marriage, I could almost hear their thoughts: "Huh? I just spent all this time sharing the nuances of long married life, and now you want me to sum it up in a couple of words?"

But it was in answer to this question that I often heard this lesson: Accept that marriage is hard. The good news is that it isn't always hard and that it can provide some of the most splendid emotional experiences life offers. But we must accept this interplay of smooth and rough patches, or we won't make it through married life. The experts know that marriage necessarily involves learning how to deal with stress—and possibly for long periods of time.

Perhaps no one put the complex mix of joys and challenges as eloquently as Eunice Schneider, who, when asked to rank the happiness of her fifty-three-year marriage on our scale, replied:

> I would say very happy. But you know what? I even have a hard time using the word "happy." I think "happy" is not the right term; it's a word that doesn't apply to a marriage. I think you can find joy—there are joyful times. There are times of disillusionment; there are times of romance. So to me, it's like a roller coaster of romance, disillusionment, and joy in a marriage. And I'd say for the most part, we've reached a point now that we're here with almost fifty-three years in this marriage, that it's a level of contentment. So I don't know if happy really even fits that.

What makes marriage hard? Sometimes it's unpredictable difficulties, like a serious illness or a financial disaster. However, according to the experts, the most stressful aspects of marriage are predictable and occur to most couples. Paradoxically, the stresses often result from events we consider positive—having children is the classic example. In this chapter, we will look at five major stressors couples experience: children, balancing work and family, in-laws, dividing household chores, and money issues. In each case, the experts offer clear advice to make these challenges easier. To top it off, the final lesson provides specific tips from the elders for coping with the day-to-day stresses of married life.

LESSON ONE
Children: Put Your Relationship First

Is anyone really ready to have children? For many of the major transitions in life, we have a period of preparation, or what sociologists call "anticipatory socialization." For example, everyone who goes to college has had long experience as a student, and many high school students have spent enough time away from home that dorm life is not a shock. For marriage itself, most young people have lived together, so setting up a new household is not the novel life experience it was for newlyweds in earlier generations.

Ah, but having a child? It is a fundamentally different thing. Even experience with one's younger siblings or professional work in child care can't adequately prepare a couple for the impact a baby brings to a marriage. Sigmund Freud famously used the phrase "His Majesty the Baby" to convey the degree to which a child manages to rule the household by his (or her, of course) mere presence. The arrival of children is a source of immense joy, but also of major readjustments and stressors in their parents' relationship.

I asked the elders this question: "For many couples, the arrival of children can place stress on a marriage. What advice would you offer for dealing with the effects that children can have on a relationship?" Because this is a book about marriage, the focus was not on child-rearing (although they have plenty of advice about that, too). Instead, I wanted to know: What can couples do to maintain a close and intimate relationship in the face of the time demands and competing commitments brought about by this new member of the family? And as children grow older—and bring with them new and changing pleasures and stresses—how can partners preserve the positive relationship qualities that brought them together in the first place?

There is no question that integrating children into a marriage is an enormous challenge. The experts agree with Austin Little, seventy, who said: "Of course, when the kids were born, it changed my perspective of the marriage. You have to readjust." Kyle Caldwell, sixty-seven, stated it more strongly: "Oh my goodness, I have dictionaries of conflicts that have to be resolved." Kyle cataloged many of the issues that come up: "Because with children, they start school; they have disagreements; they have fights; they have bullies; they deal with teachers they don't like. You know, so it's just an awful lot of stress." Okay, kids cause stress for a marriage. So what's a couple to do?

The most important thing they can and should do, according to the experts, was quite a surprise to me. You might expect the oldest Americans to endorse unanimously the idea that children are the undisputed stars of family life and the major reason why marriage should exist at all. In the 1950s, family life became extremely child-centered, and the activities of parents at that time focused on school, homework, clubs and organizations, and neighborhood activities. Often, financial sacrifices were made so women could stay home full-time with children. Fathers worked long hours to provide a better life for their children than they had experienced. "His—and Her—Majesty the Baby" should be the motto for the experts, right?

Not so much. Despite the fact that the experts belong to the most child-centric generation in American history, their lesson for overcoming the stress of child-rearing is this:

Put your marriage first.

No matter how much they loved (and still love) their kids, the experts forcefully argue that one of the worst things couples can do is focus entirely on the children, ignoring the need for the marriage to be nurtured and sustained. In their view, you don't do your children much good if your marital relationship dries up. It's in this sense that they mean "put your relationship first." It in no way means neglecting your children, but rather acknowledges that if your partnership is suffering, your child-rearing is likely to suffer, too.

Neal Mitchell, sixty-six, gave a response that was typical of the experts:

We had great kids. But we said, "Well, our union's just as important as you kids." And they figured it out. And I hope we were good models for our kids. You've got to keep the foundation there—the two people. The kids are a result of the two people. The relationship with the mate has to be paramount, and a good relationship with the children has to come from that union.

It's important to distinguish the elders' lesson from a perennial story in the press. Every once in a while, a controversial article comes out titled something like this: "Your Kids Come Second" or "Put Your Spouse First." You may remember a few years back, when the writer Ayelet Waldman raised a ruckus by declaring she loved her husband more than her children. An often-quoted line from the essay is: "He and I are the core, the children are satellites, beloved but tangential." The article set off a firestorm of protest, with some angry commentators accusing Waldman of child neglect. Although this idea—mate over children—reappears regularly in the media, it never seems to lose its controversial edge.

That's not what the experts are advising. They take it as a given that you love your children and that you would freely give your life for them. It's not a question of loving your husband or wife more, or that you would sacrifice your child for your spouse (or vice versa). Their point is that the *relationship* between you and your partner is what sustains the family and makes a good childhood possible. One expert used this analogy: On an airplane, you are directed: "In the event of an emergency, put on your oxygen mask first before assisting others." This is the spirit in which the elders encourage you to put your relationship. Because without a vibrant marriage, childhood stressors will be far more difficult to manage.

I found my mentor on this issue in Cecilia Fowler. She leads a full and interesting life, devoting much of her time to working as a community volunteer. Cecilia endorsed the lesson "put your relationship with your spouse first." She told me:

> I have been thinking about this for many years. I was single for nearly twenty years between the time my husband and I were divorced and I remarried, so it was a long time. Then my second husband died after just six years of our being married. And that marriage was very happy.

If Cecilia could change anything about her first marriage, it would have been to put the relationship first, making sure they carved out time with each other. Her description of what happened is common to many people who experienced failed first marriages:

> Thinking back to my first marriage, we just became so mundane and boring with each other. I mean, we didn't do anything to stimulate our relationship; we just were married and that's the way it was. You know—we just floated along. That doesn't work. So my thought for young people is to try their dead-level best to keep excitement, interest, and stimulation in their marriage. Challenge your skills and your brain and your whole being together.

Cecilia pointed to the shift in attention from the relationship to their offspring as the core of the problem:

Your life is totally changed! It is not your own anymore and all of your energy goes to your children. We just fell out of love. I think the mundaneness of our lives caused that. There was no pleasure, no play, no—it was just work. If I could have a do-over, I would try harder.

The power of this lesson comes from the fact that she did have a "do-over"—her fulfilling second marriage. She is an avid gardener, and she learned to tend to and nurture the relationship just as she does her beloved plants:

My second marriage was a delight because my husband was always finding, in his words, festive things to do. Now that probably sounds old-fashioned to you. But he would like to get all dressed up to go to dinner and it was just fun. I can remember the first time we went for pizza in one of those chain restaurants and he ordered a pitcher of beer. For the two of us to sit there and drink a pitcher of beer and get all dressed up to go to a pizza place—isn't that silly? But it was fun.

This attitude is a good one for all couples. Cecilia told me, however, that it's an even more important priority after you have kids:

When things get so heavy and there's no joy—there's no excitement, there's no adventure—well, what's left except grayness? Find some way to experience joy in your marriage, and don't let having kids stop you. Even if it's a silly little thing like going to a pizza place all dressed up. That may sound ridiculous, but it's an example of a spontaneous, fun thing to do. What a great thing that is! It erases all kinds of hard work and mundane stuff that parents can fall into.

There's one more bonus from focusing on your relationship—it may be the greatest gift you can give your children. Don't forget that observing your marriage is perhaps the most powerful tool your children will have in creating their own relationships. The experts believe one of your most important contributions to your children is to model a couple that finds joy in being together. Carrying out necessary "relationship maintenance" has a direct and powerful effect not just on you, but also on your offspring as well. Begin the habit early, they say, and never give it up.

LESSON TWO

Work-Family Stress: Make Your Home a Safe Haven

You've set it all up on Friday night. Your husband is working late, so you get home early and prepare a special dinner. The candles are lit, music is on, and your plan is to have a true "quiet evening at home," where you can relax and refresh yourselves after a difficult week. Your husband breezes in and he's so caught up in his thoughts he doesn't register the special preparations. "You won't believe what happened at work today!" he begins, and launches into a long litany of work dumped on him, new deadlines, and what a jerk his boss is. You try to reorient him, and he eventually plays along. But you sense his preoccupation the entire evening, as the urge to process events at work is almost irresistible.

Or you're headed to bed on a Sunday evening, hoping you and your wife can watch a movie you recorded and spend some much needed quiet time together. She comes but brings her laptop with her—just a few things to get ready for tomorrow morning. You finally give up and doze off but are awakened intermittently by the glow of her computer screen until she finally turns it off at two a.m.

If you've been through something like this (as most couples these days have), you are experiencing what social scientists call "spillover": transferring moods, emotions, and behaviors from work to home. Occasionally, this spillover can be positive, when a great day at work brings you home feeling enthusiastic and upbeat. But more often, spillover can be a big problem for couples; indeed, according to the experts, it's one of the most persistent and damaging stressors in married life. Diane Harrison, seventy-two, summed up the problem this way:

In the early part of your marriage, a lot of your time goes into your careers. There's a lot of competitiveness in the work world, and it affects your marriage—just coming home from work and there's tensions. If there are tensions and someone's in a bad mood, that's not what you expect when somebody comes in the door, so you've got to work these problems out.

There is voluminous social science literature on spillover, work-family conflict, and related issues. And as you can imagine, a host of solutions has been proposed to help husbands and wives balance the load. Sound complicated? Fortunately, as they do on a number of other matters, the experts are happy to take a complex issue and simplify it for you. They acknowledge that both spouses often must work, and work hard. And they know that today's workplace is a hotbed of stress and tension. They realize that you can't change society, but there is one lesson you can put into practice:

Make your home a haven from the stress of work.

The idea is to expel the pressures of work to the greatest degree possible from your married life. They want you to imagine your home as a castle of sorts, with a high wall and a moat that leaves job stress where it belongs—on the job. And not just job stress—the experts tell you to leave *work* at the office. A haven is a safe harbor, a refuge, a shelter, a sanctuary. It's a place where the dangers of the outside world can't enter—including, especially, the immense stresses of the modern workplace. More than a castle, the experts are talking *Star Trek* deflector shields, through which your work life can't pass.

Merle Rowe, sixty-five, has reached a very happy point in her forty-five-year marriage, but there were earlier periods of struggle. She diagnosed the problem incisively:

When we are at home, home is our one safe place. And unfortunately that is the place where we feel like we can just dump.

You know, when you've just had a crummy day and everything's wrong and whatever—we can go home and just let it out. And when you are the unsuspecting person, it feels very personal when they come home with the bad mood and the bad attitude and the grumpy and the whatever.

The experts make an important distinction in this lesson. On the one hand, they are asking you to eliminate "dumping" the negative emotions produced by a bad workday on your partner. Francis Spencer, sixty-six, placed typical emphasis on this point:

When you leave work, leave work at work! Don't bring your job home with you. If you need to talk about it, that's fine, but sit down and talk rationally. Don't come home and explode in each other's faces about something that happened at work that made you angry. Leave that at work. Deal with it on a professional level.

They are not, however, asking you to eliminate all work discussion from your marital interactions. Such an achievement would be impossible—even more so if one or both members of a couple work at home. On the contrary, they believe that supportive and helpful discussions have an important place in couples' lives.

This point was brought home to me by George Mandel, eighty-seven, who had a very successful career in advertising. George regaled me with stories about life in the world of *Mad Men* in the 1950s and 1960s. Unlike the characters in that show, however, he stayed true to his deeply fulfilling marriage to Tina, now in its fifty-seventh year. George told me that he greatly valued discussing work with his wife:

When I was involved in a very stressful business issue, I shared my work with my wife. When I had problems, I talked them over with her. And with one word, she would sometimes save me, set me straight on things that I was worrying about needlessly. And I think that was helpful to sustain our marriage, and she agrees that she felt as proud as I did when we did well in the agency. We were connected through my work. She saw through my worries and how they were needless, and showed me I wouldn't get killed because of what happened today. I think that's a very important part of our marriage.

There is an enormous difference, however, between having a circumscribed conversation in which one partner asks for support or advice from his or her mate, and dumping all the residue of workplace stress on a spouse. In the first case, there is a reason to bring up work issues, and one is seeking a result from sharing them. It's obsessing about the job and taking out negative emotions on your partner that's the problem.

And the solution is to carve out a calm and peaceful space at home. Or if not entirely calm and peaceful (I can see those of you with small children rolling your eyes), at least one where the world of work does not permeate every nook and cranny. You need to make what at times may seem like a herculean effort, but the elders believe that adopting an attitude that "home is home and work is work" is a critical first step.

The major solution is a change in mind-set, so the critical first step is to become aware of the problem Merle Rowe raised: using the fact that we feel safe at home to simply dump everything on our partner. Sabrina Burke and her husband both worked outside the home, and she is adamant about this issue: It is *not* okay to mercilessly inundate your partner with your work problems.

If you have a bad day, don't let it out on one another; that's very, very foolish. And if you do, you have to remember to apologize.

My granddaughter has a new boyfriend and she said to me: "I've been having a really hard time at work and I've been kind of taking it out on my boyfriend. That's okay, isn't it?" And I said *no*! Even if you've had a bad day, it's not okay just to take out your bad day on your partner. Maybe a little bit, but if you do it a lot, it's a problem.

The experts argue that making your home a haven also means that whoever has been taking care of the kids on a given day should not dump every problem on the spouse when he or she comes home. Gwen Miles has learned an extraordinary amount about marriage over her ninety-four years. Her husband, Stephen, was drafted in 1942. She became pregnant when he was on furlough and was unable even to get word to him for weeks about the coming child. "That was a real tough time for me because I wanted to share that with him and ask his advice about certain things that had to be discussed." When he returned, they had two more children, and Gwen became the primary caregiver while her husband worked.

Gwen found she had to sacrifice the immediate urge to dump the day's issues on her spouse immediately when he walked through the door:

> One of the things I've learned was after Stephen got home from the war. Because he worked, he wasn't home at all during the day. At first, I had to tell him about every problem I had all day long. I have never forgotten how one day he said to me, "Oh, I was so tired when I got here, but I think I'm tireder now."
>
> And I realized that saving all those nitpicking things for him when he got home was making things worse and wasn't helping me. My advice is to handle everything you can when you are with the children. Just share the big, important problems when they get home from work. Little fights with the

neighborhood kids or each other, I would try to settle before my husband got home because I remembered him saying. "Oh, I was so tired when I got here, but I think I'm tireder now." When they come home, they can enjoy being with the family without troubling them with every little thing.

Her response was to make the home a "safe haven" from work stress. It took effort, and her husband's cooperation, but they learned to leave work issues at the office as much as possible, and to allow him to breathe a sigh of relief when coming through the door. The payoff may have saved their marriage.

I don't know how many times I've thought, "You know, the home is the safe place." And so my advice is to seek quiet and peace. To me, that's home. That is how we recuperate and get renewed.

The experts recommend that you create a conscious time buffer between work and home (using a *Star Trek* analogy again, think of a decontamination chamber before you enter the ship). Many experts believe that important issues should not be discussed right when you return from work. Instead, let everyone decompress first when they come home.

Phyllis Barton, sixty-six, shared the ritual that let her change from businesswoman to "Mommy":

I have always been a professional woman, and my kids were three weeks old when I went back to work. Work was always an extremely important part of life for both me and my husband. And, of course, our careers both had bad moments in them for one reason or another.

So we began to realize that work is important but it isn't all of life. When I came home from work I would go into the shower. I told the kids it was my time to change from work to home. I actually had a ritual of going into the shower and literally quieting down, putting on a pair of jeans, and coming back out as "Mommy." And it was a very healthy thing for me to be able to walk in the door and say, "I'm home but not yet," and go through a transition, because otherwise they immediately put me into the role of Mom and I found it very difficult.

I happen to be passionate about what I do. I've built a life around it. And my husband is passionate about what he's done and he's built a life around it. God only knows how we did it all. I'll tell you one thing that really does matter, though—we created rituals like that, ones we sort of fell into. It really matters.

The experts advise you to employ such rituals of passing from one world to another. Use your imagination to find one that works for you.

LESSON THREE
In-laws: On Good Terms, Without Surrender

"You don't just marry a person; you marry his or her family." In Chapter 1, we learned that the experts hold this to be a fundamental truth about marriage. According to them, in-law relations have such a powerful effect on a couple's happiness that you should take them very seriously in choosing a mate. Despite the fact that most dating couples do not spend much time thinking about their partner's family, it's a key component in a fulfilling long-term marriage.

Unfortunately, no one has written the definitive handbook on how to manage your partner's family, and most couples find themselves without much guidance for negotiating the potential minefield of in-law relations. But, fortunately, we have the experts, whose unique experience makes them particularly good guides. Here's why: They experienced the same kinds of in-law issues and problems you may be going through, *but often more intensely.* The boundary between the married couple and their families was much more permeable than it is today. They had the same issues you are likely to encounter—but magnified.

As I combed through hundreds of reports of in-law relations— ranging from loving and respectful relationships to "in-laws from hell"—I uncovered extraordinarily useful lessons for insulating your relationship from problems with each other's families. These "rules" for in-law relations have been tested by hundreds of the oldest Americans for decades. Given what's at stake, they are well worth your attention.

Rule 1: Your Loyalty Is to Your Spouse

Life is full of difficult decisions in which no solution leaves everyone perfectly happy. Unfortunately, that's exactly what a difficult in-law situation creates—a classic example of ambivalence that in a worst-case scenario may persist over years (or even a lifetime). Because unlike other transitory decisions you make (Mac or PC? Boxers or briefs?), it can feel impossibly difficult to work your way out of this dilemma: Wife or mother? Husband or father? My old family or my new one?

But one thing I learned to love about the experts is this: Sometimes they cut through all the complexity and just tell you what to do. Your psychotherapist may want you to work it out on your own, but the oldest Americans are more than willing to make things easy for you. Here's their advice on dealing with the supposed ambivalence of in-law relations:

In a conflict between your spouse and your family, support your spouse.

The experts are unequivocal; it is your duty to support your husband or wife and to manage your own family in a way that consistently conveys this fact. Further, you and your spouse must present a united front to both families, making it clear from the beginning that your spouse comes first.

In couples where this allegiance did not happen, marital problems swiftly followed. In fact, some of the most bitter disputes occurred over a spouse's failure to support his or her partner. Erin Rose, sixty-six, was a lot of fun to interview—witty and tough-talking, there's a bit of *Jersey Shore* in how she expresses herself. In an otherwise good relationship, in-law issues remain the stumbling block for her and her husband. When I asked Erin to describe a conflict that came up in her marriage, she told me:

Oh yeah, his mother. A lot of conflict. I had the impression she didn't like me very much. I could live with that, but my husband never stuck up for me, so we fought about it. The apron strings were tied to him, and you just didn't go against Mommy. And we fought about it because he would say, "Oh you're crazy, she never said that." And I'd go, "I don't believe you don't believe me." And arguments would start. And after it was over I'd say, you know, how stupid we're arguing about this. God forbid we get divorced over her. My husband would never say anything like, "Hey, Mom, that's my wife, cool it." I never got that.

Given the depth of this problem, I'm glad I found my mentors on this issue happily ensconced in a condominium in the Sunbelt. I loved getting to know Greg Myers, eighty-three, and his wife, Judy, eighty-one. I gratefully stepped out of the tropical heat into the cool of their comfortable home. It was late afternoon, and they offered me the opportunity to join their daily cocktail hour (sadly, for scientific purposes I was required to stay sober). Just a few minutes in their presence revealed how much this couple cherishes their marriage, as well as the energy they have invested over nearly sixty years to keep the relationship vibrant and interesting.

Greg and Judy came from similar backgrounds and found they were highly compatible in every way. Judy told me, "We both had a feeling that we could communicate with one another. That was very basic and very important. And it's been that way ever since." After listing all the positives, the couple confessed that there was only one real problem in their married life.

Judy began, "Let me be honest. His mother did not approve of me. His mother said, after she met me—"

Greg broke in with a resigned smile: "Must you remind me of that?"

"Well, yes, it's part of it, it's part of our marriage. Because that's one thing we had to work out."

"She was so wounded, she's never forgotten."

"I will never forget it."

"I don't blame you, really."

Having settled the legitimacy of the problem, Judy continued the story:

> His mother's comments were: I was not rich enough, I was not intelligent enough, and I was not pretty enough. Other than that, I was okay. Greg was still living at home when we got engaged. His mother stopped cooking and cleaning for him when he was living at home after he wouldn't break up with me. Then she threatened she wasn't going to come to the wedding. She came, but she was an hour late. That's the way she was.

Those of you who are struggling with difficult in-laws: In all but a few cases, Judy and Greg have you beat. But Judy loved Greg so deeply that she made the conscious decision to not let his mother interfere with their happiness. She would do her best to get along, but both of them endorsed the rule: When push comes to shove, the child needs to stand firmly with his or her partner—and not Mom and Dad.

Over the years, there were many conflicts. But Greg knew exactly where his loyalties belonged. I suggested that it must have been difficult for him to be caught in the middle between these two strong women. He replied:

> I wasn't caught in the middle! I had this wonderful gal, and we were happy from the beginning. It was a sad distraction that my mother felt this way, but it wasn't going to influence any part of our lives. I think the problems become unsolvable if the other

spouse, you know, sides with the parent. If you're not committed to each other, it's not going to work. You have to throw in your lot with your mate. You have to side with your spouse. Rightly, wrongly, you're a unit, you need to be unified.

In a world of "gray areas," the experts make this one decision easy for you: Don't feel caught in the middle, because your place is on your spouse's side. To be anywhere else is to undermine the trust that is the underpinning of your marriage.

Rule 2: Depersonalize In-law Relationships

The experts recommend that you depersonalize negative in-law interactions to the greatest degree possible. That's where understanding comes in. By considering how in-laws' background and upbringing influence their attitudes and behavior, it's possible to take conflict less personally and achieve some emotional distance in the relationship.

Annie Dawson, seventy-seven, lived near her parents-in-law for most of her married life, and the relationship was not an easy one. But by infusing their interactions with understanding and a more positive attitude, she made the situation work:

> Rather than assume the worst, it's more helpful to assume that they are saying things to you because they want to help their child and you. Try to realize that their intentions are good and sometimes people, especially as they get older, can't change the way they deal with others in their life. Realizing those things helped me a lot in dealing with my mother-in-law in her later years.
>
> In the end you really did marry the family. So do your best to try to find the good traits of the mothers and fathers who are

involved. They are going to be upset when there are differences in opinion, but my advice is to try to look through that and think of the good characteristics of the parents of your spouse. And there are some. Try to focus on that, even though it may be difficult at times.

Rule 3: Eliminate Politics from Discussion

Here's a tip that I have personally found very useful, and it's one you can implement immediately. *Keep political arguments out of in-law relations.* It can be the biggest bomb in the minefield, and the elders say that these conflicts are unnecessary. There is no need to engage parents-in-law in political debates or to convert them to another viewpoint. Often, the urge is to make parents-in-law "really understand" what's going on in society and to show them how irrational or wrongheaded they are politically. I heard many accounts of holiday dinners and family gatherings disrupted by debates over the president, Congress, abortion, the death penalty, and on and on. According to the experts, you may not be able to avoid conflict over your in-laws' disapproval of your marriage, your job, your lifestyle, or how you raise your children. But you *can* make it a rule to take noisy and unnecessary political debates off the table. (I'm not talking here about a lively, enjoyable political discussion; I mean the kind that ends with slamming doors and a spouse crying in the car.)

Gwen Miles had a difficult in-law relationship. But she and her husband made visits much more tolerable by following this tip and cutting politics out of the interaction.

> My husband didn't care for my dad because my dad was a completely different kind of person compared to my husband. My dad was the boss of everybody and everything. He was never

aggressive; he never hit us kids or my mother. But he was a total boss. What my dad said was law and order and we all knew it. And my husband was a gentle, soft-spoken, easygoing person who would rather die than make a fuss. He was a completely different personality.

In particular, they didn't see eye to eye about the government. My dad was a Democrat; my husband was a Republican. They'd get into those arguments. So finally, I made the rule that there would be no discussions of politics when we were all together. And I said to my husband: "If Dad starts in about the Republicans, I'm going to walk out of the room and you come see what's wrong with me because I don't want to hear this anymore." I guess that was the only problem in our early marriage. Of all the big decisions we had to make in marriage, I think the most important was deciding that I wasn't going to listen to that problem between my father and my husband.

You may wish to apply this same rule to other hot-button issues (based on my own extended family, I'm tempted to include Red Sox versus Yankees). When buttons are pushed on a repetitive and sensitive topic, leaving the room is an excellent—and potentially relationship-saving—option.

Rule 4: If Necessary, Put Distance Between You and Problematic In-laws

The experts believe you should work hard on the relationship with your in-laws, even though it may mean compromise, strategically withholding some opinions, and searching for points to respect and admire. But what if nothing works? What if contact with in-laws is strained or unpleasant, and you are being asked to surrender who you are to maintain the relationship? In such cases, the experts advise you: *Keep your distance.*

Gina McCoy, seventy-three, and her husband, Cam, have been married for thirty-five years. A legacy both brought to the relationship was difficult family backgrounds, in which both sets of parents fought a lot with each other. They learned early in their marriage that they were in line for contentious in-law relationships. Gina described the strategy they employed:

> Well, what we did was move away from both sets of parents. We realized early on that my mother is very controlling and both mothers tend to take sides. And so we decided, "Well, we're going to leave." We ended up moving out West. We really got away from everybody. And then we eventually had to rely on each other and make our own decisions, and not have anybody say, "Well, why are you doing this?" and "Why are you doing that?"

This couple—and most others—did not consider cutting off relationships entirely. The experts recommend against such extreme steps, if for no other reason than your children's need to know their grandparents. According to Gina:

> But we always had our home open to the folks, and they did come visit once or twice a year, and we got back East at least once a year. I did it with the family, and then I just stayed at my parents' for a week or so and then got the car and drove over to his parents'. We were away about ten years, and I really think that the success of our marriage was because we had to rely on each other. Couldn't run to somebody and say, "Oh, look what he did, look what she did," because I tend to do that. So that's another overriding thing: You want to kind of sublimate your

differences so that your kids have a happy life with their grand-parents.

Rule 5: Remind Yourself Why You Are Doing It

This final tip from the elders is one that many have used like a mantra in difficult in-law situations. Tell yourself this: The effort to accommodate your partner's family is one of the greatest gifts you can offer in marriage. You are used to putting up with your own relatives, and you have accommodated to their quirks and foibles. But now you have to do it all over again. The closest thing to a magic bullet for motivating yourself to put the effort into in-law relations, the experts tell us, is *to remember that you are doing it because you love your spouse.*

Most important, by staying on good terms with his or her relatives, you are honoring and promoting your relationship in one of the best ways possible. Gwen Miles, married sixty-seven years, puts it better than I can:

> You may not like your mother-in-law or your father-in-law or your in-laws very much, but you certainly can love them and stay close to them. Remember that they're your loved one's family. I learned to love them. I mean, I loved them because they were my husband's parents and I loved him.

Looking over the experts' lessons for living with your spouse's family, I was reminded of a poem by Max Ehrmann popular in the 1960s (and still frequently quoted today). Entitled "Desiderata," the poem offers guidelines for a peaceful life (things "to be desired," as the title indicates). One of the maxims goes like this: "As far as possible without surrender, be on good terms with all persons."

It sums up beautifully the experts' advice for in-laws. First, a loving respect for one's partner means genuinely striving to "be on good terms" with the family that raised and loved him or her. Such efforts must not be halfhearted and can require putting up with views and behaviors you don't like or admire. However, if conflicts occur that force you to surrender your basic values, your commitment to each other, your privacy, or your day-to-day happiness, then the couple must come together in solidarity and support each other. When push comes to shove, the experts say, you need to back up your spouse. Paying attention to that principle will allow you to stay on good terms without surrender with your in-laws.

LESSON FOUR
Household Chores: Play to Your Strengths

The best kind of marital problem is one that you can solve once and for all. A major issue emerges, you make a decision, and it's done. The analogy I use is the difference between stopping smoking and going on a diet. It's agony to quit smoking (believe me, I know), but at least after a while, it's over and you can avoid cigarettes completely. With food (been there, too)—well, you have to keep eating, so the temptation to overdo it is always there. You need to get up each day and engage with the problem anew.

Similarly, in marriage there are events in the relationship that get resolved in one way or another. Deciding to buy a house, for example—you may argue about it for a while, but when it's done, it's done. Some difficult issues, like a partner's job loss, strike suddenly and demand resolution. We scramble to fix such problems, and the intense pressure of the acute episode passes.

But some stressors in marriage are chronic rather than acute. Because two people are living in the same household, these issues can't be resolved once and for all; they must be dealt with day in and day out, for a lifetime. And the biggest troublemaker in this category is the division of household labor. That fancy social science term means how couples answer classic questions like: Who cleans the toilet? Who balances the checkbook? Does my doing the yard work on weekends equal your keeping the house clean every day? Decades of research show that conflicts over who does what in the household affect many couples and are a major threat to marital happiness.

This source of stress can seem unresolvable because it's really two problems rolled into one. As scholars have pointed out, on the one hand it's a practical challenge. A household is an economic enterprise that often involves the care of dependent humans (that is, kids), and, well, stuff just has to get done. Food and clothing have to be purchased, appliances maintained, and the place kept relatively clean.

But beyond these practicalities, there's a symbolic dimension that further complicates things. Participation in household chores is seen as a symbol of commitment, even of love for one's partner. So doing the dishes becomes more than just doing the dishes—it is bound with a sense of how the relationship is going, and how much the partners care for each other. (This is why one of the experts jokingly referred to her husband's washing the dinner dishes as her "best aphrodisiac.")

According to the elders, there's an approach that can help you cut through this complexity. Although not a cure-all, it's a perspective on organizing household work that they have found useful. Couples often try to work out the division of labor through long, emotional discussions and resolutions that are hard to keep. But the experts had a different—and to me unexpected—idea that separates the emotion from a logical allocation of household chores.

They suggest you rely on what you've learned at work to address this issue. Many of the experts were in jobs in which they had to manage employees in highly stressful situations. Often, they took specialized training to assist them in these responsibilities. At some point, the idea occurred to them: Why not transfer the kinds of "people management" skills we perfect at work to our families?

The experts specifically recommend employing principles learned at work to answer the "Who does what?" question at home. They made this observation: *Much conflict over chores occurs because the wrong person is assigned to the job.* Fights about household labor are exacerbated by the fact that many couples do not assign tasks logically. Instead, they do so based on gender-role expectations, on which person believes he or she has a talent for the activity, or by just falling into a pattern without ever actually discussing who wants a particular responsibility—and more important, *who is good at it.*

I thought back to one of my first jobs, where I was supervising a large study. I hired two perfectly wonderful people, one as an interviewer and one to organize the data. It took me only a week or two to notice that our interviews were ending early and had lots of missing information, and that the data were not well organized. It turned out that my interviewer was a shy introvert, and my data manager was friendly and outgoing but had no eye for detail. All it took to solve the problem was switching them to jobs that matched their particular strengths.

The experts want you to do this kind of task analysis in your marriage and reallocate chores based on this devastatingly simple lesson:

Assign a specific task to the person who is best suited for it.

This lesson is one of those that seems intuitive—even obvious— the minute you hear it. But for many of the experts, it was a revelation. And I have to admit, it was for me as well. When my marriage began, it was assumed (due to a few lapses on my part that do not need to be revealed here) that my wife should be the one to handle our finances. For my poor spouse this task was, over several years, a miserable experience. She didn't enjoy it and as a result sometimes let things go. So I began to try to "manage" her (especially when I noticed that a bill wasn't paid on time or that we overdrew our account).

At some point, she threw up her hands and said, "Okay, *you* try this." We exchanged chore responsibilities, and lo and behold—I turned out to be very good at the job (and I enjoyed it). A simple reallocation of a task to the person who had more interest and aptitude resolved a long-standing source of conflict in our marriage.

I was not alone in this discovery. Many experts argued that one of the first things a couple should figure out is: Who will manage the finances? Olive Warner, sixty-five, learned this lesson and argues for a logical assignment of tasks in strong terms:

> In the beginning we had it really hard financially. It was horrible. And it almost ended the marriage; it got that bad. I'm very bad with money. I'm the first to admit it. We only resolved it by him taking over. I would give him a lump sum from my paycheck at the beginning of the month and that's it. That's one of the best things a couple can do: Realize that one of the partners might have better skills. Be aware of each one's talent and if it's going to enhance the relationship, then that's what you go with. And if it's the other way, where you don't match the job with the talent, it's going to tear the relationship apart.

The experts pointed out an important barrier to this kind of sensible allocation of work responsibilities. Coming from the oldest Americans, it may surprise you. They urge you not to let traditional gender-role expectations get in the way of answering the "who does what" question. Many of them learned this attitude late in life, and they suggest you adopt it sooner.

Sam Myers, seventy-six, shared his experience:

> Getting the housework done can be all-consuming. It's important that you both get involved and make it plain that you are involved. It can't be "Okay, I'll let her do it." You know what I mean? I'll tell you one thing that's been helpful in my marriage is figuring out who is best at something. For example, I like to cook and she kind of doesn't. So what we do is we alternate cooking nights. And that takes a burden off "I have to be the cook" for anybody. And a lot of our friends are always amazed by that. But for me it builds the idea that "Hey, we're a partnership and we're both committed to it."

This relates back into my first marriage, where I worked and my wife didn't. You get into specific roles and it's hard to get out of them. And I've seen that in a lot of people I know. They get into that "My role is such and such." And that's a conversation nobody wins. Our way to do it is we share stuff. I do the food shopping weekly and she takes out the garbage, you know? So we each have our things we do best, and that engenders the feeling that you're pulling your weight.

How do you get to this optimal division of labor? There's only one way, and having read Chapter 2, you can probably guess what it is: You have to talk. However, the experts' advice lets you cast the discussion in a new light. Instead of stewing angrily because your spouse has yet again failed to perform a task and then blowing up about it, they propose that you examine how tasks are allocated in a calm and rational way (easier said than done, but you need to try).

Such a conversation doesn't start this way:

"I can't stand this anymore! Why won't you ever do the dishes/feed the dog/get the car fixed/[your choice here]?"

Instead, the discussion begins:

"Here's everything that has to be done to make our home function. Which of these things are you best at and do you most like to do? (Or given the reality of housework, which of these do you hate doing the least?)"

To sum up, the experts' lesson is clear. Before your next knock-down, drag-out fight about who's doing what in your household, brew a cup of tea (or pour a glass of wine) and frame the question as who's *best* at doing what. Create a sensible allocation of tasks based on that principle, and see how it works. However, there's one more key to this lesson that you can't ignore; without it, the elders say you will be back at square one before you know it.

After you have assigned someone CEO responsibility for a task, *you have to let that person do it with a minimum of interference.* In fact, research shows that the temptation to micromanage your spouse's work in the house can be almost irresistible. Marital researchers refer to this behavior as "gatekeeping," in which a spouse gives up doing a chore but can't stop controlling how it is done. Tara Parker-Pope, in her book on marriage, provides a classic example of a husband who agreed to take over the laundry. Instead of providing relief for his wife who no longer had to do the chore, his failure to sort the laundry according to her standards created a new source of arguments for the couple.

Therefore, if you give up a chore because your spouse is better suited for it, you also have to give up being the gatekeeper for the chore. Otherwise, it becomes a new and significant source of stress. Glen Banks, seventy-six, noted that even after you divide chores according to the "who is best" rule, it's still possible to disagree about things. But he proposes that you respect the division of labor you have decided on:

> I have the attitude that it's not worth messing with. In other words, I let her design, arrange, and take care of the house any way she wants to. And she lets me take care of the yard. And she doesn't mess with the yard and I don't mess with the inside of the house. So if she wants to change things around, to some people it might lead to a conflict, but to me it's not a conflict. So, you know, it's that you agree to—"Well, you take care of this and I'll take care of that."

The payoff in trusting your partner to be the CEO of his or her domain is that you can let things go. As Rhoda Newman told me, you learn to relax and trust your partner to get things done:

If Marianne says she's going to do something, I know she'll do it. That level of security is really important. I know I don't have to think about it because if Marianne's in charge of that particular thing, she'll make sure it all happens. For example, we realized that Marianne is better than I am at handling the shopping. So of course there will be food in the refrigerator, because she's a star shopper!

No system has yet been invented for a perfect and conflict-free division of household labor. And even paying people to do the work doesn't solve all your problems. As *Downton Abbey* fans are well aware, even if servants are doing all the housework, someone has to manage the servants. However, taking a workplace approach and sensibly allocating tasks can go a long way toward reducing conflict. And the beauty of this idea is that it's pretty simple. Dixie Becker, eighty-four, summed it up neatly:

You just need to share at home. It can't just be one person holding down a job and the other person taking care of the family; it needs to be cooperative. And here's the way to do it: Whatever needs to be done, the person who can do it best is the one who should do it.

LESSON FIVE
Money: Deal with Debt

One robust research finding about marriage is this: Married people do better financially. For many couples, the presence of two incomes and the sharing of resources (one washing machine instead of two) leads to greater economic well-being for husbands and wives. But here's the paradox: Even though married couples are better off on average than singles, money issues are among the most contentious. Beyond their frequency, studies show that arguments over money are often angrier and last longer than those that occur over other topics. For a long and peaceful marriage, partners must find some way to avoid the trap of financial conflict.

So I was thrilled when the experts offered a clear and specific lesson for reducing the stress that money (or the lack thereof) places on a relationship. They start from the following simple premise: If a couple has enough money to live on, fighting over finances will be reduced. Conflicts probably won't be eliminated, because even wealthy couples argue over how to allocate their funds. However, when there just isn't enough money to go around, the arguments over how to allocate what's there can become fierce. These fights embody not just practical issues, but also deep-seated frustration at being behind the eight ball financially and not seeing any way out.

For this reason, the experts want you to stabilize your money situation so you predictably have enough to meet your basic needs. They offer a clear way to overcome financial conflict and create a saner family environment. It may take a new mind-set (or perhaps an old one, as you will see) for you and your spouse, but it's a highly concrete action you can start working on right now:

Get out of debt. And if you are not in debt, *stay out of debt.*

Researchers and counselors agree that debt is a killer for many couples, with lots of marriages in the worst kind of indebtedness—large unpaid balances on credit cards. It's not just younger couples in this boat; nearly half of people age forty-five to fifty-four are paying off credit card balances. There are more grim statistics, including the fact that the average outstanding credit card debt per family has more than doubled over the past twenty years. Other kinds of "bad" debt, like payday loans and bank overdrafts, have also invaded couples' lives more than ever before.

The way spouses wind up in debt and making huge interest payments is all too clear. Mandy and George, a typical two-career couple, look at their paychecks and feel that they add up to a lot of money. In addition, after a hard day's work, the pair want to indulge themselves. Because they see their peers outdoing one another to consume, they join in. They eat out frequently, take expensive vacations, and buy a fancier car and a larger house than they can afford. Credit cards are available, as are high-interest loans. And down that path, say the elders, lies disaster.

You can find all kinds of advice about how to deal with your finances, from how to make more money to how to invest it. But in the unique viewpoint of the experts, you should make your initial and strongest focus on paying off and avoiding debt. By engaging in some relatively simple analysis and behaviors, they argue, you can work your way out of debt—and out of continual arguments.

You must be willing to do one thing while you are reading their advice. Because times have changed (but on this issue not as much as you would think), you may be tempted to dismiss the difficult parts of this lesson as old-fashioned, saying to yourself, "What do these old folks know about financial trouble anyway? They seem to be pretty well-off now."

Well, how about this, for starters? They lived through the Great Depression. If you need to remind yourself about that piece of history, look it up. Many middle-class people didn't just have to downsize in the Depression: They lost everything. Professionals became ditchdiggers, day laborers, and farmworkers, if they could find work at all. People like you and me not only lost their houses—they also risked starving as the safety nets we now rely on were not yet in place (no food stamps or Medicaid back then). I find it shocking that, as we deal with the effects of the second-worst economic disaster in the past one hundred years, no one is asking the people who got through the *worst* one how they did it. It's like having Noah around and not asking him how to deal with a flood.

If there's one group that knows firsthand how to live well through hard economic times, it's the oldest Americans. Through conscious planning and the right priorities, they managed to stay within their means during financial crisis, to avoid debt, and to live quite happily while doing so. Because overconsumption and resulting debt are ubiquitous these days, please attend carefully—your marriage may depend on it. Here's the experts' worldview on marital finances, in three steps.

Step 1: Learn to Hate Debt

The oldest Americans hate debt (at least for anything other than a house, and even then some have their doubts). And they are utterly baffled at the ease with which younger people use (and abuse) credit. Debt for them is the true four-letter word (it's one reason, by the way, that they get so upset over the federal deficit, but that's another story).

Indebtedness makes them deeply uneasy, even afraid. And they find contemporary attitudes about it incomprehensible.

Where does this heartfelt conviction come from? In the Great Depression, they watched neighbors lose their livelihoods and their homes, making them aware of how tenuous financial security is. They saw what happened to people who couldn't pay their bills, and it instilled in them a frugal mentality. Even seventy-year-olds, born after the Depression officially ended, were affected by the experiences of their often traumatized parents.

Here are two examples from the elders showing the depth of the anti-debt mentality. And you need to imagine raised voices here— they are passionate about this issue.

Evette Cope, eighty-three:

What should young people avoid? Debt! They've got to have the instant gratification thing. I struggle with my granddaughter about it all the time because she doesn't have the patience to save for anything and racks up debt.

Darrell Ferguson, seventy-two:

I see it in my own children. What is happening with the families today, they do not live within their means. They go for the big car, the truck, blah, blah, blah. Nobody wants to live within their own means. You know what? Okay, so you can't afford a three-hundred-thousand-dollar home. Get yourself a seventy-five-thousand-dollar home. Or rent. You've got to live within your means!

Rather than accepting debt as a fact of life, learn to dislike it, to feel uncomfortable when you owe money, to feel driven to pay off loans as fast as you can. That approach spells independence, freedom from worry, and much less marital conflict. By changing your mind-set to that of the experts, debt can seem not like a natural state of being, but as a problem to be rooted out.

Step 2: Save Up the Money Before You Buy

It is remarkable how a principle that was almost universally endorsed only five decades ago now seems old-fashioned. Who patiently saves up to make a purchase rather than taking out a loan or using a credit card? And yet, if you want to eliminate debt and financial conflict from your lives, the experts exhort you to follow this simple rule: *Save up the money you need to buy things rather than use credit.* It really works, according to Everett Leonard, ninety-two:

> Well, money is always a big problem between husbands and wives, and we decided when we were very young that we weren't going to let that be a problem. And we worked it out where she got a certain amount of money each week and I got a certain amount of money each week, and we tried to live within our means and it worked out. We didn't buy a whole lot of stuff just because we liked it; we waited until we had the money to buy it and then we bought it. And so we really haven't had any prob-lems during our sixty-seven years of marriage.

Over and over, I heard: *If you haven't saved the money, don't spend it.* People in their eighties and beyond are baffled by how such an obvious approach is so widely ignored. Dave Neal, ninety-three, sees the key to avoiding debt as so obvious, he doesn't understand why there's so much complicated financial advice floating around:

> Of course, it's been rough for us a lot of times. After I got out of the service, we didn't have nothing. Imagine trying to make

a home and things like that. But, it's like, okay, we had only so much money. And we paid our bills. If there was any left, we'd go to a movie. If there wasn't, we didn't go. And we didn't sit there and fuss and argue about it or go first to the movie and then worry about the money; we just kept our bills paid.

Like financial advisers, the experts know that borrowing for certain things not only is necessary, but can also be a sound financial decision. Buying a house outright is rarely feasible, both then and now. Further, for many families it is impossible to finance a child's education without student loans. No one knows better than the Depression-era generation the security that home-ownership brings or the enormous economic value of a college education. What you should avoid is going into debt for *stuff*—things like electronics or furniture that break before you have made the last payment, or expensive vacations.

Instead, for your marital happiness you must learn patience and the ability to delay gratification. This attitude may mean, for example, setting aside a small amount each week for your annual vacation rather than paying it off for years on your credit card; buying fewer holiday gifts; and yes, even saving up to purchase a car outright rather than making payments. The experts argue that if you start this practice early in your marriage, it becomes a lifelong habit. And it's one of the best marital stress-busters available.

Step 3: Stop Comparing Yourself to Everyone Else

Finally, the experts tell you to confront the main reason why most of us aren't comfortable living with less. Namely, we feel intense pressure from our peers who appear to have more (and thus appear to be having more fun). It was easier for the experts, because when they were starting out, almost no one had more than they did. Everyone was struggling just to keep food on the table and a roof over their heads. Myra Goodwin, ninety-two, told me:

> Well, we didn't know any different. Everybody in our group was in the same boat. None of us had money and so we learned from one another how to manage. We had the privilege of having shoes given to us, and sometimes clothing and sometimes food. But we were all in the same boat, so we didn't seem to mind.

So here's a worthwhile thought exercise to end this lesson. Take a moment to consider what you would be able to give up if everyone else were in the same boat and there were no expectations that you should have as much or more than your peers do. Would you be willing to live in a smaller house, if most of the people you knew were doing so? Rent instead of own? Drive an old car into the ground rather than buy a new one? Wear comfortable but less stylish clothes? Skip clubbing for gatherings with friends at your apartments? If you find yourself answering yes to any of these questions, you will also find easy places to cut your expenses. Because getting into debt just because everyone else is—well, that's the opposite of elder wisdom.

LESSON SIX

Five Secrets for Managing Stress

Imagine a marriage without any stress at all. Go ahead, try it: What would a stress-free marriage look like? All I can imagine is a kind of barren, isolated life that avoids stressors and resulting conflict, but in which *nothing good happens*. Because most positive events in marriage—both of you finding jobs, having a child, buying a house—inevitably bring challenges with them that couples must handle.

Therefore, even the most happily married experts laughed at the idea of a stress-free marriage. Dewey Wise, seventy-three, spoke for the elders when he offered a list:

> Oh, after thirty-eight years of marriage, you see about every type of conflict you can imagine! You've got children, you've got in-laws, you've got job issues, you've got money issues from time to time. And then you just have issues of people—men being men and women being women and trying to make that all come together. When you get married, that's what you've got to understand.

In this chapter, we have looked at major sources of stress that couples encounter. These stressors are predictable—it's the rare couple who doesn't experience them at some point over the course of a marriage. In each case, the elders offered serious and thoughtful advice for how to think about these challenges differently and how to find solutions. Now let's take a look at their insider secrets for managing the stresses of marriage.

Tip 1: Hold a Monthly Meeting for the Most Contentious Topics

One problem with highly stressful issues is that they threaten to consume your relationship, becoming *the* topic of discussion that eliminates relaxing and pleasurable interactions. You go out for what should be a pleasant dinner—and then *the* topic comes up yet again. Instead, the experts suggest that for a chronic stressor in your life together, concentrate the discussion into a single, regular meeting. In so doing, you keep the reservoir of anxiety from spilling over the edges and flooding the entire relationship.

Agnes Weber, eighty-one, found that money issues could be best handled this way—something she learned from her parents:

> My parents would sit down once a month to talk money. They would call it their swindle sheet. They would go over their swindle sheet, and I never particularly wanted to be around them because it was one of the few times that they ever argued and fought. But it worked. I mean it kept the unpleasantness to a minimum. They sat down and went over what they were spending and who was doing what with their money and they had a specific night when they did it. Then it was over until the next time.

Agnes and other experts found that stockpiling all the worries, arguments, and hard feelings about a topic until the agreed-upon time, and then letting it all come out, was an immensely helpful way to handle chronic stressors. In fact, they suggest reminding each other to "hold your comments" when they come up randomly outside the designated meeting times, and writing down your concerns to bring them up in the meeting. This approach takes discipline, but it can put a lid on continual processing of a stressful situation.

Tip 2: Seek Out Social Support

How often we suffer in silence when our marriages are under stress, believing that we are the only ones experiencing a particular problem. Many elders, to be sure, were wary of sharing their problems too freely, using expressions like not wanting to "launder their dirty linen in public." However, the experts tell you to get over that fear and *reach out to trusted others.* Social scientists use the term "mobilizing social support"—that is, activating your social network to provide the kinds of ideas and assistance you need.

Archie Burton, eighty-five, and his wife found themselves in a situation so difficult that they nearly reached the limits of their coping abilities. Shortly after buying a new house, their young daughter was diagnosed with a potentially fatal illness. He told me:

> Well, during that situation it was very stressful for us. We had just purchased a home and now that my daughter was ill, it was very costly and we really didn't know anything about it at the time. Back then, it was harder for black people like us to get a handle on it and to find somebody who knew about the illness and could advise us, financially and otherwise. It was very stressful on us because we had saved up, but we found ourselves having to pay out everything that we had saved up and start over again. So you have a problem which relates to finance, you have a problem which relates to the illness itself, and you have a problem with the relationship—how we're going to manage from day to day.

A couple who prides themselves on self-reliance, they were at first reluctant to bring others into this crisis. When they finally did, however, solutions began to come forward. "We got through it because we did receive very good advice, fortunately. We got advice from my child's doctor, but also from friends of ours, so we were lucky in that respect." Their lesson is to overcome your desire to just "handle it on your own."

> Neither one of you can go into a shell and say, "We're going to do it our way and we're going to do it ourselves." You're going to have to depend on family members. You're going to have to depend on friends you can rely on to help work things out. So yeah, we had our problems—whew! We had them. But we were able to work out all of them with the advice and help of friends and family.

Tip 3: Spend Time with Good Role Models

We've just seen that friends and family can be helpful. But they are not beneficial, according to the experts, if they drag you down further rather than provide solutions and encouragement. Research shows that people who associate with more positive individuals are more likely to be happy. The same applies to your marriage. When you are experiencing a hard-to-solve problem, seek out couples who are particularly good at handling the challenge in question.

Violet Marsh did just that a number of times, and found it invaluable:

> Sometimes if you know a couple that is doing well and has a good relationship, they can tell you how they succeeded and how they're doing things. Maybe that will help you open up the doors of communication and start talking, too. A couple that you know are getting along well and things are working for them, invite them over for dinner. Have a bottle of wine, have some dinner, and chat. Relax and see if they can offer some suggestions.

Rather than commiserate with someone who is mired in the same problem as you and can't find a way out, associate with successful role models who can provide inspiration to find solutions. Jeremy Bennett, age eighty, emphasized this point:

> If you're hanging around with negative people, find some positive people and hang around them instead. You know, success imitates success. So if you see people who seem to have a very successful happy marriage, well, you hang around with those types of people. It does rub off. Avoid the ones with a defeatist attitude—get out of there before they drag you down.

Tip 4: Give It a Rest

Looking back over long experience, the experts have learned an invaluable secret to married life. It may seem unrealistic. It may even seem like magical thinking. But they recommend one particular strategy for some stressful situations: *Wait.* Looking back over the marital journey, it is astonishing how many things just got better over time. The seemingly unbearable stress of your teenager's nastiness; the difficulty staying engaged in home life when work is difficult; the anxiety of limited financial resources—if a decision is not absolutely urgent, the experts say you may simply want to let the problem rest for a while and revisit it later.

Judy Ray, sixty-seven, was fed up and considering a separation. The problem was her husband's drinking; although not extreme, how often and how much he drank bothered her greatly. She discussed the situation with a wise older relative. Judy told me:

> She gave me excellent advice. She said, "There's no reason you have to make a decision right now. You're very angry, upset, and frustrated. You don't have to make a decision now; give it a year.

And if you still feel the same way a year from now, then go ahead and do it." And a lot changed in a year! A lot changed. In our case, we came to a compromise, and he drinks a lot less.

I have given that advice to other people, that you don't have to make a decision now; you can wait a year. It's difficult for one person to understand how the other person feels, but giving it a year allows both parties to examine what they want out of life. Have we backed each other into a corner, you know?

It doesn't need to be a year; depending on the situation, a week or a month of "letting it go" may be all you need.

One gift of being married for decades is that it makes you an expert in taking the long view. In particular, the oldest Americans know for a fact that bad times pass. Simply getting through them, while resisting the temptation to give up, may be the best strategy. Charlotte Buchanan, at one hundred years old, knows the importance of patience in solving problems in a marriage and urges you to consider whether a problem is one that may just go away in time. I will give her the last word on the long view—because she certainly has it!

Allow time sometimes just to pass, because sometimes, as you know, a problem will just disappear if you give it time. Communicate with patience. Have long-term patience. Take the longer view of marriage and wait, because these things often do resolve themselves. Don't be afraid of the future and staying together in the future. Test whether a problem is temporary and may go away on its own, or if you have to accept that it will never change, and recognize the difference.

Tip 5: Focus on the Day at Hand

The experts point out that some stressful situations are compounded by what psychologists call "awfulizing"—taking an overly pessimistic view and focusing on the most awful outcomes possible. Such a situation seems particularly frightening because the couple looks out into the distant future and can't see an end in sight. One answer to that anxious mind-set is to adopt the time-honored expression "one day at a time." Indeed, there may be no alternative to such a viewpoint if a marriage is to survive a chronic stressor.

I'd again like to call on one of my foremost marriage mentors, Lucia Waters. Considering the love, security, and joy in her fifty-five-year-long marriage today, it's hard to imagine the immense difficulties she and her beloved Stanley experienced in their marriage. But they found the mantra of "one day at a time" to be a lifesaver:

> We had a period of time where we had kids in college and kids in high school and I had returned to college, too. And my husband, Stanley, was trying to keep everything going at his business. He hit a point where he simply became overwhelmed with everything and he became depressed, which for him was very unusual. But you could just see it on him. And he found it really hard to talk about. He said he'd go into his office and sit down and put his head in his hands and think, "How on earth can I carry on?"
>
> But then we would look at each other and say, "You know, one day at a time. That's all we have to do. We aren't going to worry about anything. Let's just get through the day." We'd tell ourselves that in the morning and line up what we had to do and make sure the kids had the support they needed. We'd remember to tell each other we loved each other. Whether we did or not at the time I don't remember! It was kind of overwhelm-

ing, but I'm an endless optimist, which is really a good thing. We would concentrate on each day, and it really helped.

Experiment with the idea of "one day at a time" rather than let your minds—and discussions—veer off into the vast range of disagreeable possibilities. In my interviews, one word came up over and over: patience. Older people know that not everything needs an immediate fix, that people take time to come to the realization that change is needed, and that in a lifetime commitment one can patiently try different approaches to dealing with the predictable stresses of marriage. That's the benefit of the long view, and it's one we can adopt at any age.

CHAPTER 4

Keeping the Spark Alive

In marriage, there has to be a spark there right from the beginning, the capability and the desire to share experience and to find empathy in the person you're with. It's the willingness to learn from each other and appreciate the other's qualities. To keep the spark alive, it's carving out time together. Actually doing fun things rather than saying, "We'll have time to do that later. I'm just too busy right now." Find out ways to make it fresh. Go to a rock concert if you've never been to one and you only go to classical music concerts. Volunteer for something that ten years ago you wouldn't have even thought to do, as a way of opening yourselves up to new experiences. Travel—take your partner to a different place and experience a new culture. These kinds of things are definitely possible and very satisfying as you get older.

—Frederick Black, 73, married 38 years

Two more dinners, two more chances to ask people what they longed to know from America's elders about staying together happily for a lifetime.

After a heroic effort, I finally found a time when six mothers of young children could have dinner with me. As we sat down, they told me they were thrilled simply by the excuse to have the night off. The women in this group had been married around ten years and were very eager to talk about the challenges of juggling marriage, children, and work.

On a different night, I joined one of my favorite contemporary institutions: a book club. The members were women in their late forties to early sixties. Most of their children were grown and some members were watching their offspring make marriage decisions, so the issue was on their minds. Many people in the club were married twenty-five years or more.

Underlying the discussion in both groups was a powerful (and for some, troubling) question. It's one I also heard when I spoke with men and with twenty-somethings, therefore it became a key question I posed to the wisest Americans:

"How do you keep the spark alive over decades of marriage?"

It seems everyone wants to know how life can possibly stay interesting, new, challenging, and yes, *fun*, for thirty or more years. That's the idea of the "spark"—the little something (what the French call "je ne sais quoi") that makes a marriage exciting to wake up to each day. It's the loss of this same spark that hit movies are made of—a couple starts out passionately in love, falls into stultifying routine, and wakes up one day to find that they have nothing in common besides the same address and a couple of children.

In my book *30 Lessons for Living*, I talked about a discovery I made. Looking back over their lives, many older people described what I came to call "the middle-aged blur." From around age thirty to age fifty, the dizzying combination of building a career, raising children, and maintaining a household all runs together in a jumbled rush. When this phase winds down, people come up for air and are stunned by the time that's passed. It is daunting to keep the relationship spark alive during that busy and stressful time.

However, it is as great a challenge to maintain a vibrant relationship in the decades after children leave home. People think of marriage as inextricably bound up with raising children. But here's news for you: With the ever-lengthening life span, you and your partner may spend twice as many years together *after* children are launched as you did with kids at home. You had Megan and Jason by the time you were thirty-two, and they're gone by the time you turn fifty. *Hello*—we could be talking about forty more years as a couple. What's that going to be like?

After talking to hundreds of long-married elders, here's what I learned: *It can be wonderful*. We've already heard from the experts that marriage is hard, and one of the hard parts is keeping the relationship fresh, alive, and interesting. But nothing made me more optimistic about the next thirty years of my own marriage (knock on wood) than listening to couples for whom life together never lost the spark.

People like Eunice Schneider, who has been married for fifty-three years. Her first date with her future husband took place when they were sixteen years old. She went to college and he went into the service; when he came out they immediately got married. She recalled fondly: "We were good friends first. He made me laugh a lot and he still does. I appreciate his kind of humor, so it's been good."

When asked about how to keep the spark alive, she turned thoughtful, reviewing more than half a century of life together:

It wasn't always easy. In fact, it started out kind of bumpy, because our families didn't get along. Later, there were times when
financially we had major issues, but that also brought us closer
together because we worked together. There were times when we
locked horns about it, but we always talked about everything,
always made sure we faced whatever the problem was. We never
ran away from our problems.

And the spark? She went on:

For me, it's been an absolutely exhilarating trip through life,
sharing it with somebody else. And that sharing has been the
essence of who we are and what we do. We just plain old have a
great time. And that is really important when life is full of all
the twists and turns—the broken backs and the sick sisters and
the mothers who die and all the traumas and battles that come
with raising kids.

But at the end of the day there's a great sense that this is the
best hug I could have and the most wonderful kiss there is, and
let's have some fun, and you wanna go play golf? And we have
so much opportunity that to not treat it as a gift is really a
shame. Marriage is a wonderful trip if you can find a great
friend to have it with.

In this chapter, you will encounter more examples of experts who
made this difficult but ultimately wonderful trip. Fortunately, real
life is often better than the grim fictional portrayals of washed-out
marriages. The elders who succeeded in sustaining vital and passionate relationships are living proof that it can be done. They offer five
lessons for keeping the spark alive, as well as once again providing
five "trade secrets" for making things interesting over many decades.

LESSON ONE
Think Small (and Positive)

I love gift-giving holidays and birthdays. I may be one of the few people over the age of fifty who eagerly looks forward to my birthday—
I'm stuck on the idea that it's my special day (it still feels to me like I
should bring in a plate of cupcakes when it rolls around). And I will
admit that I'm a lover of birthday presents. But as I studied the experts' advice for how to keep the spark alive in a relationship, I
learned something new and different about the idea of a gift.

Think about it for a minute. As your birthday approaches, you
drop hints about what you would like. Assuming you have a sensitive
partner, you wind up with that new laptop, bracelet, or golf club—
and possibly a nice dinner. But did that experience help you keep the
spark alive? My guess is that, overall, the effect was neutral, because
we expect this kind of treatment. It would have a very negative effect
if we did *not* receive a birthday gift, but getting one simply fulfills our
expectations.

But what about these scenarios?

You walk downstairs one spring morning and on the table are
freshly baked blueberry muffins and a vase of daffodils from the
garden.

You're supposed to pick up the kids after work, but your husband
e-mails you saying he knows you've got a busy day so he'll get them
instead.

You mention your interest in going to a concert you have read
about—and your wife surprises you that weekend with a pair of tickets.

The dog is scratching at your bedroom door at six a.m. on a cold, rainy morning. It's your turn to walk him, but your partner quietly gets up and lets you sleep in.

According to the elders, gifts are expected on the official occasions and probably necessary. But what keeps the spark alive is the unexpected kind gesture. In fact, there is nothing more effective in keeping a relationship warm, supportive, and fun than *making a habit of doing small, positive things.*

The idea behind this lesson first hit me a number of years ago when I began my search for the life wisdom of the oldest Americans. Antoinette Watkins, eighty-one, told me about her marriage, which was troubled in the early years. Through hard work, talking, and counseling, she and her husband of fifty-five years attained a warm and loving relationship. When I asked her what she believed was the most important change she made, she thought for a few moments and said:

> There is one practical piece of advice I have given to my children. This is just one little jewel that I passed along to them. And that's when you wake up in the morning, think, "What can I do to make his or her day just a little happier?" The idea is you need to turn toward each other and focus on the other person, even just for that five minutes when you first wake up. It's going to make a big difference in your relationship.

The elders strongly endorse the power of small, frequent, positive actions in keeping the relationship spark alive. We should focus less on big-ticket items when we think of giving our mate something (often spending more than we can afford for items that may be quickly forgotten). Concentrate instead on giving small "gifts" throughout the week or the day. The buildup of these positive gestures can have a transformative impact on a marriage.

Darren Freeman discovered that the key to happiness in his marriage is "being loving and caring and doing things for the other person." But he immediately added:

> In my case it is being spontaneous. Going on trips by saying, "We are going to go out on a certain night." Not tell them where you are going, and then you take them out to a special place for dinner. Not necessarily overloading them with gifts during Christmastime and so forth, but just throughout the years giving them little things. Like if I notice that she has shown interest in something while we were shopping, then going and buying that and bringing it home and saying, "Here, I got you something special today!"

He feels that men in particular need to develop this habit of doing small, positive things:

> Do something special—not just sitting there drinking beer and watching the television all the time, but sitting there listening to music on a quiet evening, spending downtime together, having a glass of wine, or having a candlelight dinner at night. Things like that pretty much maintain that spark. And hugging and kissing and saying how beautiful she is today, or "What a lovely outfit you have on," or "You have such good taste in your clothing." Being complimentary and not being negative about things—that's the key to it all.

How can you make the strategy of doing small, positive actions work for you? The experts suggest three types of gestures that, when done frequently, have a major impact on the relationship: surprises, chores, and compliments.

Surprise Your Partner

We just heard Darren highlight an important feature of small, positive gestures: The effect of these acts of consideration are enhanced when they are unexpected. Jeanne Beauchamp, seventy-two, and Rachel Strauss, seventy-four, talked about the element of surprise in their long relationship. Jeanne told me, "Well, I think it's really important to do little things that are a surprise. Whether it's giving your partner a card or going out to celebrate a special event like a promotion or a special anniversary."

Rachel added: "Or going away for the weekend!"

Jeanne agreed:

> We might go up to an inn for an overnight, just to see what it's like up there. Just little getaways we would do. And little surprises. Like I buy you flowers. Doing things spontaneously, like you know you're planning to have dinner at home, and it's almost four and instead you say, "Let's go out for dinner. Let's go somewhere special."

Earlier in this book, I mentioned couples who are like a ray of sunshine—you just want to bask in their warmth. Mitchell, eighty-seven, and Emma Haynes, ninety-one, are one such pair. Their fifty-eight years of marriage have been happy ones—and the spark has never died—in large part because they have both injected spontaneous, positive moments into the relationship. Even though Emma now spends part of her time in a wheelchair and Mitchell is recovering from a stroke, the vibrant energy in the relationship shines through. When asked about how they keep things new and fresh, here's what they told me:

Mitchell: Well, you pull different things out of your hat that she doesn't expect and that'll help. You know, I'll say out of the blue, "I'll buy you dinner." And that is great.

Emma: Yeah, and you did other things, like this works great with me: bringing me flowers. That always worked. Or when he would do things . . .

Mitchell: Unexpected things . . .

Emma: Yeah!

Mitchell: Things that you know she likes. You know, you don't wait for Valentine's Day to buy her candy.

Emma: No!

Mitchell: And you do it on your own and you make it spontaneous. One time I was so spontaneous you started to cry. I bought flowers one day and she lost it.

Emma: No, I couldn't imagine why he was giving me flowers.

Mitchell: Bless her soul.

Emma: And I went, "Oh my, that's so sweet." So you have to do little things that are unexpected. And not only flowers; over the years he would unexpectedly buy me a little piece of jewelry. And you can imagine that made me feel good.

Mitchell: And I learned about the expression of affection.

Research in the field of positive psychology underscores the importance of unexpected pleasant events as contributors to daily happiness. Giving your spouse a pleasant surprise also conveys something special: your knowledge of him or her. To successfully surprise someone—even in a small way—demonstrates a deep understanding of his or her likes and dislikes. So it's double the pleasure: There's the enjoyable gift or event and the assurance that your partner knows you intimately.

Do Their Chore

We talked in an earlier chapter about the division of labor in a household. In many relationships, partners have firmly established responsibilities. It might be the separation of the inside/outside of the house domains, a schedule of who prepares dinner, who cares for a pet, who picks up the kids. The experts say that one of the most effective small, positive actions is spontaneously taking over for your mate (especially if it's an odious chore).

Nina Hogan and her husband both worked throughout their marriage. One of the best gifts they gave each other was stepping in and helping out:

> In your marriage, he looks out for you and you look out for him, you know? And you make sure that you do things for him and he does things for you. Say if he has a day off and you have to work that day, and you come home and he's cooked something—that just makes you feel so good, you know? And you have to do the same for him. Like cleaning out the garage or making sure the garbage is taken out. This guy is working—if you have a day off, just clean out the garage, even if it's "his" chore! The guy is just so grateful, you know, that you've done those kinds of things.

Tracey James, sixty-eight, contrasted this approach to giving big gifts—and told me that freely offered chore assistance wins hands down:

> Frequent smaller acts of kindness greatly trump large rare acts of kindness. Taking out the dog when it's raining, going to the dry cleaner because I didn't get there and not being angry about

it—that really trumps a dozen roses. If you give me a dozen roses on Valentine's Day, that's one day out of the whole year. What am I supposed to think about in August when I'm not thinking about that? But if you have carried up the laundry or made the beds or emptied the dishwasher and I go to the dishwasher and you've done that, I can see that right away, and I'm grateful and that's part of my grateful day. That makes a big difference to me.

Because chores can be so contentious in many households, taking over someone else's tasks because they are busy, tired, or need something to cheer them up is "money in the bank" for positive feelings in the relationship. And it costs nothing at all!

Give Compliments

Showing admiration and appreciation for your partner represents another small but very positive action in a marriage. This point was often brought up in a sad context: The failure to give and receive positive feedback and compliments was one of the most common regrets of the elders. Janice Jenkins, eighty-three, told me:

Well, we of course are quite old now, and when we were young it was common for people not to be demonstrative. So neither I nor my husband were very much into showing our feelings or our emotions much. That is one thing that I would do differently. I would try to be more affectionate and then I think he would have eventually learned how to be also. I knew that he cared about me and everything, but it was just the small little things that weren't there, just through everyday life. I really missed that. I could have done something about it, but I did not really realize that at the time. And as the years went by it was just a pattern that never changed.

For those elders who made a habit of complimenting their spouses, the payoff was a warm atmosphere of mutual appreciation. The men I interviewed believed that this mind-set was easier for women than it was for them, and they acknowledged that it takes work. Richard Anderson, sixty-nine, summed up the view of many male experts:

> Let each other know that you care, like write a surprise love note or something. You know women and men get married and a lot of times one or the other takes the other one for granted; yes they love them, but they go about their business. They don't show that they care and that they love the person. Women need to be shown or told that they are loved; men don't tend to need that as much as women do. You know, say, "Hey, sexy!" or "Hey, you know why I married you," and that kind of thing.

What does a life of sincere compliments mean? I got used to tearing up now and then when I heard a particularly poignant marriage lesson from one of the experts. But one story was especially moving and stayed in my mind for days after our interview. Clara Osborne loved her husband and loved everything about being married. Now age ninety, she is still adjusting from the death of her beloved Arthur three years ago. How are compliments remembered? Like this:

> Here's what I want to tell you about compliments. Some friends and I just went to see a movie called *Quartet*. It was a nice movie. Maggie Smith was in it, and so that was wonderful.
> But the one scene that I really cried over was where Maggie

Smith had gotten dressed in a beautiful gown and her ex-husband was standing there. He said, "You know what, my dear, you look so beautiful tonight!" And she said, "You look so handsome!" And that was exactly what Arthur and I said to one another every time we were ready to go out. He told me I was lovely, and I told him how handsome he looked. I was with two of my friends who had the same memories about their husbands, and they were sobbing just like I was.

That's the feeling a lifetime of little compliments, surprises, and favors brings you. Sometimes you have the urge to stop analyzing and just *do* something to improve your relationship—well, here it is. Try upping the number of small, positive things you do for your partner. According to the experts, it can create a cascade of positive interactions that will improve and enliven your marriage.

LESSON TWO

Become Friends

You meet someone and the spark ignites. What we usually mean by "spark" is a powerful physical sensation. (The elders aren't afraid to call it lust.) That feeling is famous for coloring our thoughts and restraining our reason—and it's the way most relationships start. But when it comes to the elusive issue of keeping the spark alive, I discovered what seemed to be a contradiction in the experts' advice. Eventually I came to call it the paradox of physical attraction.

Is physical attraction necessary at the start of a relationship? You bet it is. The elders affirm that attraction was essential for their relationships to move beyond an initial meeting or two. Drop your ageist stereotypes: People in their nineties are as likely as those in their twenties to aver that a physical pull puts in motion the events that ultimately lead to marriage.

Gladys Hunt is a witty and wise ninety-two-year-old. She was married to her husband for sixty-four years and is now adjusting to widowhood. Her marriage was a wonderful one, she told me. "My relationship was such a close companionship. My husband, Edward, was so bright and so supportive of me that I grew tremendously through this marriage." Gladys and Edward spent a lifetime discussing politics, enjoying involvement in the arts, and sharing their varied intellectual interests.

But when it came to an initial commitment to a relationship, Gladys surprised me with her frankness. When asked what drew them together, she pointed to physical attraction first and foremost.

Their physical attributes are important. I was twenty when we met and looks were very important to me. And he was very good-looking. I don't care what anybody says—the physical aspect cannot be avoided. It is nature's way of bringing people together. And that's important. I honestly didn't want to sit across the breakfast table from someone I didn't find physically appealing.

A couple of decades younger, Preston Barker, seventy-one, agrees with Gladys. The importance of physical attraction is simply "a given."

Obviously you've got to be attracted to each other, but that's a given, you know? If you're not attracted to each other, how does it even get off the ground? Early in our relationship, physical and mental emotions were high. We were excited that we found each other. I married a very attractive woman. I didn't think I was as attractive as she was, but she picked me.

Okay, so why do I say there's a paradox in physical attraction? Because every one of the experts who validated the importance of physical attraction eventually provided a qualification: Physical and sexual attraction are not enough to keep a relationship going over the long term. No sooner had an elder endorsed the need for some kind of passion than he or she added a cautionary statement: Once the relationship is established, *there has to be something more*. People change, physical appearance changes, and other satisfying dimensions must emerge—things like companionship and shared interests—or the spark will go out.

What they are talking about is friendship. Because in the experts' view, if you want to be married for a lifetime, friendship must become as much a part of your relationship as romantic love. And this is difficult to see in the early stages of a relationship. No one put it as well as Lydia Wade, seventy-three, who counted her husband as her best friend. When asked for her most important marriage lesson, she didn't hesitate:

> Be friends, like each other. I think it's hard when you're young and hot on one another to back off and say, "Do I like what is behind these hands and these body parts?" But that is the piece that doesn't wear out, that grows and deepens. The sexual aspect deepens, too, in its own way, but it becomes less important and the friendship becomes more important as the years go by. It will be challenged by kids and hardships and losses of parents and changing interests and patterns, but an abiding friendship is at the base of a solid marriage. I think you really have to like each other and you have to like being with each other. The friendship needs to be there.

But friendship and romance may seem like polar opposites. We see our friends as having different functions from our lovers—in one case there is passion and sex, and in the other there is the ability to have fun, hang out, relax, and be yourself. Popular culture also makes that distinction. For example, the iconic film *When Harry Met Sally* is devoted to the question of whether men and women can be friends, and how romance fits in that picture. It's summed up in Harry's classic line: "What I'm saying is—and this is not a come-on in any way, shape, or form—is that men and women can't be friends because the sex part always gets in the way."

The elders are unequivocal: For a long and happy marriage, the precise opposite is true. You and your partner must make a transition into companionable friendship or the relationship is unlikely to last. It's not that romance and passion die—many of the elders (as we will see later in this chapter) still value sexual activity very highly. But whether it's after one year or ten, you have to learn how to become friends—and preferably best friends.

What do the elders mean by having your spouse be your friend? You have to *like* your partner as well as love him or her. From the experts' responses on this issue, I learned that there are two components of friendship that greatly enhance a marriage. It's never too early to start putting these two behaviors into practice—and to become best friends.

Friends Know How to Have Fun

Remember the "middle-aged blur"? From hundreds of interviews, I learned that there is one enormous risk during that time period: forgetting to have fun. You probably had fun when you were dating; in fact, that's probably what you focused on. After you got married and had kids, sometimes you still had fun—but more often on those occasions when you went out with your friends and not with your spouse. It's extraordinary how grim day-to-day life in marriage can become, unless the couple sometimes focuses on having fun—just the way friends do.

I found no better example of this attitude than Winifred Austin, sixty-seven, who has managed to have fun with her husband for over four decades.

> When I'm away from my husband, and I travel a great deal, I miss him dearly. And when I'm with him, we never can have enough time together and we truly feel like we're nineteen and we're off to have another adventure. There was one day we went bike riding and then drove two hours to an outdoor concert, listened to Beethoven, and managed to drive home all on a Sunday. I said, "We're out of our minds!" He said, "Yeah, I know.

Isn't it fun?" And so, if you have a hell of a good time together and laugh a lot, those are really good feelings. If you overthink everything, you'll probably have a hard time of it. Have as much fun as you can, and don't think about it too much. That's my two cents based on forty-four years of marriage.

A key part of having fun is being a good companion. You need to ask yourself, Am I good company to my spouse? If we are doing an activity together, am I crabby or stressed—or am I making the effort to be a friend? After so much hard work together, the experts remind us that it can take a shift in perspective to become good companions again.

Faye Garner, sixty-nine, believes that it is remarkable how many couples simply forget to have fun. If you want to keep the spark alive, that is a huge mistake.

Having activities, interests, things you enjoy together, whether it's going to a movie or whatever, just having shared fun and adventures over the years is the main thing. And don't be too hung up on duties. An older man once told me that his wife had died and he was regretting all the time she spent cleaning. Instead of going out and doing things, she had spent her time cleaning. Putting things off until later is a mistake, especially having fun. Don't delay something you want to do because you need to be working in the yard, or skip having fun because something needs cleaning up, or it's not quite looking right, and what will the neighbors think? Letting rules and chores get in the way of having fun in your marriage is something a person will regret.

Sometimes the advice from the experts sounds like hard work. That's why I love this one: Give yourselves permission to stop worrying about getting things done, and make sure you have fun! Friends don't bog down in the mire of daily life; they think of enjoyable things to do, and they do them. That's what friendship in marriage means.

Friends Are Open to One Another's Interests

The second key to building friendship within a marriage can be summed up as "if you can't beat 'em, join 'em." Among unhappy couples and divorced elders, resentment of a spouse's independent interests shone through. The partner's passion for an activity was seen as a threat to the relationship. For example, in one couple the wife became a devotee of the martial art aikido. She went off to workshops, bought books and manuals, and planned to undergo training to become a teacher of aikido. Her husband sat at home becoming increasingly angry and hostile while she pursued this interest.

The long and happily married experts used a different approach: *Join in.* Ask yourself the question: What's more important—how you spend your leisure time or your marriage? If it's the latter (and they hope it is), then at least try—and if possible adopt—your partner's interest. It's better than sitting at home and stewing angrily.

You may recall my stories about the "tough old guys" in an earlier chapter. Well, Ernie Grogan fits the description. Now eighty-eight years old, Ernie grew up in a rough Detroit neighborhood. He had to prove himself over and over: "We had gangs at that time. We had a lot of fights against different neighborhoods. You think you know it all when you're a teenager; nobody can tell you anything."

Ernie escaped the gang world through sports. "I signed a contract to play professional baseball at age seventeen, and when that happened I was done with that life. I was away from the gangs, and that made me real happy." He traveled the country in the minor leagues for three years, then joined the army and fought in the Korean War. Upon discharge, he found good but hard work in a factory. This rough-and-tumble life made marriage initially a challenge for him. But with effort, it's become the centerpiece of his life.

> We've been married fifty-six years coming this July. Marriage is a hell of a good thing, the best thing I ever had. My wife's treated me good and if I didn't have her, I don't know where the hell I would be. We've seen some tough times and some good times. I mean we lost a child; she almost lost her life at one point. But through it all, we've been very happy, not rich, but very happy.

When asked why it's worked so well, he uttered two words I never thought I'd hear from a guy like Ernie: "opera" and "ballet." But he believed that a loving marriage meant learning to enjoy his wife's interests. He shook his head in amazement when he said:

> I went to operas. *Operas!* I didn't like operas, but my wife went to baseball games and she didn't like baseball, so we just split it up together. I learned to like things that she liked, and she learned to like things that I liked. I didn't want to go to the opera; it's a sissy thing. But I went, and you know what? It wasn't bad. I didn't want to go to the ballet; I thought, it's terrible. I went; I liked it. Baseball games—she went, didn't know anything about it, but she had a good time with the crowd. That's what it means to give and take; it lets you be married and really enjoy it.

Annie Roberts, sixty-eight, and Deborah Jordan, sixty-seven, have the kind of relationship where love shines through their conversation. Both have had serious illnesses in recent years that limit their activities, but they maintain a positive outlook on life and savor their time together. Listening to their specific and a bit unusual interests, I wondered how they created a friendship in their relationship. The answer was a tolerant, amused attitude toward their partner's passion—even if they did not entirely share it.

Annie told me:

One thing I have to tell you is about interests. Do you like country music? I don't know where this came from—I grew up next to Yankee Stadium!—but I adore country music. She lets me put classic country on and she lets me listen to it.

Deborah laughed, and said, "And I don't particularly like it."

Annie responded: "But she never says, 'Could you just get that music off?' Sometimes she'll say, 'Could I put classic rock and roll on?' And I go, 'Go ahead. Put it on,' because I know there's a limit." Deborah explained her friendly tolerance: "She loves it so much that it would be mean. You know, she lives and breathes it. In fact, she reads books on it and everything. So what are you going to do?"

Then Deborah revealed her passionate interest, which made me sit up in my chair: "I love aliens. I love to talk about aliens and parapsychology and science fiction. Annie listens to my rhetoric, too, so it goes both ways."

Annie jumped in:

That's right, she loves science fiction, which wasn't my thing. But I've learned to like some science fiction. And if I hadn't met Deborah, I never would have watched a science fiction movie. I had no use for them. But through Deborah watching them and enjoying them, I learned—it's not so bad. Hey, *The Day the Earth Stood Still* is a masterpiece!

You now have the keys to the experts' idea of marriage as friendship. First, you focus on fun in the relationship. Second, even if it's with a laugh or the occasional raised eyebrow, try embracing a partner's interests rather than resenting them. This is what we do with friends. And it works in marriage, too.

LESSON THREE
Sexuality—the Spark Changes

In this lesson, I want to begin by sharing a revelation with you. It took me months of pondering my interview data from hundreds of long-married elders, but I finally got it. It's a question I know is on your mind (especially given that you are reading this book). But it's one that everyone is afraid to ask—indeed, we don't know anyone we *can* ask about it.

Yes, it's about sex. I could hear the question from my discussions with younger people—even if they didn't come out and say it:

"How can sex possibly stay interesting for a lifetime?"

I have good news for you. I'm going to allay your worst fears and help you relax about the idea of sex in the later years of marriage. I will tell you the spoiler right now. The message from our elders is: Don't waste your time worrying about sex in later life, *because it's pretty good*. But first, here's the revelation. Ready?

The reason you are worried about this issue is because sex between people a lot older than you always seems kind of gross. I don't know if this characteristic is bred into us through evolution, if it is the product of ageist stereotypes, or what. But if you think about it, we have a lot of trouble imagining people a lot older than we are having sex. I will now prove this fact to you.

Imagine yourself at age eight. You get out of bed and sneak downstairs to get a snack. Your eighteen-year-old babysitter and her boyfriend (where did he come from?) are engrossed in making out on the couch. And what did you say to yourself?

Yuck.

The eighteen-year-old babysitter goes home that evening a little earlier than expected, and her fifty-year-old parents are making out on the couch. What does she say to herself?

Yuck.

And that weekend, the fifty-year-olds watch a movie that involves two eighty-year-olds making out on the couch. What does that couple say?

Yes, you guessed it: *Yuck.*

The problem I discovered with younger people thinking about sex in later life is that they envision themselves now, at their age, somehow with an eighty-year-old. But the revelation is this: *It's just fine when you have grown old together.* You've learned what your partner is like (and likes), you are comfortable with each other—and you're older, too. The beauty of staying married for a long time is that you enjoy each other, and giving each other pleasure is fun. And there is absolutely nothing yucky about it.

Alfredo Doyle, seventy-seven, captured this phenomenon succinctly. He pointed out that when you are aging together, a lot of things just seem pretty much the same:

> Somehow as you get older you kind of get blind to the infirmities that affect the other party. And you always see them the way they were. You don't see aging. It's a wonderful thing. I don't know if the brain is wired for that, but that's the way it is. You just need to have a spark to begin with. And whatever it is you're doing, just keep doing it. We're in our midseventies, and we still have a fine sexual relationship; it's wonderful. You make do with what you've got, basically.

And the experts assure you that you are likely to feel the same way.

I have some credibility on this issue, because I don't know anyone who over the past few years has talked to as many very old people about sex as I have. At first it was awkward, but after the first two or three elders eagerly embraced the topic, I was no longer embarrassed. It's something they have thought about a lot and still think about. And, of course, they have some lessons for you about it.

No, not *those* kinds of lessons. We're not going to go into specific techniques and tricks to keep this particular kind of spark alive (although a few of them did venture into that area in our interviews). And I am not going to offer advice on the physiological changes that affect sexuality and how to address them medically. A physician is the best source of information on that topic. Instead, we'll look at the experts' general advice about sexuality in a long marriage that involves respect, communication, and adaptation to change.

First, let's be clear: Many elders continue to have sex, and most believe that it is important to keep up a sexual relationship. Although younger people often hold a negative image of the "sexless older years," research shows that in marriages (or long-term committed relationships), rates of sexual activity are actually quite high. For married people whose health does not interfere with intimacy, the vast majority of people age sixty-five and over are sexually active.

And that's what the elders will tell you. Diane Harrison speaks for many of the experts:

> I think sex is very important because it's kind of the glue that keeps the spark alive in a marriage. The one special expression that a married couple has is through sex—sexual intercourse—through keeping your bond just very close and very tight. It's that expression that makes your spouse know that they're loved and well cared for and you put all the other things with it.

To be sure, there are elders—just as there are people at any age—who are sexually incompatible or for whom their sex life is contentious or unfulfilling. In some cases, physical illness leads to lack of sexual interest or ability, causing distress for one or both partners (and again, such maladies can occur at any age). But the majority of the experts in long marriages found that sexuality can remain interesting and fulfilling into the ninth and tenth decades of life. The experts believe that young people are just plain mistaken when they worry about the "sexless older years."

As Rachel McCormick, eighty-six, told me:

> If you're really physically and sexually attracted to somebody and your head is working right, then you should be able to feel that all the way until the end of your life. And what fun that is! I don't know whether young people hear that kind of thing. They think, you know, when you get to have gray hair that the sex just removes itself from your life, but that's not true. Not at all.

So for many couples, sexual activity doesn't stop. But there's more good news: As you grow older, the idea of sex expands. It grows to include—and even to emphasize—a much wider range of loving and supportive behaviors. The experts used the term "intimacy," which they believe goes beyond sexual intercourse itself. In their view, sex can continue to be a great experience. Over the course of decades, couples also come to greater appreciation of physical and emotional intimacy as the source of the enduring spark.

I learned that when sex takes on this broader definition, for most elders in long-term relationships the spark never dies. This was the insight of Michael Bowers, seventy-seven:

> Intimacy should always be there. In the early days, the romantic element of marriage takes over, but I don't think intimacy ever loses its luster, its interest. In fact, even as you grow older, there's no lack of intimacy. It may be simply a hug or something, but I

don't think that age by itself should mean, "Oh, we're too old for that." You're never too old for anything. If it gives you enjoyment, why not? If you feel comfortable, go for it.

Throughout my interviews, the experts showed a sense of relaxation about sex. Many described the deep joy of emotional and physical intimacy with a partner of many years, adding that having sex itself was additional spice in the stew—or a tasty side dish, as Gertrude Bennett put it:

> How important is sex? Well, when I was young, I thought it was ninety percent! But at seventy-one, it's a very lovely side dish. And I do think it's important—yes, I do. At our age, it's not as much the hot romance kind of thing as it is for young people. But there's a certain wonderful friendship that exists if you have the basic foundation for it; if you've made that, you've got each other. And it's quite nice! Of course this is a woman's viewpoint, but the comfort of touch, a hug, a kiss— those are things that mean I love you.

Or as Beverly Elliot put it: "The great thing at our age is that sex is not about procreation; this is purely about recreation!"

However, I don't want to paint an overly rosy picture for you, because for some older people, physical limitations do change the sexual relationship. But it was precisely these elders who pointed to the continuing fulfillment an intimate relationship provides, even when sex itself changes. Ed Maleski, eighty-eight, told me:

> It is important, but it depends on exactly what you consider important. In some older couples, women lose some of their interest after menopause. That happened in our case. And when

I was in my seventies, I had a prostate cancer operation. So I got my problems there. So we didn't have real sex for quite a while, but we touched each other and we caressed each other. We just didn't feel that that problem drove us apart. In a way, it strengthened our togetherness. So, yes, I think that sexuality is an important part, but it is based in love, in trusting each other and your common ground. And the sex part can be satisfied in different ways than the actual sex act.

Despite such problems, the pleasures of touching, holding, cuddling, kissing—all were emphasized by the oldest experts, even if these elders wouldn't register any longer on a survey of sexual frequency. An active sex life was always very important for Rebecca Gibson, eighty-eight, and her husband. Like many elders, sex and intimacy came to mean much more than intercourse:

> We always had a marvelous sexual relationship that lasted all of our lives. If you are there for your mate and spoil him or her a little bit, that doesn't hurt. You know, like cater to your partner; make him or her feel better. And sexuality remains important for the whole marriage. Even if you can't complete the sexual acts, cuddling and touching are very important. I know there are plenty of people who are older who really don't care about sex anymore, but for whom touching the person is important, cuddling, being with them.

I was surprised to hear that, for many of the elders, intimacy is as satisfying as (or even better than) when they were younger. They tried to convey—sometimes with difficulty—the sublime pleasure of physical intimacy with a partner of fifty or more years. It's one of the best arguments for making the sacrifices needed for a long marriage.

As Roxanne Colon put it:

The romance and the love is there. And sometimes it's better, it's more—I don't know. It has a sweetness to it more than when you're young. Just holding each other and you know, cuddling. It's a beautiful thing. Because as you grow older, you grow older together and it's a different love. It is sweet—I can't put it into words. But it's a different love, you know?

Samantha Jones described the beauty inherent in this transformation:

Sexuality is important, but I think we evolved so that as you get to be an old person, holding hands is an incredibly intimate experience, or holding each other. It doesn't have to be intercourse. It doesn't have to be the kind of passion that explodes when you're young. It becomes a—it's not exactly a gentle or more peaceful relationship, but it's a more comfortable kind of connectedness that is deeply physical and deeply emotional and terribly difficult to live without.

It was by no means only women who described intimacy as being as good or better than when they were younger. Mason Speare, seventy-seven, described his feelings, based on his forty-year marriage, in a way I found deeply moving:

I think what happens is the spark changes. You know, initially there's a lot of physical attraction and that continues. But it changes over time so that the romance or whatever you want to call it becomes actually much more profound. It's less, what's the word—frenetic, maybe. For me anyway it's really wonderful just to be able to sit together reading or watching TV, and I'll just hold her hand or touch her arm or whatever. There's a kind of a quietness there that's quite deep. It's very fulfilling. You feel a peaceful intimacy that's in a way really more meaningful than the frenetic thing.

Like many elders, Mason is concerned with the misconceptions younger people have about intimacy and aging, which are so different from his experience:

In our culture, we are so afraid of aging and accepting the changes that it brings that we try to fight it. Also in this hypersexualized culture one of the ways that we think we're going to stay young is by being sexually active all the time. I'm not saying that sex is not still pleasant and pleasing and something that one wants to do. But maturity means that you understand that's only one piece and that there are other things that are, in a way, actually more satisfying than that. Not allowing that kind of mature transitioning is a problem.

So here's the lesson you must learn, whether you are a twenty-five-year-old pondering marriage or a sixty-year-old wondering about the future. The sexual side of things—barring a troubled history or serious physical problems—is probably going to be good enough to keep you happy, and it may be much better than that.

There are lots of things to worry about in life. But fretting about sexless later years, according to the experts, isn't one of them. Some elders were baffled that this question would so preoccupy younger people. Horace Watson, seventy-eight, shrugged and said: "My thought is that the spark just stays alive, you know? If you really care for your partner, then you don't have to worry." And Ed Maleski shook his head and laughed: "Well, the sex thing is something that a lot of young people are kind of worried about. I've never really understood why so many people are worried about it!"

The experts' message is that we should rid ourselves of the false images our culture and media feed us. A couple needs to develop a deep, caring, and communicative relationship throughout their life together. More than any product, therapy, or medication, this base of loving concern is the best way to keep the spark alive as we grow older.

LESSON FOUR
Give Up Grudges

When is a piece of advice about marriage an empty cliché, and when is it profound—and practical—wisdom? In interviews with hundreds of long-married older people, one prescription for a happy marriage was offered by almost everyone. So before I continue, take a break and go find someone over seventy who's been married a long time. Now say to him or her: "Give me three pieces of advice for having a happy marriage."

I'm waiting . . .

Okay, you probably didn't do it. But if you had, I can almost guarantee what one of the pearls of wisdom would be: *Don't go to bed angry.* By the two-hundredth or so time I heard this statement— often worded in identical terms—I found myself obsessed with what this seemingly all-important advice actually means.

Again and again, that's what people married forty, fifty, sixty, and more years told me: Resolve your differences before you wind up in bed at the end of the day. As I probed the experts in my interviews, I found out that there was in fact a deep meaning born of long experience behind this statement. It's this important lesson for keeping the spark alive:

Don't hold grudges.

For long-married elders, going to bed angry is a warning sign of an even greater danger: holding grudges in a marriage for long periods of time. They told me that there are few things that are more certain to extinguish the spark of marital happiness. Arguments and bad feelings that linger over days are something to be concerned about. Lan Tung put it this way: "One thing I always said, 'Don't carry any argument overnight. Talk it over before you go to bed.' And if it's something that you carry over and over for several days, I think that is a big red flag for your marriage."

Many of the experts learned not to hold grudges. Rick Lamb, seventy-seven, and his wife, Julia, eighty, began their life together keeping fights alive for weeks. Then Julia had a revelation:

> I woke up one day after I hadn't talked to him for a day or two and I said, "Why am I doing this?" I mean it's over; it's done with. I can't change it. He's done or said something that I don't agree with. But that doesn't mean that I can't talk to him or I don't want to talk to him because of what he did. We aren't going to die over the fact that we're disagreeing. It's actually just an obscure event that occurred. And it's over with. Forget it.

Debra Duncan shared advice from her unusual marital experience. Her first marriage of thirty-six years was stable but unhappy. Her husband was a poor communicator who kept resentment smoldering rather than resolving it. When she moved into an assisted living facility several years after his death, the last thing she expected was to fall in love again. But that's what happened, and at eighty-seven, she's in "the happiest marriage I could ever imagine."

Thinking of two very different husbands, she told me that going to bed angry is often part of a larger dysfunctional pattern:

> When you wake up, first of all you may not have had a good night's sleep if you're both angry, because you were tossing and turning. So you're starting out another day on the wrong foot. If it drags on to the next day and goes on to another and another, people find themselves so entrapped they can't get out of it, you know? They feel like they're in a spot where they just can't change

and they've got to stick to the anger. And if the other person has the same feeling? That's the end of that marriage.

So even though you don't agree, you can say, "Well, gee, honey, maybe we can work something out in the morning. Let's have a good night's rest and then talk about what the differences are and see how we can come together in the middle somewhere."

One problem with a grudge is that it lurks in the background, waiting to emerge when provoked. If you are juggling child care, for example, it may be about who gets more free time. If it's about money, you may find yourselves coming back again and again to the question of whether to buy a larger house. Or it might be the age-old "Do we spend the holidays with your family or mine?" If you look at your own relationship, my guess is that there is at least one argument like this that continually resurfaces.

The experts have had long experience of dead-end fights that emerge from grudges but never get resolved. Some conflicts seem to be arguments just for the sake of argument—symptomatic of stress or tiredness. Perhaps we have short relationship memories, but we can often take up these fights as if we had never had them before, investing all of our energy in a battle that's been fought many times before.

Ralph, sixty seven, and Nadine Perkins have reflected often on the dynamics of their forty-two-year marriage, analyzing and working on their marital conflicts. Ralph told me about how they approach arguments and grudges that go on for too long:

This may sound like a flip thing, but it works for us. We came up with it at some point along the way. We call it jokingly "Fight number 17." It's when you have had the same fight over and over, and now all of it comes down to this one. Giving it the name of "Fight number 17" puts it in perspective. It means we've had this one at least sixteen times before. We've decided we don't even bother to have it anymore. We see it's coming and we just shut up and don't even start with it. Because it's not going to get anywhere.

My theory is that in every marriage there is one of those issues, your own "Fight number 17." There's a place at which you're just two very different people and you have to acknowledge that and figure out how not to go there.

Nadine added:

And we finally decided that all of our fights could be distilled down into one fight and the name of this fight was "My stuff is more important than your stuff." But it's the same fight. And we learned how to have that fight and how to really have it and then be done with it and get on with whatever we were doing.

Thus, when the experts exhort us not to go to bed angry, underneath this slogan is an extremely valuable lesson: Most things that couples disagree about aren't worth more than a day's combat. They urge you to feel pressure at the end of the day and let it push you toward a resolution whether you feel ready or not.

As I listened to their advice about letting hurts and conflicts go, I realized that the experts were talking about a profound issue in marriage: forgiveness. The long and happily married couples often made forgiving each other a top lesson. Forgiveness does not happen just once or twice in a long relationship, but it should become a regular practice, because it is impossible to live together for decades and not aggravate, hurt, or upset your spouse.

Based on this fundamental truth, Cyril Hackett, seventy, proposes we become good at two things:

Be quick to apologize and quick to forgive. If you do something wrong, make an apology in a fitting, appropriate way; you don't need to debase yourself. And when your husband or wife makes a mistake and apologizes, be quick to forgive. If you're married for a long time, both of you will make mistakes. We need our partner to be quick to forgive us and not bring it back up again. Don't keep reminding your mate, but just let it be forgotten. Tell them, "Don't worry about it," or something equivalent to that. Let them know, "You're forgiven," and smile and move on to the next thing.

Devi Banerjee, eighty-two, has a rule after fighting with her husband, Bhanu: Be the first one to ask forgiveness.

There are small things that you quarrel about and you fight about and you wind up sleeping on the couch. When you are sleeping on the couch, you lie there thinking that it is the other person's fault. And both of you are thinking it's his fault, her fault, and that he should be doing that, or that she should be doing that. "You didn't pick up the child today." "It was your turn to make dinner." That kind of thing.

My advice is to be the first person to say you were wrong. Let me be the first person to say I'm wrong, and to give a good kiss. Let me be the first person to say I'm sorry. Why should I wait for my partner to say he's sorry? Let me be the first person. And when this happens, often he says sorry before I have time to say it! So that's the attitude we should have.

And the elders aren't alone in their belief that forgiveness can work wonders. Research also suggests that a continual willingness to forgive can help heal marital problems, both large and small.

Delores Neal, who is grateful to wake up each morning next to Dave, her husband of seventy-four years, provided a wonderful image I'd like to leave you with—that of "cleaning out each day" and starting over:

> Remember not to go to bed angry at each other. And that's hard to do when you're young, especially if you've had an argument or something. But remember before you go to bed, to say, "I love you" and you know, the next morning things are a lot brighter. Not to carry things over into the next day. Clean out each day as it comes along. Try to clean each day so when you shut your eyes at night, you've cleaned up everything.

LESSON FIVE
Get Help

When you spend as much time as I have with very old people, you meet couples who cause you to impulsively go "*awww*." I'm sure you have seen them—an older pair who have weathered the storms of life and settled into a love that shines out from them. They smile, they laugh, they tease each other, they hold hands. When you talk to them, they freely tell you that every day together is a gift—like Doug Mason, eighty-five, who exclaimed, "We still stick together and want to be with one another. So it's a real utopia for me; I couldn't be more blessed!" Sounds like one of those sentimental greeting cards, right?

Except that for many of these joyous couples there was a time—months or even years—so miserable that the relationship nearly ended. A surprising number of the experts who made it to the finish line with an intact and fulfilling marriage considered calling it quits. In a few cases, couples who divorced eventually remarried years later, deciding the breakup was a mistake. Typically, the decision to stay was agonizing and required hard work on the relationship. Both members of the couple were usually very glad they stayed together— in fact, the "near miss" strengthened some relationships.

Every elder was posed the following question: "I would like you to imagine that a young couple has come to you and said that they're considering calling it quits. What advice would you have for them?" This question was thought-provoking and they offered a range of suggestions. But their first and unanimous recommendation truly surprised me, considering the source. From the youngest experts in their early sixties to the centenarians, there was one strong piece of advice for what to do if the spark feels like it's dying (or dead): *Get counseling.*

I hardly expected the oldest Americans to endorse marriage counseling for troubled couples. They did not grow up in the midst of our "therapeutic society," where it is normative rather than stigmatized to seek professional help for life's problems. I assumed they would see marital therapy as unnecessary, frivolous, or as a "lot of bunk." The elders surprised me, as again and again I heard "see a counselor" as their top lesson for what to do when you're at the end of your rope. This lesson came not only from those who did seek marriage counseling, but also from many who did not and believe that it would have greatly helped them.

You may be thinking that this advice is obvious. If so, it will surprise you to learn that most couples having marital difficulties wait years before seeking counseling and, astonishingly, that only a small percentage of divorcing couples have received help from a therapist. Overall, research shows that the vast majority of couples do not seek out counseling, even when it would benefit them. Therefore, the elders' message is of the utmost importance:

Do not separate or divorce before you have made a genuine and wholehearted attempt at marriage counseling.

Because statistics show how many couples fail to use this option, my guess is that some of you are right now making that same—and according to the experts, wrong—choice. You may be throwing away a fulfilling, lifelong relationship with that decision. I was convinced by the story of Molly Woods, seventy, whose marriage was very difficult in the early years.

There were times when I wanted to go crying home to Mom and Dad because I was not happy and things were very tough. By the time we were twenty-one we had three children, and we had no money for anything. We had high school educations and my husband worked construction. He got up in the dark and worked and came home in the dark.

Things came to a head in their midtwenties:

> To be very blunt about it there was one point in our marriage when things were not going well and we were extremely unhappy with each other. I had a houseful of kids, plus I was babysitting. My husband was working six days a week. Sunday was the only day he could be home—but he started playing golf on Sunday. Then he would come home and watch football and go to bed and get up and leave the next day again. That was how things were going at the time. It was not just one thing—it was all these little things that were piling one on top of another.

In near desperation, Molly proposed to her husband that they see a marriage counselor—and to her surprise, he agreed. That one decision made all the difference:

> So we decided to see a marriage counselor. She talked with both of us together and talked to us individually, and that's really all it seemed to take. It did not go on forever. We worked out what was going on and we got through it and I think our marriage was stronger after that. We were scared to realize how close we had come to ending our marriage!

With the counselor's help, they learned the communication skills they needed, in a safe environment. When asked about her relationship now, she replied: "I am extremely happy." Both she and her husband have been through health scares that have made them even more appreciative of their relationship. She laughed when she described their level of closeness—remember, this is a couple that came within a hairsbreadth of divorce:

> I can read his mind: He will be reading, and I will get up and say, "When do you want the popcorn?" He looks at me and says, "Pretty soon." And it does not even occur to him that he did not ask for popcorn but I just knew that he wanted it. This is going to embarrass you, but I also know exactly when he wants to have sex. And he is seventy and I am almost there, but we still enjoy it, maybe not as much as when we were first married, but we still do. I know that guy is mine like you won't believe.

She insisted I pass this message on to younger couples in trouble:

> Go talk to a counselor and try to work it out if at all possible. I would tell people to find professional help to help them get them through whatever is going on.

The experts recommend counseling in particular for one of the most devastating problems in marriage: infidelity. Elsewhere in this book, we've talked about danger signs in relationships—behaviors, like violence, that the experts consider deal-breakers. To my surprise, infidelity for many of the elders did not fall into that category. Rather than a zero-tolerance policy for an affair, both men and women suggested that the specific situation and the context in which it occurred were important. A number of couples overcame an act of adultery—but most needed some kind of outside help to do so.

Eveline Meldin, seventy-eight, has been married for forty-nine years to Rick. Learning that he was having an affair broke her heart—and nearly broke the marriage. She told me:

Rick was unfaithful and that was an unhappy time. But it was also a key turning point in our relationship. I had to decide whether I really wanted to stay in the marriage. I found that when I thought about ending my marriage, I couldn't imagine a life without him. But the affair changed the course of our marriage. I thought of him differently. And it affected my self-esteem. It was hard facing friends and relatives, thinking what they were going to say about it and how they were going to think about me as a person.

Eveline and Rick sought counseling to repair their relationship. This experience helped Eveline stop blaming herself. She reported, "I realized that his infidelity says nothing about me as an individual, but it says more about him as an individual, about the choices he made and how immature these choices were." By getting help, both partners gained new insights about themselves and what caused the affair.

It turned my thinking around and that helped me. That changed a lot in our marriage and it made me a better person. And it made him a different person in the marriage because he had to think about things differently. We needed to do our homework. We needed to learn how to make it work. In any marriage or relationship, you just need to constantly work on it. I'm glad we stayed together, but we needed help to do it.

The experts believe that counseling isn't just for overcoming a crisis. For Anna Sherman, seventy-one, it is an important "tune-up" to keep the spark alive, helping create a successful forty-year marriage to her second husband, Isaac. Her first marriage of eight years ended in divorce. She found compatibility in her second marriage, but nevertheless experienced a rough patch. As the relationship progressed, a deadening routine set in, and she and Isaac felt that they were drawing apart. That's when they made the step to go to counseling:

> Well, over the years Isaac and I fell into the trap of becoming like ships passing in the night. You know? Careers, being busy, going through periods of time without really connecting on a deeply personal level. You have to work to avoid that. And we found we couldn't do it by ourselves. We've had to go to a counselor and get some strategies and work on those strategies for a while, which has helped over the years.

They have used counseling several times in their relationship:

> We have done it more than once and it's been very, very helpful. It helps for a while, and then you tend to slip back into your old patterns of doing things, the way you have of dealing with each other, and you have to say, "Okay, I wasn't going to do that anymore." And I would do it again if I live long enough. I probably will, if we should need another tune-up!

I don't think I can make the point more clearly than these two experts, and I assure you that around seven hundred more of them feel just the same way. Whether they have used it, they believe that an "iron law" of marriage is this: *Don't assume the spark has died before you give professional help a serious try.* Even if it doesn't work, they told me, you will have the assurance that you did everything possible.

There's a second part of this "iron law" that is equally important: *If your partner suggests counseling, you must say yes.* In the experts' view, that's part of the deal. All too often in marriages, one partner simply refuses to see a counselor. They claim it won't work, that it's too late, that it's pointless. If that's happening to you, show your partner what the elders have told us in this chapter. For many, it rekindled the spark and led to a lifelong, happy marriage—rather than a divorce. According to the experts, if you got into the marriage in the first place, it's your responsibility to give professional help a try before you get out of it.

LESSON SIX

Five Secrets for Keeping the Spark Alive

I consulted the experts for their "trade secrets" on keeping your marriage fresh, vibrant, and exciting for a lifetime, and once again, they did not disappoint me. Drawing on many decades of experience in and out of marriage, here are five tips for keeping the spark alive.

Tip 1: Look Sharp!

We've heard from the experts that physical appearance is an important element in beginning a relationship. It's also an important way to help keep the spark alive as the years go by. The experts believe we should remain as physically fit as possible. Note that the key phrase here is "as possible." The elders do not want anyone to try to conform to an impossible standard of physical appearance into their seventh decade and beyond (or at any age, for that matter). And take note: Not a single elder of more than seven hundred suggested "antiaging" products or plastic surgery. The few who mentioned these options did so in a highly disparaging way.

But they do endorse the idea of making the most of what you've got when it comes to your physical appearance. Most experts agreed that staying in good shape is a key to maintaining the sexual spark. Kathryn Summers, eighty-nine, noted:

> I think you need to care about yourself and care about how you
> look and so on. If you care about yourself, then you will care

about how you present yourself to your husband, your loved one, and that in itself helps keep the spark alive.

Sherri Grass, eighty-eight, put it even more bluntly:

Don't just settle down and say: "Well I'm married now. He's mine; I don't have to worry about it." Keep yourself the size you should be; don't let yourself get out of shape and all of that. That's not attractive to the other person. We followed that rule, and we have never had any sexual problems.

Interestingly, both men and women tended to be harder on members of their own gender. Like the women we just heard from, Taahir Karim, seventy-seven, took his fellow males to task on this issue:

I have found that men have less consciousness of their personal appearance and its effects on women. I think you have to be aware of the fact that if you keep yourself up—your personal appearance, your personal hygiene, and your personal attractiveness to other females—that will make her hold on tighter. She values you a little more than if you let yourself go and become sloppy. You go to the bathroom and you urinate and everyone in the house hears it, or you expel wind in her presence. If you look like a bum, if you don't buy clothes that fit you—well, you just destroy her image of you.

Lamont Bennett agreed. At seventy-three, Lamont is a handsome and well-dressed man who takes pride in his appearance. The idea that his wife believes he is still attractive to other women, he says, adds spice to the relationship. He chuckled through his answer:

She calls me the gray fox. She says she gets worried when I'm out too much. They don't let you go. I mean, you could be as old as

Methuselah, and she's still thinking about you out there. Hey, but that's all right, that keeps everything cool, you know? I'm thinking: I'm glad you think that way about me—you know, like I still got it going on!

My idealized view of the elders had me expecting that they would focus only on inner beauty and disregard physical appearance, but I was wrong. Their tip isn't complex: To keep the spark as alive as possible, stay in the best shape possible and take reasonable care of your appearance. There's no reason why you, too, can't keep it "going on"!

Tip 2: Hit the Road

In my book *30 Lessons for Living*, I learned that one of the important pieces of advice the oldest Americans have for the young is *travel more*. Many of the elders grew up in small towns or self-contained neighborhoods, and they came to relish the excitement and adventure of travel. Much more than the purchase of material possessions, travel experiences were among the most cherished memories and the highlights of their lives.

This principle also applies to keeping the spark alive. Indeed, one of the most frequent answers to the question of how to keep a marriage exciting was: *Travel more*. For Debra Palmer, seventy-three, it was the single recommendation for keeping the relationship lively:

Travel! Different circumstances change your way of thinking. When you're home, things become placid and routine. You just take everything for granted, but when you go away for a few days, the sparks all come back again. It does make a big difference. You recover the feeling that you're so glad to be together. In our late fifties we were able to go to a different country for a year, and we had a blast. We were two people fumbling around learning a language and just having a grand time. We were constantly doing different things.

And don't think that what's needed is expensive adventure travel. Most of the experts had limited incomes, and they nevertheless used travel to perk up their relationship routine. They camped, they took bus trips, they stayed with friends and relatives to save money. You don't need to raft the Amazon or trek the Himalayas (of course, if you can afford it, more power to you!). Instead, modest trips that take you out of your normal routine are what counts—and are well worth saving money for. According to the experts, when things feel like they are getting stale, hit the road.

Tip 3: Reach Out

Many long-married couples told me that a secret to maintaining the love in their relationship is sharing it with others. They found that engaging together in volunteer service activities greatly enhanced their marriages, providing them not only with shared experiences but also with a common sense of purpose and meaning. They frequently described such service as a natural extension of their affection and commitment—a desire to share with others the joy they find with each other.

My mentors on this issue were Herman Dawson, seventy-nine, and his wife, Annie. This couple is active physically and socially, engaged in travel, adult education, and relationships with a wide network of friends. But what has really kept the spark alive in their relationship is reaching out. Annie told me:

Another thing I would pass along is to get outside of yourself—it can really help you appreciate your partner. With older people, it's very easy to become self-focused; you think about

yourself and your ailments. In marriage it's important to be able
to focus outside yourself, to have compassion for other people,
and be involved in the world and think about how you can help
others. The more self-focused you are, the more you just sort of
dwell on negative things.

Herman agreed:

Those of us who are retired who have more time should get out
there and try and help some other people. You feel good and
realize how fortunate you are.

Annie explained:

For a number of years, Herman and I have tutored in an inner-
city school, teaching children who are behind in their reading.
And it's been a very revealing experience for us. We live in a
suburb, and some people ask how we can go to the city. But
they don't have any idea how other people live in this world and
all the problems that come with poverty, and what poor children go through. So that's a value that we have both shared
that's made our marriage stronger since we've retired. Working
with people that live in poverty and understanding what they
go through—it makes you that much more grateful for all the
family ties you have and material things and a partner that
loves you.

Based on the experts' advice, it's hard to think of an activity that
can bring a couple closer than volunteering. It involves a challenge,
seeing the world in a different way, and the opportunity to feel pro-
ductive and good about yourselves. Doing it together provides a
shared experience that can deepen the relationship, providing you

with new friends and new things to talk about. You may not have thought of community service as a way to keep the spark alive, but it may in fact be one of the best options available.

Tip 4: Embrace Change

Because marriage divides itself into several long periods, it often seems very stable—almost as if nothing is changing in the relationship. My brother David, who is a psychological researcher, has found in his studies that people construct their lives into "chapters"— segments that organize the passage of time in the life course. While we are going through a particular chapter—say, the "child-rearing chapter"—we perceive our marriage as a stable and unchanging entity. But of course it never is.

As I spent countless hours poring over the marriage advice of the oldest Americans, I kept hearing an important phrase: *the inevitability of change*. A marriage is always changing—even if so slowly that we can't observe it. Looking back over the long arc of married life, the experts firmly believe that marriage possesses this fluid quality— and we need to embrace it.

Lora Medina, seventy, told me that seeing marital happiness as an endpoint is an illusion. "The important thing is to acknowledge happiness as a moving goal. That regardless of what you do there's more to be done because you're still alive. It's a relationship that grows and changes and you have to accept that." Other elders focused on the *process* of married life. Bob May said: "I would tell anyone anticipating marriage that marriage is a process. It's not a product. It's a beginning and you don't know the end." Aiming for a permanent state of marital happiness, according to the experts, leads to dissatisfaction. Instead, we need to accept and adapt to change.

For many people this idea—that a marriage is continually changing even if a couple does not perceive it—can be frightening. However, a willingness to change, and to change together, was the hallmark of couples who were successful at keeping the spark alive. Rather than view life transitions, job changes, the arrival and departure of children, or retirement as frightening and unwelcome threats, these experts see them as interesting and exciting, and as opportunities for growth. It's that perspective that helps ensure a marriage will remain vibrant until the end.

The beauty of this perspective—gained through hard-won experience—is that it puts temporary discomfort, stress, unhappiness, and setbacks into proper perspective. Taking the long view, the experts ask you to view marriage as an opportunity for growth—*because change keeps the spark alive*. Rather than being afraid of a partner's new interest or expanding horizons, they tell you to embrace it. Instead of being fearful about life course transitions, such as the departure of your last child or retirement, it's precisely these things that move you as a couple, that shake you up, and that make life exciting. Sometimes, the experts say, you can only ride the wave together—so enjoy the ride!

Tip 5: Go on a Lifetime Date

Every once in a while, an expert would manage to pin down an idea in just a few words, leaving me shaking my head and saying, "Why didn't *I* think of that?" I had an inkling that there was one last tip for keeping the spark alive, but I couldn't quite put my finger on it. Many of the experts emphasized a special kind of attitude toward the relationship. It's not just your actions, I began to realize, but also your general frame of mind. Those elders who developed a worldview about the relationship that emphasized freshness, excitement, and joy managed to get over the gray and listless periods. But how to sum up something that ephemeral?

Then Leigh Murphy, seventy, offered this wonderful tip that can shift your thinking about what marriage should be. When asked her most important lesson for marriage, she told me:

> Each of us had a ten-year marriage prior to this marriage, and we had some experience about what the challenges were. So we made an agreement when we got married. Actually my husband proposed this idea: that we would fashion our relationship as if it were a date. And that we would be on this date and then we would take breaks from the date. Just like when you're dating as a teenager and you go on a date, but then you have to take a break and go home to do your homework. Then, you know, you see each other the next day.
>
> Well, we decided we would have a lifetime date, where we would take breaks for sleep and kids and work or illness, you know? All the things that come along with life. But the context for what we were doing was this date idea. That was really a wonderful way to frame our relationship.
>
> Because you think, oh, I'm on a date! I've got to keep up and look good and plan fun things. So the lesson is to keep the positive emphasized, and not be whipsawed by all the stressful things that happen in a relationship. So we have had a lifetime date and that's worked out really well.

There's no better way to end our exploration of the elders' advice for creating a marriage in which the spark stays alive. Never forget what life was like when you were dating—and keep that spirit for a lifetime.

CHAPTER 5

Thinking Like an Expert About
Love and Marriage

Be prepared to come into this relationship for a lifetime. It's the most important decision you'll make in your life. And don't give up too easily. I would say hang in there when it gets tough. Don't take it too seriously, always keep a sense of humor. You don't want to start feeling sorry for yourself. And don't expect things to happen overnight—they don't. Remember the things you loved about this person when you met and fell in love. Realize that the marriage can grow and become more beautiful, really. And that you can be happier than you ever dreamed of.

—Lucy, 94, married 60 years

I've been writing and speaking about the practical wisdom of older people for nearly a decade. When I give talks on the life lessons of the oldest Americans, it never fails: I get The Question. I've had a lot of practice answering The Question over the years. And that's a good thing, because I bet you've asked it yourself while reading this book. It goes like this:

"Don't people have to live their lives before they can really believe these lessons?"

I've found that many people appreciate the idea of elder wisdom, even though they have little opportunity to ask older people for it. But the question they raise is whether elder wisdom is, well, *for elders*. In my book *30 Lessons for Living*, I argued that by virtue of their vast personal and historical experiences, older persons possess a unique perspective on life. This book was written to answer the question, "What do older people know about having a happy and fulfilling marriage that younger people don't?" And that's why I call them the "experts" in this book—they are experts on living. But can younger people learn from their expertise?

As you might guess, I am absolutely certain they can. It is of course difficult for a twenty- or thirty-year-old to have the same sense of a limited lifetime as a ninety-year-old. And younger people have not experienced signature events like the Great Depression or World War II. But they can learn to "think like an expert" in some key ways. And in so doing, they will enrich their lives.

I have never forgotten the words of Malcolm Campbell, seventy, one of the first individuals I spoke with when I started collecting the life lessons of the wisest Americans ten years ago. He talked about his career spent as a driven workaholic, which contributed to the dissolution of his marriage. Late in life he discovered how to live in the moment, savoring the beauty of daily experience. After a moving description of this later-life transformation, he said wistfully: "I wish I had learned this in my thirties instead of my sixties—it would have given me decades more to enjoy life in this world!"

It is in this spirit that I offer my final chapter. You have traveled with me on a journey to understand what older people—and especially those in relationships spanning decades—can tell us about doing better in love, relationships, and marriage. We've followed the course of a marriage, from finding a partner, to learning how to get along with each other, to dealing with the stressors of the middle years, and winding up with keeping the mysterious spark alive for the duration. Along the way, the elders have offered dozens of insights, ideas, tips, and strategies—perhaps you have given a few of these a try already.

In this chapter, we approach the experts' ideas on marriage from a different angle. Each of the lessons in this chapter focuses on a key word or phrase used by most of the experts in answer to the question, "What are the most important lessons about marriage you would like to pass on to younger people?" Often these answers were so deeply ingrained in the elders' worldview that they seemed self-explanatory. But I persevered, pushing them to explain these core attitudes for a happy marriage. I wanted to pass along to readers their unique way of seeing and understanding the world of love and relationships. In these final lessons for loving, we will explore what it means to "think like an expert" about marriage. I firmly believe this wisdom can help make marriage a more joyous and fulfilling experience.

LESSON ONE
Respect Each Other

While digging into the deep core of elder wisdom about love and marriage, I kept hearing a tune in the background. Hmm, what *is* that, exactly? Ah, yes, there it is—the booming voice of Aretha Franklin, telling us that what you need in your relationship is "a little respect when you get home." Sometimes my opening question about the most important advice for a successful marriage was answered by the single word "respect." I heard it over and over, but I have to admit that initially I wasn't sure what the term meant to the experts or why it was so important.

If you think about it, the idea of respect feels foreign to a love relationship. Growing up, we are told to respect our parents and our teachers. Later, we learn about respect for the laws that govern our society, for property rights, and for religious leaders. There's a formal quality to respect that seems opposed to the bonds of romantic love and emotional intensity that make a marriage. But after hundreds of interviews, I learned that respect is important *precisely* because it provides a necessary check and balance on the passions that boil up in married life.

Perhaps you have noticed one paradox that keeps coming up in the experts' advice on marriage. On the one hand, marriage is the closest adult relationship most people experience. We open up to our spouses, revealing secrets and flaws no one else ever sees. We allow ourselves to become dependent on another person, which inevitably gives him or her power over us. It is precisely these strong bonds of attachment, intimate knowledge, and dependency that provide us with a unique ability to wound our husband or wife. The paradox of marriage is that we can hurt the one we love and do so more effectively than in any other relationship.

And that's why, according to the experts, respect is absolutely necessary to a marriage. Respect elevates our partner to a position of safety, because it involves attitudes that rein in our raw emotions (that can so easily be stirred up in marriage). It balances passion by placing front and center appreciation and admiration for one's partner. When we respect others, we focus on their dignity as a person; we hold them in esteem; we even revere them. The elders tell us that such respect must be present to make a marriage last; when it goes, usually the marriage does, too.

My mentor about respect was Tim Briggs, ninety-four. When young people ask me—sometimes incredulously—whether it is really possible to stay happily married for a long time, I blurt out: "Well, yeah!" I've seen it so many times by now that the sense of astonishment has worn off, and I've come to accept the simple fact that people can live together, grow together, fight together—and be happy for fifty years or more.

But I have to admit that I'm still a bit awestruck by people who are in their eighth decade of marriage. And it's hard not to be impressed by Tim's story, because it's not far from the truth to say that Tim and his wife, Heidi, have known each other for their entire lives. Tim explained: "We were both born in the same hospital in 1920— and in the same room! Our mothers were in the same room. Heidi is one day older than I am. We're both ninety-four years old. That's a little story for you." He added with a laugh: "But of course we didn't get married right away!"

They met again when they were fourteen years old, were married at age twenty-one, and they've been together ever since. Unable to keep the emotion out of his voice, Tim told me: "I've always loved my wife—in fact, I love my wife just as much now as I did when we got married." And how happy is their marriage after all these years? Recall that in the interview people were asked to rate their marital satisfaction using categories ranging from extremely unhappy to extremely happy. Hearing those options, Tim asked: "Couldn't it be even better than 'extremely'?"

The secret to seventy-three years of happy marriage? According to Tim:

> Being married—the number one is love. But absolutely number two is respect. Heidi and I respect each other very, very much and that's why we've lasted so long. Anything she says to me, I agree with ninety-nine percent of the time because she is generally right. Of course being married seventy-three years we've had our little arguments together, but most everything she did, I agreed, because I realized how smart a woman she is.

Respect pervades Tim's view of Heidi. Their marriage was challenged during his military service, but Tim describes his wife's efforts as almost heroic:

> I was in the navy in World War II and Heidi had to take care of herself. And not just herself, because when I went in, we had a little boy who was two years old. She took care of herself and him. She knew she had a job to do and she was very good at it.

Like many couples of their era, Tim worked while Heidi managed the household. But this did not reduce her to second-class status in Tim's eyes. Instead, he profoundly respected her efforts. He stated proudly:

> Well, she ran a beautiful house; she was a wonderful person; she took care of our wonderful kids. And I was never one to say, "I'm the boss of the house and you'll do what I say." You know what

I mean? We had none of that! You treat each other every day just like when you were first married. And our children learned from that. Show your kids how you live. Show them the respect the two of you have together and they'll take it from there.

According to Tim, Heidi, and the rest of the experts, mutual respect is at the core of any successful marriage. But what does it mean, exactly? I learned that respect is partly an attitude (but as we will see shortly, that is only one part). In a marriage, this attitude of respect means allowing your partner to be an individual and not an extension of you. Eula Zimmerman, eighty-eight, summarized this expert opinion beautifully:

> It's important to respect each other. That means valuing the other person's self and contribution to the world. The basic thing is to let the other person be who they are. I've seen people who become very unhappy because the other person doesn't do what they think he or she should do. However, respect means that I value you and your opinions and your beliefs even though I may not agree with you. Respect means freedom, not control: I give you the right to be yourself.

Although valuing individuality is important, there's another important component of a respectful relationship: admiration. The experts suggest that you step back and do an inventory of everything your partner is doing *right* in your relationship. Frances Barton, seventy-two, described the stressful and contentious experience of dealing with her mother-in-law's declining health. One phrase from her husband turned the situation around:

> Well, Ervin's mother is in a nursing home now, but she lived with us for a year and a half before we were to that point. I re-

member the day we took her over to go into the nursing home. Most unexpectedly, when we got back home, my husband just turned to me and said, "Thank you, you did a great job." That meant more to me than anything. So you just have to pull together. Expressing something like that shows you're both pulling in the same direction.

Thus, to demonstrate respect, acknowledge your partner's positive contributions and openly admire them.

As I immersed myself in their views, I learned that respect is much more than an attitude—the elders also see it as *a set of behaviors*. Respect translates into clear actions that you can begin practicing right away. If you want to show respect to your partner, the elders told me, create a mental checklist for three important behaviors. As you are reading, ask yourself, Where do I stand on this "respect checklist"?

Respect Means That You Pay Attention to How You Say Things

The content of what we say, according to the experts, is often less important than the tone of voice in which we say it. It's easy to communicate using an irritable, exasperated, or disparaging tone of voice—and often we are not even aware of doing so. Instead, we need to convey respect. Delia Allen, eighty, told me:

Well, I think sometimes tone of voice is very important. You say what you are thinking, and it comes out like: "Oh, you always do it the wrong way and I don't like it!" Instead, you have to moderate how you say things. Sometimes it takes a little practice to do that. Just how you say something, using at least a neutral tone of voice, and if at all possible a friendly one, really helps.

As we saw in Chapter 2, courtesy and politeness are key ways of demonstrating respect. A significant amount of marital conflict can be avoided by modeling spousal communication on how we interact with other people we respect: a mentor at work, a respected member of the clergy, a beloved teacher. It may sound simple, but the experts tell us that by conveying respect in our tone of voice and our choice of words, we build an excellent foundation for a long marriage.

Respect Means That You Listen— and *Show* You Are Listening

According to the experts, perhaps the most frequent disrespectful behavior committed by spouses is the failure to obviously listen to one's partner. We don't get off the computer, turn off the TV, or put down the smartphone when our spouse approaches us with an issue for discussion. Myrtle Casey, seventy-four, makes the important point that one must not only listen; being respectful means *demonstrating* that you are listening:

> Listen to the person. Listen with your mind, not just with your ear; show them that you are understanding what they are attempting to say. Let the person finish what they are saying and try to understand what the spouse is saying. Listen with your entire self, and not just to say, "I'm listening to you, okay, what else?" Don't be quick to cut the other party off and say what you need to say, or get your point across. Just take the time and let the person finish what they have to say, and show you are listening in a very positive way. And if it really isn't the right time,

politely say, "Dear, I'm running a little late, can we discuss this another time?" something like that. But just don't be rude; be very courteous to each other.

The experts suggest this technique: Imagine you are listening to your boss or that you are in a job interview. In those situations, we use the clearest signals we can muster to show that we are genuinely interested—and we certainly would not check our phone in the midst of the conversation. Demonstrating fully engaged interest is a key, the elders say, to introducing the principle of respect into the conversation.

Respect Means Not Going to Extremes

As an argument escalates, there is often a temptation to "drop the bomb." Our sense of courtesy and decorum goes out the window and the urge to attack sets in. It's precisely in that moment when the elders' advice—don't use language toward your spouse that you wouldn't use with someone you respect—can be immensely helpful.

Leah Stone has been married for fifty-one years. Communication was difficult early in her marriage. In particular, as the women's movement began, her goals started to expand. She wanted to reenter the workforce although her children were young. Her husband was traditional and felt ashamed that other people might believe he wasn't a good enough provider. Leah sought outside help from a counselor to deal with their disturbing arguments. She brought home one important skill that served her well: Stop yourself before you make an unkind or impolite remark.

I have never been afraid to say what I'm thinking, and that has been part of the problem. But I learned to choose my words, because I realized I never wanted to say something that I was going to regret, such as calling names or bringing up some stupid thing from the past. I try to make my point without being nasty or mean or lashing out. I do this especially in the heat of an argument, because you say things and they're never going to get taken back.

The principle of respect means not insulting or belittling the other person. Just one of these behaviors can entirely derail a disagreement that is on its way to resolution—so the experts say: Don't ever engage in them. It's tough to do, but it's necessary. If you combine the three behaviors on this checklist with an acceptance of each other's individuality and admiration, you have gone a long way toward thinking like an expert.

LESSON TWO
Be a Team

What makes being married different from being single? The answer lies in both the joyous quality of marriage and its greatest challenge: merging the lives of two fundamentally separate individuals with their diverging interests, personalities, and life experiences. When starting out in a relationship, many people imagine that bringing two lives together will be as easy as deciding whose apartment to move into and what to do with the extra couch or television. Actually, according to the experts, creating a shared emotional and economic enterprise is one of the most difficult human experiences. As Cheryl Sims succinctly put it: "If you want to stay married you have to learn to compromise. Because you're two totally different individuals trying to live one life."

The challenges are exacerbated by the direction of contemporary Western society. Sociologists have pointed out that American values promote an individualistic way of thinking and behaving, such that individual satisfaction, self-development, and meeting one's own emotional needs are seen as the primary aims of life. Marriage threatens that individualism and asks—in fact, demands—that we overcome it.

Every once in a while a cliché turns out to be correct, and in this case one phrase captures what people both love and sometimes hate about marriage: that "me" must become "we." As Whitney Rhodes, seventy-five, put it:

You have to forget the "me" factor. It's compromise and team effort. You have to say: "*We* have a problem, can *we* talk about it?" Learning to work together and making it a team effort is one of the most important things you can do in marriage. But today it's very difficult, because the "me" factor becomes much more important than the "we" factor. What worked for us—and what I'd recommend to young couples—is working together: having the same goals and values, wanting the same things out of life, and being willing to negotiate if they differ.

How do we accomplish the feat of placing ourselves under the demands of an entity—The Couple—that's bigger than either one of us while maintaining our individuality? The experts offer a guiding concept for how this alchemy can be accomplished: *the team*. They urge you to apply what you have learned from your lifelong experiences in teams—in sports, in work, in the military—to marriage.

Rick Freidson's life was shaped by his service in World War II. Now eighty-seven years old, he remembers as if it were yesterday the gunshot that shattered his leg and his nightmarish experience in a German prisoner of war camp. But he also learned what it means to function as a team, where using your own strengths while cooperating with others was literally a matter of life and death. When it came to his marriage, the idea of the team was responsible for a satisfying relationship lasting over sixty-five years:

> This is a team operation. I came to marriage with a very special perspective, having had that World War II experience. In the army, each person realizes that he's not alone. There's a common goal. And I find that to be the most exciting part of the whole marriage thing. Approach marriage as a shared experience, one where you are on the same team.
>
> It's a whole different approach to problems in life, because you solve them together, not unilaterally. I can't say: "Okay, we're doing this" or "We're doing that." With the team, it's:

"This is what I think—what do you think?" And that's where
we are in our marriage. You don't even realize you've done it,
but you find yourself being able to subjugate your own feelings
for somebody else's.

The experts used sport analogies to convey teamwork in marriage.
Sally Jenks, sixty-four, and Kimberly Carter, sixty-seven, lifelong ath-
letes, applied lessons learned on sports teams to their relationship.
According to Kimberly:

> It's really important that when you have something that has to
> be worked out, view it like the two of you are on the same team.
> Even though your first gut reaction might be I'm right and she's
> wrong, and I'm going to explain to her so she understands why
> she's wrong, you have to move to thinking of it as: "*We* have a
> problem and let's try to solve this problem together." Because,
> when we solve it together, it's going to be good for the team.

Teamwork in marriage can also extend to deciding when to get
help, just as an athlete in trouble turns to a coach. Sally told me:

> Before giving in to your desire to do what you think you want
> to do, you have to think if that's good for the team. If we get to
> a point where we can't communicate and we don't feel like we're
> on the same page, we both feel it's okay to get someone to help
> us. That's not a sign of weakness in a relationship but a sign of
> strength. You say: "We're on a team and we have a problem—
> can you help coach us to make us a better team?"

I learned an important lesson from one elder who failed to show the
team spirit and paid the price. Milo McCrarie, eighty-one, was married
for fifty-three years to Celeste until her death three years ago. Although

he still deeply mourns her, he is consoled by memories of their long and vibrant relationship. The couple's activity was undiminished into their late seventies, as they traveled, ran a business together, and continued to pursue their careers until shortly before Celeste passed away. Milo sums up the success of the marriage in a single word: teamwork.

> You have to adjust to the other person's wishes. You've got to be honest with your spouse; you can't hide anything. That creates a workable marriage. You're not a unilateral person when you make a decision. You have to make joint decisions and that's what we always did. Don't get me wrong—we both had our own beliefs and we could be stubborn. But at the same time, we were never afraid to talk about our opinions and work them out together. I mean, that's what a marriage is. You solve these situations between the two of you as a team.

Milo learned this lesson the hard way. He believes he violated the team spirit once in his marriage, and from that moment on, he vowed he would never do it again. To understand this cautionary tale, you need to know about Milo's passion: He is a devoted skier who still hits the slopes as often as he can in his ninth decade. Unfortunately, this was one activity that his wife never shared. He became emotional as he explained why:

> There's only one thing that I ever did that I really regret. We were about forty, and Celeste asked, "Why don't we try skiing?" I said, "Fine." I'd never skied before in my life and so we went to a nearby ski resort with our kids, and we all skied. Anyway, I didn't respect her because she was not as athletic as the boys and I were. We left her on the bunny slope, and after two or three days the boys and I were up at the top of the mountain and she was left alone. So she quit.

I tell everybody, "Don't do what I did. Don't be the macho man and forget about your spouse. Because you've lost a partner on the ski slopes for the rest of your life." But if you take the time to learn together, you're going to have a partner forever. I should have stayed with her, helped her, enjoyed it with her. But instead, by going off on my own, the interest was gone. I tell everybody that and a lot of people listen to me. And I truly believe that—that's the way you cooperate with your partner.

Teamwork is never so important as when trouble hits. Indeed, the experts say that it's hard for a marriage to survive stressful events without teamwork. When life gets tough, the team approach means saying—and believing—that there is no such thing as *your* problem; there is only *our* problem. Any difficulty, illness, or setback experienced by one member of the couple is also the other partner's responsibility.

Thinking about this advice, I was reminded of how athletes think about an individual team member's difficulties. For example, if a baseball player is in a slump, his teammates don't say, "It's his problem, let him deal with it." Instead, they support him and help find solutions. I remember reading about the New York Mets star first baseman Ike Davis, who underwent a serious batting slump in 2013. His teammate David Wright put it this way:

> The biggest thing is he knows this clubhouse supports him. This team and these guys in here support him. We have his back. Hopefully, the next thing we're talking about is how hot he's getting and how he's going to carry this offense like he did the second half of last year.

It's in this sense that problems in marriage also require a team approach. Each partner has the other's back and works with him or her to find a solution.

But when problems strike, the team approach can be all too easily abandoned. One member of the couple may resist involving the other, wanting to solve it all on his or her own. In so doing we lose the opportunity to strengthen and deepen our marriages. In my interviews the happiest couples framed their responses as "we," even when the problem occurred to only one member of the couple. When asked about a difficult period in her marriage, Eunice Schneider described how they dealt with her husband Ray's job loss:

> Ray was a barber, and he lost his business. But it didn't just happen to him—it changed us completely. The one thing we did was to look at it as an opportunity. I remember we said when he lost his job: "Let's have faith and believe this door is closing because something better is out there for us. It's devastating right now, but it's going to be better." And it was! He started a whole different career and it turned out to be better. So it really turned out to be an opportunity in disguise for us.

It's not "Ray lost his business" or about what "he tried to do"—it's what *we* did. The problem and the search for solutions were met head-on and solved as a team.

Dennis Myers, seventy, and his wife encountered every parent's worst nightmare—and fought back as a team:

> Our second child developed cancer. She was thirteen years old and we learned that she had a malignant brain tumor. We had to deal with her, and we also had to deal with our relationship and the relationship with our other two children. When you face that kind of a problem you have two choices. You either deal with it as a team and your love becomes deeper and your respect for the other becomes greater. Or you run.
>
> Obviously, this caused stress in our marriage. Fortunately,

our daughter, although she went through many operations, survived. So we have been able to not only overcome the impact of life-threatening disease in our family but we have grown closer as a family. It has drawn us together, and my wife and I have learned a lot about each other.

For Dennis, the team approach turned a tragedy into a powerful experience that melded the couple into a unit. He suggests everyone be prepared to work together when trouble hits, because this is what marriage is all about.

You do it as husband and wife. As parents, that's what you signed up for, you know. That little pledge that you make when you stand in front of the priest, rabbi, or minister—where you say, "For better or for worse, in sickness and in health"—those words should not be taken too lightly. Because in the course of a long-term marriage, something will happen and you have to be able to take the responsibility together.

The more I heard about it, the more I became intrigued by the team concept. I realized that when experts described unhappy marriages, more often than not it was because the spirit of teamwork was overshadowed by the feeling of individuals out for themselves. Alison Myers, seventy-two, has been married for fifty-four years. Although she cares for her husband, the relationship has never been fully satisfying. At this stage of her life, she appreciates the companionship of a mate, but as she put it: "It hasn't been all a bed of roses either."

The core problem in her relationship was the failure to work together as a team. She told me:

He was never on the same page as I was; he never has been. With my husband and me, it was a power play. Who's going to

be the boss? And that's wrong. You can't do that; you have to
work at it together. My husband feels he is supposed to be the
master of the family. But I never wanted him to be the boss and
he didn't want me to be the boss. We really should have gotten
together and been the bosses together. But to this very day, my
husband and I think completely differently. You know, if I'm
driving down the road and I want to turn right, he wants me to
turn left.

After a moment's reflection, she sighed and summed up: "For people
nowadays, I recommend that the two mates do it differently: Work
together as a team because that's the only way a marriage can work."

The experts offer the idea of the team as a powerful metaphor for
married life. Rather than a pair of individuals seeking their own interests and fulfillment, the team implies sharing a goal that requires
a united effort. Few things are worse than a pervasive sense of lone-
liness within a marriage; if both partners need to make it on their
own, the experts ask, why be married? Instead, the marriage itself, its
success and its happiness, becomes a transcendent goal. The team
metaphor is a particularly helpful gift from the elders, because it acknowledges spouses' individuality—two separate people who unite
their unique strengths as a team of lifelong partners.

LESSON THREE
Make Time

What's something older people know that younger people don't? No, I'm not talking about who won the World Series in 1954, or who Lucille Ball or Bob Hope was, or what a "rotary phone" might be. I'm asking what our elders know on a deep level and with a much greater degree of certainty than people in their twenties, thirties, or forties. After spending ten years studying the practical wisdom of the oldest Americans, I've learned they share this one piece of knowledge:

Life is short.

In *30 Lessons for Living*, this point was the most important lesson the elders wished to convey: Even a very long life seems short when you get to the end. Looking back from the later years, all of the experts will tell you that your most important resource is *time*—and if you are not aware of that fact, you risk squandering your own precious lifetime. Money, they say, you can always get more of. Time wasted, on the other hand, is gone forever.

Social scientists have studied the heightened sense of a limited time horizon experienced by people beginning around age seventy. Interestingly, they find that the realization of having a shorter time on Earth doesn't depress people as much as it helps them make better choices about how they spend their remaining days. As we reach life's last decades, we are more likely to focus on people and activities that are truly rewarding and enjoyable, dropping unpleasant associates and unfulfilling responsibilities. We become aware of the irreplaceable value of time.

It should therefore come as no surprise that when the experts think about marriage, they consider decisions about time and how to spend it. For younger married couples, time for each other feels very limited. But from the elders' viewpoint, it's not a question of having time; instead, it's one of *making time*. They argue that the busiest couple can choose to carve out time together—and yes, even in the midst of dual careers and raising children. To think like an expert, you and your partner need to become much more aware of time as a scarce and precious commodity.

In preparation for my interviews, I asked a number of young people about how much time they spent as a couple. I was surprised at what I heard. These thirty-somethings described themselves as spending almost all of their time in work or children's activities (the array of which is stunning). Many reported that they rarely do things on their own (some actually couldn't remember the last time they had gone out by themselves). The elders advise that this pattern is a terrible mistake in a marriage—and one most people regret when they reach later life.

They focused this advice in particular on parents with children still at home, as busy mothers and fathers are often the major victims of the time crunch. And their advice couldn't be clearer: No matter how artificial or contrived it seems, you *must* carve out time to be by yourselves, away from the children. And not only physically away—you must also force yourselves to be *mentally away* from your offspring.

Bryant Walker dealt with this issue successfully in his relationship, but it took a real wake-up call to alert him and his wife to the seriousness of the problem:

> Children consume so much of a parent's attention that before a
> couple realizes it, they have nothing to talk about to each other
> aside from the children. One time my wife and I went out to
> dinner and we sat there at the table and we tried to talk about
> something other than the children and we had nothing to talk

about. That's a bad place to be, and it's very easy to get there, because taking care of your children is regarded as proper parenting. It's easy to ignore the major things that brought you into the marriage in the first place.

Sound familiar? Bryant, like many other experts, sees a single solution to this problem:

The only way I know of to counter this is a concerted effort to make some time for a couple to be alone with each other and do something they both enjoy, even if it's just a Sunday drive, a dinner at a restaurant, going wine-tasting together, something at least every few weeks. But to accomplish this one has to make an effort to plan the event—otherwise something will always get in the way. In other words, it has to be given importance and moved to the top of the list. Marriages definitely need to be actively worked at when you have kids.

If you don't make time, carve it out, cast it in stone (or choose your own metaphor), the experts tell you that it just won't happen. Many elders used a specific phrase for this time you must make together: "date night"—a time to be husband and wife, not just mother and father. Although my wife and I didn't use this term, we did use the idea. Even when we were nearly broke, we scrimped and saved for two hours of a sitter's time for our infant daughter and a trip to a local chain restaurant. A few times we simply walked around a mall. We now recall those "adventures" as more liberating than later long vacations. Once you start doing it, I promise you will never go back.

The important thing is not the content of what you do. Trying to create elaborate and meaningful date nights is probably a recipe for failure. Judy Reeves, eighty-one, and her husband, Greg, eighty-three, made this rule after the birth of their first child:

A lot of our friends learned a very important lesson from us. Every Wednesday night for years, we had a babysitter, so every Wednesday was our dating night. There were times at the beginning that we took our returnable bottles, cashed them in, and with the quarters went to McDonald's for a hamburger. But it was our time. And it was our time away from kids so we could talk, and so we could just be alone, the two of us, communicating. Was that ever important!

The point is to decide on a regular time and stick to it. And remember: Most of the experts had worse finances starting out than you probably do. They followed the date night rule with little or no money. It can be as simple as a short drive or even—in a pinch—staying at home, as Lorena Riley, seventy-two, told me:

The thing that we always clung to: We always made time for ourselves. During the lean years, we lived in Buffalo and we'd go to Niagara Falls, which is twenty minutes away. Or we would do date night right in our own house. I'd get the kids in bed early and we'd have dinner and spend the evening together and I would threaten the kids if they stuck their head out the door— I'm joking! But they were to stay in bed and go to sleep. In other words, we made time together a priority. We always did.

But it's not just parents who fail to spend time with each other. In contemporary society, there are enormous and continual demands on our attention. It sounds like an easy answer to "make time" for each other. But what about during those tough periods in a couple's life, when work and challenging life events cause both partners to be stressed to the limit? Mona Underwood, seventy-seven, experienced such a situation. She and her husband, Mack, went through a "pileup" of stressful events over the course of six months:

There was one point in our marriage when we had quite a lot of bad things happen all at once. My father was dying of cancer; my best friend was dying of cancer; my cousin's daughter was murdered. It was a peak time in Mack's career on top of all that. It was a kind of "system overload" for us.

Mona emphasized that it is in precisely this kind of situation where the need to make time is greatest. One barrier, Mona told me, is that people become too grandiose in their thinking about making time for each other, feeling they have to plan a major event. Instead, you should "think small," creating a short escape from ruminating about your life's difficulties:

> When things seem like a mess, take even a little time together away from housework, away from your profession and earning your living. Take time just to be together, to do something fun— I don't know—go out and have a cup of coffee and talk, go for a walk, bird-watch—do something away from work together for even an hour or two. Maybe light some candles once the kids are in bed and agree not to talk about work and other problems, and snuggle and put your arms around each other. Making time for yourself as a couple—that's really important.

To carve out your time together, be creative. If money for babysitters is a problem, the experts recommend finding a couple with whom you can trade time away from the children. Again, be sure to make this a regularly scheduled event, following the principle that if you have to arrange a time every week, you probably won't. And don't forget about grandparents. Cecilia Fowler suggests that younger couples make as much use of their parents as possible.

> My children brought their children to me to babysit when they were infants up until about ten years old. And I am very close

to them now. So don't spare your grandparents! Most grandparents want a close relationship with their grandchildren, but to do that, you've got to spend time together. Everybody wins. Leave the kids with Grandma and even let them stay overnight. That's a good way to get your date night!

I have one more recommendation from the experts about how to make time for fun, shared activities, and pleasure in your relationship. But let me warn you: This will be a controversial point. I suspect some readers will say, "No way!" Or even, "You're out of your mind!" You may think this advice is old-fashioned. But remember: When you picked up this book, one of your reasons was to have your worldview challenged by people who have lived in a very different way from you. So keep an open mind when I tell you this key piece of advice for creating more time together:

Disconnect from your electronic devices when you are away from work.

According to the experts, staying connected 24/7 to work via your laptop, tablet, or smartphone is a form of insanity. They argue that many people do it simply because the technology is there, not because they have a genuine need to continue to work after they get home (remember—it's your haven). And they are pretty much unanimous about this—including very successful people who worked in high-powered jobs. As Darrin Carter, seventy-seven, asserted, with a conspiratorial air as if we might be overheard: "*We all think that, we older people.*" He explained:

> I see so many people today, they come home after working all day and then they get on the computer and work half the night. Well, gee, that's a tremendous stress on a marriage. So they're really working probably fourteen hours a day rather than eight hours a day, which we didn't have, of course, because we didn't go home with a phone in our pocket. They couldn't even reach

us half the time from work even if they wanted to. Cell phones alone have created tremendous stress on people in their marriage because everyone can be contacted instantaneously.

I know so many people working all day and working half the night. And I think, "Aw, poor people, that's terrible. Do you have to do that?" You talk to the people and they say, "We've got tight deadlines. We've got to get this done." Well, that's a tremendous stress on the family. The worst thing to happen is too much communication. It is really destroying everyone and hurting marriages badly. We all think that, we older people, that this instantaneous communication is going to really hurt marriages.

The experts acknowledge that creating a perfect separation from the electronic connection to work is not possible. We live in an age when technology has made it possible for us to work anytime (all the time) and anywhere. The omnipresence of the laptop, the tablet, and the smartphone creates a demand that we be continually available to everyone—and often at the expense of time spent with our spouse. But even though that's the way things are, *it doesn't make them right, or the right way to live.*

That's precisely why you need to listen to the experts on this particular issue. What seems to you like an age-old reality is actually extremely recent. Even twenty years ago, electronic connections were not so seamless that everyone felt obligated to stay in work mode on evenings and weekends. Don't get me wrong: The experts worked hard—*really* hard. But hearing their experience, you may be convinced it's worth it to maintain a strong barrier between the demands of digital communication and your married life. Experiment with "wireless free" weekends, days, or (if you are truly addicted) an evening or two. Turn off your phone on date night. And stop bringing work to bed. From the standpoint of the experts, when you gaze back from the end of the journey that is marriage, you're not likely to say, "If only I'd spent more time online . . ."

LESSON FOUR
Lighten Up

Once upon a time, my wife and I avoided a monumental fight. We were flying cross-country with our six-month-old daughter. We settled in, the plane took off, and all was well. As I held my daughter in my arms and began to doze off, she kind of, well—exploded. I don't know if it was motion sickness, a stomach problem, or what, but if you are eating at the moment, feel free to put the book down. She engaged in a striking feat for one so young: simultaneous projectile vomiting *and* explosive diarrhea. And to make things worse, I hadn't put her diaper on properly, so it was in no position to do its job.

Everything went all over me. I took the sodden bundle that had become my daughter and literally tossed her at my half asleep wife, bellowing "Ew" and "Yuck," and things like that. I bolted straight to the restroom, where I cleaned myself up. I returned to my seat to find our neighbors looking askance at us and our daughter wrapped in a blanket the flight attendant provided. No sooner did I sit down and encounter my wife's icy stare than I realized we were on the verge of a totally ruined vacation. And then . . .

We both started laughing hysterically. We couldn't stop. The shock, the embarrassment, the smell, the looks of veiled disgust on the faces of nearby passengers—it all just seemed hilarious. They probably thought we were insane, but it became a great, funny story for years after—and the vacation was spectacular. I thought of the experience when I heard many of the experts offer this way of thinking about marriage: *Lighten up.*

An attitude of *lightness*—relaxing, embracing humor, forgiving easily—is the great stress-buster. Sometimes an oppressive heaviness can take over a relationship. For many of the elders whose marriages dissolved, there was often a moment when one partner suddenly took a look around and asked, "How did our relationship become so grim and so serious? Where did the fun go?" In long marriages, simple issues can become highly emotionally charged; a small disagreement is seen as indicative of catastrophic failure or a nagging worry permeates every nook and cranny of the relationship. Nothing is ignored and everything is taken seriously, brooded about, and analyzed.

How can you move toward a lighter and more relaxed relationship? The experts offer three excellent suggestions, drawn from the long view of what's important in married life.

Ask Yourself: Is It Worth It?

I started this book with this assertion: There are some things the oldest people around us know that the rest of us don't. The process of aging brings key insights about living more easily in the world and with other people. The reshaped worldview that comes with time goes by different names, like serenity or detachment. One of the keys to thinking like an expert is this: When looked at from the standpoint of eight or more decades of living, *most of what wives and husbands fight about just isn't worth it.* If you balance the specific disagreement against love for your partner and a desire to maintain a positive atmosphere, it often makes sense to lighten up and let it go.

To be sure, deep-seated value conflicts or terrible betrayal can strike at the heart of a marriage at any age. But the experts note that around 90 percent of our arguments are, to quote the famous *Seinfeld* phrase, "about nothing." They are products of irritation, stress, or differences of opinion where there is in fact no objective "right" or "wrong." Don't wait until you are their age, but instead do one thing right now. Ask yourself before entering into a spousal argument: *Is this really worth it?*

My interviews were filled with the realization that the cause of an argument is rarely worth the resulting energy, disruption, and bad feeling. For example, Joe Thornton, sixty-nine, described his experience:

> I will give you an example. We recently had to fly somewhere, and my wife dropped her wallet down between the seats in the car. We got all the way to the checkpoint and she did not have her ID. We had to get out of line, catch the bus, go to the car in the parking lot. We found the wallet and got back to the airport and we had exactly ten minutes to get on that plane.
>
> Well, that is stressful. You know, I could have been mad and yelled at her and she could have yelled back at me and it could have turned into a major issue—but why? So we miss the airplane, you know, no biggie. You know it costs a few dollars to change, but is that worth it? Killing a marriage? No. You just have to talk, and sometimes she swallows an issue and sometimes I swallow an issue. We just do it together.

For Lowell Lambert, seventy-two, the realization came through the usually peaceful activity of gardening:

> Recently, my wife got to pruning around the house and she pruned some things back that I valued. So I went to her and I told her that I didn't want her to prune anything more until she asks me. That didn't go over real well. She cried and said that I'm too controlling. I was about to get mad, but then I asked myself, "What's more important in my life: those trees or my marriage?" It took about twenty minutes to think this out, and then it became evident that this was not a big deal. I let it drop because our marriage is more important by far.

So take a giant step back before you lower the boom on your spouse. That simple question—*Is it worth it?*—can save you and your spouse many long hours of unnecessary argument. Rather than spiraling off on an often repetitive fight, lighten up on the issue of the moment. One time-honored technique can help you. Ask yourself, "Will winning this argument matter to me when we're eighty?" Usually, according to the experts, the answer is a resounding no.

Humor Helps

Another component of lightening up is the positive use of humor in the relationship. The longest-married couples often described themselves as laughing together throughout the years. As in my opening example, many potentially stressful incidents can be seen as funny, and joking about them has at times almost magical properties to bring an out-of-sync couple back into equilibrium.

Jordan Sherman, married for sixty-six years, told me:

> It's fortunate that we have so many things going for us, and our sense of humor is a big part of it. We laugh at most everything. I try to turn everything into a joke and she really laughs. Humor helps to resolve a conflict. If I think of something that I know is ludicrous for the argument we're in, but it's funny, she'll laugh about it and I find it calms things over.

Delores Neal and her husband, Dave, are a sprightly pair, active and enjoying life into their nineties. They learned early that humor helps to keep the relationship light and fun. She told me:

> We can laugh at each other. We've always been able to laugh, even to this day. He's a joker, which has helped a lot. And so he

does a lot that's funny, and my two sons are jokers, too. So there I had the three of them against me—until I got my daughters-in-law and then I brought in my own forces! Anyhow, he's got a wonderful sense of humor.

Now I want you to imagine this scenario. Here is a couple who are both ninety-three years old, residing in an apartment in an assisted living facility. He's had a heart attack or two, and she's got some trouble with her vision. Both admit to me that, well, they're really old. And what kinds of things are they doing? Stuff like this:

For instance, Dave the other morning cracked me up. I get up before he does, about half an hour or so, and I'll sit in the kitchen with my coffee. So he got up and he knocked on the bedroom door. I couldn't see him because the door was closed, and he knocked. Well, I thought it was somebody at our front door. And I said, "Come in!" And no one came in. So he knocked again. And so I thought, maybe it's somebody that doesn't know us. So I get up and start towards the door, and then he peeks out from the bedroom and yells, "I got you!" That just happened this week!

Lightness and laughter, according to the experts, should last a lifetime.

Do the Unexpected

Some of the heaviness of marriage, the elders say, comes from predictability. Life together falls into a routine, which although sometimes comforting can also become boring. So to keep a relationship interesting over sixty or seventy years, the experts offer another tip:

Every once in a while, do the unexpected. That's what Lindsey Nelson, eighty-six, told me: "I think you're missing something if you don't do something different every now and then. You know, don't make it same old, same old!"

My favorite role model on this issue is Margo Stiles, seventy-six, whose passionate marriage to Pierre is based on the element of surprise. Her sense of adventure began when they were young and had small children at home. Fearing things might get stale, she told me:

> I had a very close neighbor. One day I said to her, "Pierre's getting home about four p.m. Can the kids come to your house?" She said, "Sure!" So the kids went over there. Pierre came home from work and he opened the door and I was lying on the floor, wrapped in Saran wrap with a big bow on me. He had a lot of fun unwrapping the Saran wrap. And we've laughed about that for years.

As they grew older, Margo continued to base her romantic life on one principle:

> Spontaneity! I read once a long time ago that when your husband comes home from work, don't ever let him know what he's going to find on the other side of the door. And that's what I do. Sometimes if Pierre's gone out, when he comes back there'll be some silly thing waiting for him. So he looks forward to that. Ever since the Saran wrap episode, he jokes, "I'll drive around the block just to get excited about what's going to be behind the door."

Cecilia Fowler found the secret when she remarried late in life. She pointed out: "In a marriage, when things get so heavy and there's no joy, there's no excitement, there's no adventure—well, what's left except grayness? You have to find some way to experience joy in your marriage." Then she hesitated, not quite sure whether to go on, and then laughed:

> Well, there's one example, but I'm scared to tell you! One day my husband and I had to go to Boston to pick something up. I thought I would trick him, so I just wore my long raincoat and that was it! He discovered that because the thing fell apart on the way! I'm telling you, we laughed about that forever! It was just a silly thing, but it kept things going. It kept things alive and he would do things like that, too—just silly stuff that a kid might do, you know? And because we were old and probably should've been behaving better, it was far more humorous, you know? It was funny.

This sense of adventurous play characterized the marriages of elders who successfully maintained passionate relationships into the later years. To keep things interesting, they suggest you figure out your own ways to surprise your partner, catching him or her off guard every once in a while. A key to thinking like an expert involves letting go of some of the heavy issues, injecting humor and spontaneity, and letting lightness and freedom into the relationship.

LESSON FIVE
Accept Your Partner as Is

Although I believe that the long and happily married have much to teach us, I'm also keenly aware that some wisdom we accumulate over the life course comes from things that turned out badly. I therefore sought out—in addition to satisfied and joyous couples—elders who have experienced the dark side of relationships. I was fortunate to find one set of mentors who have seen firsthand the mistakes young people make and their consequences. In New York State, there is an inspiring program that supports a very admirable—and often highly stressed—set of elders: grandparents who are raising a grandchild. This group of experts generously shared their wisdom with me, based on their often painful family experiences.

They had one thing in common: a child who made a bad decision about a partner and suffered a disastrous relationship. The situation deteriorated to the extent that the parent (most often the mother) was left with a child for whom she was not able to care. In many cases, her partner abandoned the family. And so the grandparents stepped in, entering into a volatile (and at times even dangerous) situation.

We shared coffee and cookies around a folding table in a local community agency. The group consisted of grandparents ranging from their early sixties to their late eighties, representing the economic and racial diversity of the area. The meeting was an exciting one, filled with insights, laughter, tears, and very lively discussion. But there was one point during the session when things became especially animated. At this point in the transcript of the recording, our poor transcriber wrote in bold capitals: EVERYONE TALKING AT ONCE.

What was it that had group members jumping over one another to affirm the biggest mistake people make in mate selection?

Let me present a bit of the conversation:

> *Interviewer:* How can people avoid having major regrets about choosing a partner?
>
> *Respondent 1:* Don't go into a marriage or any committed relationship thinking you're going to change the other person!
>
> *Respondent 2:* I think that's human nature to want to change somebody. But if I want to change you, what got me to like you in the first place? They're not going to change because the other person wants them to change or makes them change!
>
> *Other respondents at the same time:*
>
> That is so true!
>
> I think it's really true!
>
> Absolutely!

Whew! Well, I got the point. Having had their lives turned upside down by their children's questionable choices, these elders wanted me to put one lesson in big, bold letters:

Give up trying to change your partner.

And they weren't the only ones. Almost all of the elders I interviewed made this cautionary statement: Getting married based on a plan to change your partner is a terrible mistake. This view was equally strong across all groups: African Americans, Hispanics, and whites; same-sex and heterosexual couples; the wealthy and the economically struggling; those in their sixties and the centenarians. Treating your spouse as a do-it-yourself project is a recipe for failure.

However, many people do assume they can change their partner's problem behaviors, annoying traits, choices of friends, and even connections to family. Most of the elders had made that mistake themselves, and they have seen it in their children and grandchildren. Some of them even suggested that perhaps it is a part of "human nature"—a basic belief in the ability to change our partners that flies in the face of objective reality.

Most impressive is how unequivocal the experts are regarding this truth about love and marriage. Here are a few typical responses:

Darren Freeman thinks the idea is frankly ridiculous:

> Changing someone after marriage? It never happens. The guy may not pick up his clothes; he may not put the cap back on the toothpaste; he may burp or fart a lot or have other bad habits. You just have to roll with it and accept the person for who they are. Some women don't like to cook, some women are good cooks, some women are bad cooks; some women are great housekeepers, other women don't care about it; some women always like to look nice and others don't. And all these apply to the man, too. Don't try to force your likes or dislikes on somebody. Because all the things that annoy you—either you can accept them or look for somebody else.

Lan Tung says she and her husband have given this advice often:

> Don't ever try to change people. You got to accept that and not try to change your mate. Nobody is one hundred percent perfect. You have to go in saying, well, if she's a few pounds too heavy, that's okay, then I get more woman to love. Don't say that when I get her, then I can put her on a diet.

Brian Devries, seventy-one, has been in two happy relationships. After his partner of twenty years died, Brian met Graham; they have been together for fifteen years and were married two years ago. Brian learned that a key to relationship success is dropping the expectation that you can change your partner:

What you see is what you get. And even after fifteen or fifty years, it's going to be the same. You might still nag about the same thing, but you didn't change it. Now, you may do something one way, and you realize that your husband doesn't really like it, so you don't do it. But you haven't changed your idea about it—neither has he. Don't be inclined to change somebody. That doesn't work.

What I found remarkable about this lesson is that the experts do not allow for any wiggle room—no one offers a "but on the other hand . . ." Also striking is the unusually strong language in which the experts endorse this advice. Very rarely are they as blunt as, say, Lonnie Curtis, seventy-one, whose other answers were quite moderate:

Keep in mind, you are not going to change the person you marry. If you think you're going to marry someone who is just not quite on the same page you are and you're going to change them, *you're a fool.*

It's hard to misunderstand that one! There was a sense of frustration among the elders about the unwillingness of younger people to accept this fundamental fact about marriage. Quite a few of them had offered this advice to family members and friends, only to have it rejected. One culprit may be our optimistic, do-it-yourself culture, where our houses, our diets, and our bodies become "projects" to be worked on. There also is what some have termed the "triumph of hope over experience." We are so much in love or desperate to settle on a partner that we indulge in the false hope that we can change our mate into someone new.

To help younger people combat faulty and dangerous thinking, following David Letterman, I offer you a list of some mistaken assumptions the experts mentioned: *The Top Ten Things You Tell Your-*

self About Your Partner That Won't Come True. (Male and female pronouns are randomly used—these apply to both genders!)

> She won't drink so much after we've been married for a while.
>
> He just thinks he doesn't want kids, but that will change.
>
> I'll put us on a budget so she can't keep racking up credit card debt.
>
> I'll get him on a diet and to the health club so he'll lose that gut.
>
> She hates my family now, but they'll grow on her.
>
> After we have a kid, he'll feel the pressure to go out and get a good job.
>
> After we have a kid, she'll stop working all the time.
>
> He'll get more communicative and open about his feelings after we've been married a few more years.
>
> It bothers me that she's a slob now, but I'll get used to it.
>
> He hit me that one time because he was under stress—that won't happen again.

The elders want you to resist this kind of thinking and to stop every time you find yourself saying, "I don't like X about John/Jane, but I'll make him/her change." They tell you bluntly that such thinking, in their terms, is "foolish" or "stupid."

By now, you may be objecting: "But married people do in fact change, don't they?" And the experts affirm: "Yes, indeed they do." It's important to be clear that the issue is not whether a person can change in marriage. Rather, the point is that *you* cannot change your partner. Instead, your mate must want to make a change and carry it out independently. You may support your partner in an attempt to make a change, and you may change together (for example, you both go on a diet to reinforce each other). But what's misguided is the idea that you can push your husband or wife to change in the direction *you* have chosen.

Edwina Grant, sixty-six, had this experience with her husband, who was a noncommunicator but slowly opened up a little over the course of their marriage.

> I talk and he doesn't. So when he got mad at me, he got mad at everybody, me and the kids, and he wouldn't talk to anybody, that's his nature. And I guess you can't really make someone change in that respect. That's their personality and that's the way they are.

But Edwina encouraged her husband to talk about how he was feeling. Rather than insisting on a change, she was able to get a conversation going that made him want to change:

> You get to know a person and how they're going to react to things. Once you know that, you talk to them and you try to reason things out. Then they get to thinking, "You know what, maybe I *do* need to do these things we talked about." Later on, they think about it for a while and then they want to make a change.

Tina Hubbard, seventy-seven, articulated this point beautifully. Married for fifty-two years, Tina and her husband, Steve, seventy-eight, have reflected extensively on their marriage, changing course and fine-tuning the relationship as needed. Steve is a minister and has learned much from counseling couples both before and during marriage. For Tina and Steve, the issue is one of acceptance of change and helping it occur in a partner:

> The key is accepting, and trying consciously to draw the best out of the other person. It's helping the other person grow into their gifts—not your gifts as you want them to be, but spotting *their* gifts partially developed, *their* skills partially developed, and encouraging them to grow into the person that God uniquely made them rather than you trying to make them uniquely your robot. You can spot what their gifts are by pulling the best out of them and helping them grow.

Ultimately, rejecting the urge to change your partner is positive not only because it almost certainly won't work, but also because it lets you relax. Acceptance can bring a sense of peace to the relationship, allowing you, as Tina said, to look not for problems to fix, but for your partner's undeveloped gifts.

No expert put it better than Yvette Mills, sixty-six. Her marriage has not been a perfect one, but she learned from it the wisdom to accept a partner instead of exerting futile attempts at control.

> Respect the person you are married to. You do not change grown people. Love each other unconditionally. You wouldn't hold a bird with your hand wrapped around its neck unless you meant it harm. You hold your hand open and the bird can fly in or out at will. That is the way, to me, you must act in your relationships. Respect each other, hold each other in high esteem, have faith in each other. The other person can change; it's just that you can't make them. We don't know how to fix people and we can't fix people. People fix themselves.

THE LAST LESSON
As Long as You Both Shall Live

For reasons that I cannot entirely explain, my wife and I began to run marathons in our fifties. Maybe it was to combat a midlife crisis or—even more likely—because running long distances allows me to eat as much as I want. We enjoy this activity, although we usually find ourselves at the back of the pack with the people dressed like clowns, pushing baby carriages, or jumping rope for twenty-six miles.

One thing I noticed in marathoning is the suspension of time while running. The gun goes off to start the race . . . then something happens that feels like a long moment of being out of breath and in discomfort . . . and then there's the finish line. The race for me is so absorbing that I don't notice a lot while I'm running. Looking back, however, is a different story. I remember in clear detail what happened between the start and the finish. There was pain (definitely), exaltation, stress, hope, and joy at the finish line—all of which I understood only when the race was done.

In this book, people who are near the finish line of married life opened their homes, hearts, and minds to me—and to you. A treasure trove of relationship advice emerged from the question, "What lessons have you learned about marriage that you would like to pass on to younger people?" Capturing our elders' wisdom was an extraordinary adventure—by turns inspiring, poignant, funny, and difficult—not unlike the marriages of the elders themselves. I hope joining me on this journey was an adventure for you, too.

I live with the frustration of trying to convey on paper interviews that are so rich and so deeply moving. It is nearly impossible to find the right words for the moment when a very reserved man, married for sixty years, breaks down in tears while expressing his love for his wife and his gratitude for her support and sacrifice over their lifetime. Or the look that passes between a husband and wife of seventy years, as she takes his hand and gazes into his eyes while reminiscing about the day they first met. Or the astonishment and pride of Sheila and Irene, who at age seventy-five and after fifty years of waiting finally celebrated a legal marriage. Or the ninety-eight-year-old man providing loving care for his one-hundred-year-old wife as dementia inexorably takes her away from him.

From this vast reservoir of experience—as a group the experts have accumulated around twenty-five thousand years of married life—there's one last lesson I would like to offer you. It's the biggest leap of all—the decision to make a commitment to one single person for an entire lifetime.

You might ask: Is that idea old-fashioned? If you listen to the dire media reports about the "death of marriage," you might easily assume that matrimony will soon be a thing of the past, gone the way of pay phones and manual typewriters. It may surprise you, however, to learn that this stereotype is not true. In fact, surveys show that not only do the vast majority of single people want to get married, but they also hope their union will last forever. We may be a throwaway society in other ways, but when it comes to love, most people are looking for a lifelong relationship.

But for a long marriage, there's an ingredient that no therapy, no treatment program, and even no religion can provide; the partners must do it themselves, day after day, and year after year. The last key to thinking like an expert about marriage is *commitment*. The experts tell us that you must enter into a marriage believing it will last forever. And they also reveal why that outcome is worth striving for.

There are rituals that still retain their power despite the massive changes that have occurred over the past century. These ceremonies maintain a transcendent quality; they pull us out of our usual mode of thinking and make us consider the big picture in human experience. Such events usually involve special language. Regardless of how jaded we may have become, the formal phrases can affect us profoundly.

The words of the marriage rite never fail to strike me with a sense of awe. If you have listened carefully to traditional wedding vows, you, too, may have experienced a shiver down your spine at their momentous implications. For most of life's decisions, we do not think of long-term consequences; our time horizon may go out a year or two, but rarely extends to a decade and certainly not for a lifetime. We don't go into a new job vowing to keep it for the rest of our natural lives, or buy a house swearing to live there forever.

But hundreds of thousands of Americans every year stand in front of a member of the clergy and say some version of this ancient pledge:

> To have and to hold from this day forward
> For better or for worse
> In sickness and in health
> To love and to cherish
> *As long as we both shall live.*

Where else do we publicly acknowledge that we will die someday, let alone promise to keep doing something until that happens? Do we really mean that commitment and what it implies? One thing I learned is this: Most of our elders *did* mean it. From all cultural backgrounds, ethnicities, and religious perspectives, the experts believed— and still do—that marriage is a "forever commitment."

Lai Lian told me that from their wedding day on, she and her husband believed that marriage is an unbreakable bond:

In our minds, there was no such thing as getting unmarried. That was it. You're married, that's it, by hook or by crook, there is no such thing, there is no word for "divorce." Because you're married forever.

Ranjit Singh, eighty, from a different tradition and cultural background, also believes couples should enter into marriage seeing the commitment as unbreakable:

Marriage is two people living together and becoming as one. Marriage is between souls that become one. That means the most important thing before thinking of marriage is that we have a commitment. One must be sure in his or her mind that the partner is for you and for you only. Sometimes people think, oh, if the marriage doesn't work out, we can get a divorce any time. But marriage is not a contract on paper that you can annul any time if it doesn't work out. Never start married life with that notion.

The emphasis on commitment was similarly strong from elders in the study who spent much of their lives in a committed but unmarried relationship. Timothy Salter, eighty-nine, and Jerome Jaffee, ninety, have been a couple for sixty years, sharing a fascinating life in theater and the arts and in the company of a vibrant circle of friends. They married two years ago at the prompting of a minister friend, who, Jerome told me, "really wanted to officiate at a gay wedding." But the marriage only reinforced what was already a lifelong commitment—and one made firmer, they told me, because marriage was not available. Timothy said:

Our commitment to each other had to be stronger, because it wasn't backed up by the legal things marriage gives you. You

have to have a strong relationship, because there's no legality
to it.

Jerome added:

> I read about prenuptial agreements where people only commit
> to ten years, that kind of thing. You already have a divorce in
> mind, which I find very strange. Commitment doesn't work
> that way. After we fell in love, it became the relationship for my
> entire life. You don't want to separate. I don't know that you
> enter a relationship thinking that you're going to last for sixty
> years. But you do just feel: "I want to go on. I don't ever want
> to separate. I don't want to go my own way."

This, then, is the last lesson from the experts:
Treat marriage—at every stage—as a lifelong commitment.
This must be your attitude, however unrealistic it may seem at
times. Knowing that for many people, marriage can and did last a
lifetime makes that goal an attainable one. The elders counsel you to
live with the belief that your vows represent an ironclad commitment; they feel that is the only way to approach marriage. They of
course understand that some marriages—in particular those where
verbal or physical abuse is present—must come to an end. But they
exhort you in most circumstances to try, try, and try again to honor
the initial commitment before leaving the marriage.

In my efforts to understand the experts' view on commitment, I
came to a revelation. They are talking about marriage as a "discipline." As that word is used in fields from spiritual development to
business management, it does not have anything to do with the idea
of punishment—far from it. Rather, a discipline, as one writer puts
it, is a developmental path where you get better at something by
mindfully attending to it and by continual practice. Most important,

it is a lifelong process—you don't "arrive" at success, but rather you spend your life mastering the discipline. In all disciplines—from learning a martial art, to running a marathon, to meditating—short-term sacrifice is required to reap the long-term rewards from your effort.

When the experts talk about commitment, it's this kind of discipline they have in mind: persevering, working out creative solutions for problems, and seeking help when necessary. The mental image of a lifelong commitment—where it is not easy to get out—makes partners work intensely to overcome challenges. Lora Medina told me:

> My generation was not accepting of divorce, and my husband and I were of that mind-set. Because that wasn't an option in our mind to separate, you really figured things out. It wasn't, "Well, it's not working out and I'm not happy right now. Let's give up." It wasn't an option, so therefore we needed to figure things out.

Sheldon Chapman, eighty-eight, whose marriage went through difficult periods, agreed:

> We have had some pretty hard arguments, believe me. You've got to deal with it and not to have in the back of your head that you're going to split. You've got to get that out of your head. That whatever it is that goes on, you're going to stay together and work it out.

The elders are clear that no one can make a commitment at a single point in their lives, then simply relax and forget about it. Commitment is enacted every single day, as part of the discipline of marriage. Mae Powers, seventy, has had a rocky road in marriage, but she chose to remain in the relationship for forty-two years. She summed up the meaning of commitment:

It's continually committing, actively deciding to stay together. During the rough times, you have to decide to recommit yourself to the relationship. My husband and I joke about having "gotten married" many times. Things happen that cause people to question their relationships, and then they have to make a decision to recommit or not recommit, and how to recommit if they decide to do so. So when I recommit to staying together today after a huge blowup, it's with the knowledge of all of those limitations and what I have decided I'm willing to live with.

Searching for a way to characterize this attitude among the experts, I found myself using the word "spirit." That is, many of them have a spirited approach to the discipline of marriage, to get better, to forgive, and to innovate. There's a spirit of initiative to overcome problems and an indomitable attitude to move on despite challenges. I saw many examples of this kind of spirit, but if forced to pick just one, it would have to be Lucy Dale, ninety-four.

Born in 1919, Lucy chose to serve her country in World War II, joining the women's division of the U.S. Navy (known as the WAVES). Tall, statuesque, and sophisticated (there's a bit of Lauren Bacall there), Lucy is another one of the elders we'd all like to be when we "grow up." Right after World War II ended, Lucy wound up in San Francisco. Out for a night on the town with a friend, they were seated next to two young men, one of whom was named Sam. She told me:

I felt footloose and fancy-free. I was in uniform, the war was over, everybody was happy, getting on with their lives. And I thought, "I'll go out with Sam, but it'll only be because he's good company." Well, I found out he was more than just good company. In just a few months, I was married to him!

The early years of her marriage, however, were not easy. She traveled with Sam to the oil fields where he found work. "That was a hard thing for me, because it was a little town, and I had come from a city and was used to a different life entirely. And being stuck there was not a good situation. I was unhappy, but he loved his job, we lived close to work, and it was very economical living there. And the years just went by, and pretty soon I had my boys."

I knew that her overall assessment of the marriage was positive, so I asked at what point things improved. With a rueful laugh Lucy told me:

> After twenty years, they got better. It was a long time. And I had very little patience. But I surprised myself. I stuck with it. Oh, I left him mentally several times! I was really unhappy. But I told myself: I've invested so much that I'm not going to walk out and let some other woman get all the benefits! And I didn't feel it was fair to the boys to take them away from their father. They would be resentful and it just wasn't right. And that's one of the main reasons I stayed.

Lucy was committed to the relationship, so slowly but surely she worked with her husband to make needed changes. They moved to a city and she found work she enjoyed. After the children left home, they discovered a mutual love of travel, camping throughout the United States. "Oh, our marriage got much happier. We did a lot of traveling and I had no thoughts of ever leaving again." Based on her long experience, Lucy offered this advice:

> Understand your partner's interests, even if you don't particularly care about them. Try to get involved, because two people together can make it so much better. This is where the marriage grows, by having interests in common, really caring about what

makes the other person happy. Think of how you want your life to be. You want it to be fuller, happier. You have to feel relaxed around your husband, able to tell him your innermost thoughts. And trust—to trust each other is so important. Basic trust and confidence that this is the right person for you.

The marriage lasted sixty years until Sam's death, and it reached its full potential later in life, leaving Lucy with a sense of completion and fulfillment. But I just can't let the story end there, because what happened next is a great second act.

Lucy moved back East to be closer to her children, moving into a senior living community. Call me ageist, but I was surprised when someone a few years shy of one hundred blurted out:

Oh, and I have a fabulous boyfriend! Suddenly this fellow appeared from nowhere, and he's really the nicest man I've ever met. Nathan's so thoughtful, so kind. He worries about me. He says he loves me all the time. I mean, I can't ask for more.

Then Lucy gave me a bigger shock. I asked her whether she and Nathan planned to get married. She let out a laugh and said, "Oh, no! I'm older than he is, by five years. He's eighty-nine, I'm going on ninety-five. I'm what the young people call a 'cougar.' And cougars don't get married!"

Wow—there's a quote for you. She laughed harder at my obvious surprise.

Lucy came to embody for me the spirit of the elders and the potential for love at any age. She told me, "I feel so grateful, so grateful. And it's pretty wonderful—love at any age is terrific. Don't be afraid of it. If you're alive, there's always room for hope, always."

Listening to Lucy and other experts, I was reminded of a time when, as a child, I spent a vacation in a wonderful old hotel on the coast of Maine. In the garden was a sundial, thickly overgrown with vines. Exploring one day, I saw that an inscription circled the top of the dial. Clearing away the debris, I read: "Grow old along with me! The best is yet to be." This line—by Robert Browning—sums up how many of the elders see the later decades of marriage. They do not downplay the difficulties of growing old together; in particular, declining health challenges couples as they move into their late seventies and beyond. But for many of the experts, these infirmities—and the eventual end of which they are harbingers—lead them to savor the time they have together.

Sound idealistic? For me, seeing was believing. Nothing convinces you of the value of making a lifelong commitment like being in the presence of couples who have done just that. Most people who make good on the "marriage is for life" assumption freely admit having considered splitting up at least once over the decades (and often more than once). They've lived through sloughs of unfulfillment, periods where passion waned and nothing appeared to replace it, and bouts of simmering resentment. But they hung in, they endured, they worked feverishly on the relationship—and they won out in the end.

They won out by reaching a level of fulfillment that is difficult to describe. I've introduced you to a number of such partners in this book, and perhaps you have seen it in an older couple you know. When you are in the presence of two people who have weathered life's predictable and unpredictable storms together and emerged as true and inseparable partners at the end of life, there's a feeling of "Ah, so *that's* what it's all about . . ." I had the opportunity to observe this apotheosis of married life many times, and each time I came away inspired and enriched.

When people make it the whole way, it's so good that it's better than almost anything else you can imagine. It's better than the excitement of dating; better than the heart-pounding passion of a new relationship; yes, even better than the lure of trading the old spouse in for a new model. It's good enough that it may inspire you to give your marriage a second, third, or fourth chance. Because to wind up at the last years of life in the arms of someone you fell in love with sixty or seventy years ago is sublime. It's a part of a well-lived life that is so transcendental that for many elders who are there, it defies description. There are some life experiences for which you need the whole thing to reap the benefits, and marriage is one of those.

A book has to end somewhere, and the best way I know how is to offer you one more time the words of one of the true sages I encountered. The story of Clark Hughes is an unusual one: He never expected to get married because he began his career as a Catholic priest. After nearly twenty years he realized that the priesthood was not the right path for him. His decision was finalized when he fell in love with Monica; they have been married for thirty-two years.

For Clark, the lifetime commitment of marriage leads to growth and development. Without the security of commitment, marriage does not fulfill its purpose of making us more complete and fulfilled human beings. He told me:

> What I observed over thirty-some years of marriage is the growth that comes with it. It's surprising, the depth of it and the breadth of it. When you look back, you've been changed inch by inch and you've become a different person over the years. I can say to myself, "I've become the real person I was meant to be." And if you ask, "Well, was there some sudden turning point in the marriage?" There wasn't really. It was that little day-in-and-day-out shaping by the experience of living in love with someone. Think of the way a plant grows. It's just organic. Every day adds on something and copes with something and something comes that shapes you.

Clark sees married life as a process of development that allows people to reach their full potential, both in good times and in bad. During the interview, Clark revealed that he had recently received devastating news about his health, but his marriage provided the strength he needed to meet the challenge head-on:

> My wife and I have found that the marriage has allowed each of us to develop more into the unique people we are. We learn from the way she sees me, the way I see her. I'm facing cancer. She's living and dying with me now, as I have to go through tests and treatments, and I am with her in the things she faces and suffers. To me, this is really living. Really living to me isn't who's got the bigger house or something like that. You come to see that those aren't the important things in life. It's your connections with the other people and with your family and it's the difference you can make in the world.

The result of a marriage philosophy based on the discipline of commitment?

> It's the deepest fulfillment I have ever known, to really experience being loved and loving somebody. It develops slowly. It isn't suddenly like you really love them. This would be my final word of advice to couples: I learned from my wife how to love her. Yes, you teach one another how to love.

The beauty of this elder wisdom—gained through hard-won experience—is that it puts temporary discomfort, stress, unhappiness, and setbacks into proper perspective. Taking the long view, when marriage is seen as a lifelong opportunity for growth, problems become vehicles for new insights and a deeper relationship.

When two twenty-five-year-olds stand at the altar, no one in the congregation pictures them sixty years hence, retired and surrounded by children and grandchildren. When we look at the eager young couple, the broad sweep of so many decades of life together is far from our minds. But there is joy and beauty in the security of a long and committed relationship, unfolding over time, with its triumphs and tragedies. What I learned from the experts can be summed up in this statement: Marriage for a lifetime is a unique blend of joys and challenges—*and it's worth it*. My hope is that the elders' advice can help you enjoy the journey—as long as you both shall live.

ACKNOWLEDGMENTS

This book is based on over seven hundred interviews with older people from throughout the United States. Such a complex project cannot take place without the hard work, commitment, and goodwill of many individuals. It was a pleasure learning how many people so deeply value the wisdom of our elders that they generously offered their assistance.

The most important contributors to this book are the hundreds of older women and men who shared their advice. They opened their homes, hearts, and minds because they believed their experience could help younger people better navigate the complexities of love, relationships, and marriage. I can only hope I have transmitted their lessons in a way that honors their contribution.

I am profoundly grateful to the members of my research team at the Cornell Institute for Translational Research on Aging. Special appreciation goes to Leslie Schultz, who organized and managed data-collection and coding activities, providing a calm presence in the midst of occasional chaos. I would like to acknowledge the contribution of Mary Loehr, who conducted many in-depth interviews, as well as persons who assisted with data transcribing and coding: Marlo Cappocia, Tina Chen, Chenda Cope, Christine Januzzi, Jennifer Parise, and Lauren Stutzin.

The surveys reported in this book could not have taken place without the outstanding work of the Cornell University Survey Research Institute. Thanks are due to Yasamin Miller, director; Darren Hearn, manager; and interviewers Chris Dietrich, Vanessa McCaffrey, Stephanie Slate, Caitlin Brinckerhoff, Albert Capogrossi, Seth Carl, Clara Evangelista-Filler, James Monahan, and Suzy Trautman.

I am deeply indebted to individuals who nominated wise elders for interviews. Special thanks go to Dr. Kevin O'Neil and Sara Terry of Brookdale Senior Living, a premier provider of senior living communities across the country. Their facilities opened their doors to me and provided many memorable interviewees. I am also grateful to Mandi Block and her colleagues at Country Meadows Retirement Communities, who provided me not only with interviewees but also with a chance to experience senior living firsthand via a stay in one of their communities.

Tremendously helpful were leaders at senior centers in New York City, who took time out of doing some of the most worthwhile work on the planet to connect me with their members (thereby increasing the diversity of the sample): Isabel Ching, Hamilton-Madison House; William Hamer, Abyssinian Development Corporation; Evelyn Laureano, Neighborhood SHOPP and Casa Boricua; and Suzy Ritholtz, Services and Advocacy for Gay, Lesbian, Bisexual & Transgender Elders (SAGE).

I am also grateful to friends and colleagues who nominated interviewees for the study. In addition to lending a supportive ear throughout the project, Eddie Cope's many connections allowed me to give Indiana's elders a voice in the book. I am also grateful to the following individuals for their assistance in identifying respondents:

Matthew Estill, Mary Beth Grant, Carol Hegeman, Marie Nicholson, Jane Powers, and Denyse Variano. Several individuals helped organize the group discussions with younger people that shaped the questions we asked the elders about love and marriage: Sheri Hall, Cynthia Nicholson, John Paton, Sarah Pillemer, and Christina Stark.

Thanks are due to colleagues who commented on the manuscript in draft form, including Sheri Hall, Martin Schumacher, and Myra Sabir. Risa Breckman and Jane Pillemer reviewed the book based on their expertise as psychotherapists. I am particularly grateful to Peter Wolk, both for his invaluable advice and enthusiasm about the book, as well as for exposing me one night to the game of craps, thus helping me uncover the elders' key insight about "evening the odds."

I am deeply thankful for the support of my colleagues at Cornell University who have engaged with me over the years in discussions relevant to my work on elder wisdom: Cary Reid and Mark Lachs of the Weill Cornell Medical College and Cornell University's Corinna Loeckenhoff, Rhoda Meador, Anthony Ong, Nancy Wells, and Elaine Wethington. My long-term collaborator and friend J. Jill Suitor, of Purdue University, has also greatly enriched my understanding of marriage and families.

Janis Donnaud is the best agent anyone could have, and I consider myself very lucky for access to her ideas, advice, and good sense. I also would like to express appreciation to my editor, Caroline Sutton, both for encouragement of my work and for invaluable editorial insights.

Two elders in my own life served as continual inspirations in my efforts to understand and apply the life wisdom of older people. Ruth Harriet Jacobs, gerontologist extraordinaire and my undergraduate mentor, first trained me in the qualitative methods used in this book. In recent years, she provided advice about the project and suggestions for interviewees. Helene Rosenblatt worked with me as a research assistant into her early eighties and continued thereafter to serve as a sounding board for my ideas. Last year, the world lost both of these extraordinary individuals. I hope this book lives up to what they taught me.

Words cannot fully express my gratitude to my family, who offered concrete advice, suggestions, and stress reduction throughout the project. My wife, Clare McMillan, provided unflagging support, patience, and some of the best copyediting around. My daughters, Hannah and Sarah, and son-in-law, Michael Civille, helped me keep young people's concerns in mind as I explored the elders' advice. Finally, this is a book about family life, and my understanding of the joys of an extended family would not be possible without the enduring support of David and Jane Pillemer, Stephen Pillemer and Helen Rasmussen, and Eric and Wendy Pillemer.

How the Study Was Done

At various points in this book, you have read about the "seven hundred elders" who provided the material on which the lessons are based. You may have wondered about who they are and how my research team and I captured their wisdom. In my earlier book, *30 Lessons for Living*, the methods I used to gain and organize the advice of a large number of older Americans were so successful that I replicated many of them in this project. In this appendix, I refer to the several related data-collection activities as the "Marriage Advice Project."

In some ways, the methods of the Marriage Advice Project followed standard methods of social science research. The project involved surveys designed to obtain a diverse and representative sample, in-depth interviews with a structured set of questions, and systematic coding to extract the main themes from the interviews. For this book, however, the ways in which I interpreted the results and presented the findings differed somewhat from a formal social science approach. In this appendix, I will share with you the methods used, and where they follow or depart from academic research.

THE MARRIAGE ADVICE PROJECT

Like most research projects, this one began with a review of the literature. I examined the large body of research on predictors of marital quality, satisfaction, and longevity. I also read a lot of books on the topic, all of which offer advice for a long and happy marriage. As I noted in the introduction, I quickly learned that there was very little literature on older people's advice about marriage, despite their long and varied experience. A handful of studies of long-married couples exists, but I uncovered none that focused specifically on older people's lessons and advice about how to have a happier and more enduring relationship.

A few books have been published on long-married couples. However, these books relied on small and unrepresentative samples and focused heavily on successful and exemplary older couples. It thus became clear to me that a big gap existed in our knowledge about marriage and similar committed relationships. Specifically, no one had done a large-scale survey of older people about the lessons they have learned about love and marriage, with the goal of making their advice available for people of all ages.

I knew that I had a topic ripe for further exploration. I therefore designed an in-depth interview study of a large sample of elders, ranging from couples married happily for decades, to unhappy but stable unions, to widowed and divorced elders, to long-term cohabiters (including same-sex couples). Unlike past research, my goal was to ask these experts directly and in detail about the kinds of advice they would offer younger people about getting and staying married in a complex and difficult world. To collect the data for the Marriage Advice Project, I (assisted by my research team) carried out the following activities.

Exploratory Studies

When researchers begin a new project, we like to get the lay of the land. We often try to narrow the focus of the project, anticipate problems, and avoid potential dead ends (like questions that lead to uninformative answers). In the Marriage Advice Project, I sought two kinds of information in shaping the study. First, I was interested in the kinds of answers older people would give to questions about love and marriage. I therefore invited elders to contribute their lessons on this topic to our website. We received over one hundred detailed responses, which helped us to design the project interviews.

I also wanted very much to know: What are the burning questions young people have about love and marriage? What would they like me to ask the oldest Americans? I work with young adults (and have some in my own family), so I have a sense of what concerns them about courtship and committed relationships. But to learn more, I conducted focus groups or individual discussions involving approximately forty men and women, ranging from college students, to young professionals, to young parents, to middle-aged individuals. These people offered suggestions for the advice that would be most relevant to their situations, which in turn shaped the interview questions we used.

The interview began with a general question about the kinds of lessons the elders had learned about love and marriage that they would like to pass on to younger generations. We then asked detailed questions about advice for choosing a mate (and how to avoid the wrong choice). The interview next tapped their advice about specific domains of married life, including lessons they had learned about communication, handling conflict, adjusting to children, dealing with work and financial issues, and managing in-laws. Questions covered the role of sexuality in marriage, as well as how to keep the relationship vibrant and interesting over many years. Respondents were also asked to imagine they were approached by a younger couple who were considering splitting up: What advice would they give? Individuals who had been through a divorce were asked for advice about how others might avoid a breakup.

The interviews lasted on average nearly an hour and in some cases went on much longer. It never failed to amaze me how deeply interesting the respondents found the interview and the degree to which they were willing to open their hearts and minds to our interviewers. The interviewees reported greatly enjoying the opportunity to share their marriage advice, and when asked if they were willing to be recontacted for additional information, over 90 percent said yes—a strong indicator of positive feelings about the experience.

National Random Sample Survey

With the assistance of the Cornell University Survey Research Institute, we conducted the interviews with a national sample of individuals age sixty-five and older. Respondents were selected at random and interviewed by trained interviewers on the telephone. Two categories of people were oversampled in this survey. We targeted currently married couples, because we wanted to make sure we had advice from ongoing relationships; and African Americans, to ensure diversity in the sample. A total of 388 older people participated in the national survey.

Systematic In-depth Interviews

The goal of the national survey was to avoid "sample bias" by selecting people at random from the general population. This procedure ensured a broad spectrum of individuals from all regions of the country and from different socioeconomic statuses. It provided an excellent portrait of the range and kinds of advice older persons give about getting and staying married.

However, the study also required a more in-depth and detailed method of interviewing, with purposive selection of respondents. I had learned two things from my previous studies of advice from elders. First, although they may have led interesting lives, there are some people who have difficulty translating that experience into lessons for younger people. I therefore needed a sample of people who were considered to be good at giving advice. Second, we found that we can obtain even richer and more detailed information from longer in-person interviews, for which the individuals have been able to consider the questions in advance.

Therefore, in this phase of the research we interviewed individuals who were nominated because of their perceived wisdom about love, relationships, and marriage, and the questions were provided to them to ponder prior to the interview. I asked elder service agencies and organizations, professional colleagues, and others to nominate older people for interviews. I conducted approximately 110 of these interviews personally, and the remainder were carried out by another trained and skilled interviewer.

Many wonderful interviewees were recommended by Brookdale Senior Living, a leading national provider of senior communities. A very important source helped me create a diverse sample: senior centers in New York City that served African American, Latino, and Chinese elders. Another senior center that serves the gay and lesbian elder community introduced me to long-term same-sex couples. A total of 152 respondents were recruited for the in-depth interview studies.

Legacy Project

Over the course of three years, the Marriage Advice Project collected a very large amount of new survey data on older people's marriage advice. I was very fortunate to have another source from which I could draw to further enlarge the pool of elder wisdom. As described in *30 Lessons for Living*, beginning in 2004, I created the Cornell Legacy Project. In the Legacy Project, we surveyed over one thousand elders about their advice for living for younger people. Some of the respondents in that survey provided highly detailed advice about love and marriage.

I selected the most detailed of these interviews and included them in my analyses for this book. I did so for a very important reason. Sadly, the members of the "Greatest Generation"—individuals who went through the Great Depression and experienced World War II (either in the service or on the home front)—are rapidly leaving us. In a few years, they will all be gone. Fortunately, when I began collecting the Legacy Project interviews, many more members of that generation were still alive. I deeply wished to share the perspective of these elders, and I was able to use 172 Legacy Project interviews to inform this book.

Analysis

All the interviews were tape-recorded and transcribed, resulting in thousands of pages of transcripts. Then came the fun part: making sense of what seven hundred highly experienced older people had to say about every aspect of love and marriage you can think of. Fortunately, modern technology can provide some help. Using the helpful program Dedoose, my research assistants and I coded all of the interviews into relevant categories. This process allowed me to settle on the thirty lessons you find in this book. However, I did not rely on statistical techniques and quantitative analyses in analyzing the data. Instead, I followed the widely accepted sociological approach of qualitative and narrative analysis. I read the entire interviews and the coded excerpts dozens of times, identifying major themes and the examples and anecdotes that illustrated these themes.

This project, like all academic research studies, was reviewed and approved at Cornell University for the "protection of human subjects." This process ensures that ethical procedures are followed in the conduct of the research. For the sake of anonymity, all names in this book are pseudonyms, created by a random name generator.

HOW THIS BOOK DIFFERS FROM A SOCIAL SCIENCE STUDY

The methods of the Marriage Advice Project followed standard social science practice. I used a representative national sample of elders selected at random, as well as a purposive sample of individuals especially appropriate for the project. The interview protocol was carefully constructed and carried out by specially trained interviewers. However, this book is not a scientific tome; instead, it is a popular book for a general audience. Therefore, some of the ways I've presented the information differ from how I would prepare the findings for a scholarly journal.

First, I have edited or reorganized some of the quotations to make them more easily readable; for example, you will find "ers" and "ums" removed. Grammar was made more standard, and I have not indicated missing segments of quotations (sparing you sentences like: "Hmm, well, I guess . . . when it comes to marriage . . . I mean . . . um . . ."). The quotations in the book, however, all capture the spirit and meaning of the interviews. I have maintained intact the tone and expressiveness, so you can enjoy the full flavor of the advice.

Second, the personal details about individuals are usually accurate (such as age, length of marriage, number of children). In a few cases, however, I have changed some descriptors or created composites to make the individuals less identifiable. Interviewees in this project were not promised confidentiality and were warned that it might be possible for another person to recognize them from their quotes. However, I wished to avoid some of them regretting their decision if minor details made them clearly identifiable to relatives and friends.

Third, I have taken another liberty in the interest of readability. For the Marriage Advice Project over seven hundred interviews were carried out, all of which I could not personally have conducted. However, I was involved in training all interviewers; I met with them for supervision, and I designed all the questions for the surveys. In so doing, I was able to ensure that the questions were asked exactly the way I intended. I went over the taped and transcribed interviews many times. I also conducted over one hundred interviews myself. For these reasons, I use the first person pronoun throughout the book for all the interviews that were conducted. Readers will be grateful for not reading a few times on every page: "Interviewer #5 asked . . ." I believe this decision is justified, given my extensive involvement in all phases and aspects of the data-collection process.

Finally, there is one more obvious difference between this book and a conventional academic study; namely there is more of *me* in there. I have been married for thirty-six years, which has been a fascinating, challenging, and sometimes miraculous experience. I undertook the Marriage Advice Project not only to inform the world about the elders' advice for long and happy relationships, but also to answer my own burning questions. Therefore, in this book I share with you now and again my own quest for knowledge about love and marriage and how the practical wisdom of America's elders affected my thinking and my life.

xvii   **"ultimate limit situations":** Juan Pascual-Leone, "Mental Attention, Consciousness, and the Progressive Emergence of Wisdom,"
Journal of Adult Development 7, no. 4 (2000): 241–254.

36   **lower chances of succeeding over the long term:** M. C. Morr
Serewicz, "The Difficulties of In-law Relationships," in *Relating
Difficulty: The Process of Constructing and Managing Difficult Inter-
action*, ed. D. C. Kirkpatrick, S. Duck, and M. Foley, 101–118
(Mahwah, NJ: Lawrence Erlbaum Associates, 2006); Mary Claire
Morr Serewicz, Rebecca Homer, Robert L. Ballard, and Rachel A.
Griffin, "Disclosure from In-laws and the Quality of In-law and
Marital Relationships," *Communication Quarterly* 56, no. 4 (No-
vember 2008): 427–444.

94   **as many as 40 percent of dating couples report:** Amanda Berger,
Ph.D., Elizabeth Wildsmith, Ph.D., Jennifer Manlove, Ph.D., and
Nicole Steward-Streng, M.A., "Relationship Violence Among
Young Adult Couples," *Child Trends*, 2012–14, June 2012, Wash-

ington, D.C., http://www.childtrends.org/wp-content/uploads/ 2012/06/Child_Trends-2012_06_01_RB_CoupleViolence.pdf.

98   **Demeaning and contemptuous behaviors:** Tara Parker-Pope, *For Better: How the Surprising Science of Happy Couples Can Help Your Marriage Succeed* (New York: Plume, 2011); John Gottman, *The Seven Principles for Making Marriages Work* (New York: Harmony, 2000).

116   **Ayelet Waldman raised a ruckus:** Ayelet Waldman, "Truly, Madly, Guiltily," *New York Times*, March 27, 2005.

120   **you are experiencing what social scientists call "spillover":** P. Roehling, P. Moen, and R. Batt, "Spillover," in *It's About Time: Couples and Careers*, ed. P. Moen, 101–121 (Ithaca, NY: Cornell University Press, 2003), http://digitalcommons.ilr.cornell.edu/ hr/24/.

137   **Decades of research:** Jeffrey Dew and W. Bradford Wilcox, "If Momma Ain't Happy: Explaining Declines in Marital Satisfaction Among New Mothers," *Journal of Marriage and Family* 73, no. 1 (2011): 1–12.

138   **it is bound with a sense of how the relationship is going:** Bryan Strong and Theodore F. Cohen, *The Marriage and Family Experience: Intimate Relationships in a Changing Society*, 12th edition (2013). Clifton Park, NY: Cengage Learning.

142   **Tara Parker-Pope, in her book on marriage:** Tara Parker-Pope, *For Better: The Science of a Good Marriage* (New York: Plume, 2011).

144   **greater economic well-being for husbands and wives:** Linda J. Waite and Evelyn L. Lehrer, "The Benefits from Marriage and Religion in the United States: A Comparative Analysis," *Population and Development Review* 29, no. 2 (2003): 255–275.

144 **arguments over money are often angrier and last longer:**
J. Oggins, "Topics of Marital Disagreement Among African-
American and Euro-American Newlyweds," *Psychological Reports*
92 (2003): 419–425; Lauren M. Papp, E. Mark Cummings, and
Marcie C. Goeke-Morey, "For Richer, for Poorer: Money as a
Topic of Marital Conflict in the Home," *Family Relations* 58, no.
1 (2009): 91–103.

145 **debt is a killer for many couples:** Penny Wrenn, "Real Couples
Dish: Debt Counseling Saved Our Marriage," *Forbes*, October 9,
2013, http://www.forbes.com/sites/learnvest/2013/10/09/real
-couples-dish-debt-counseling-saved-our-marriage/.

145 **nearly half of people age forty-five to fifty-four are paying off
credit card balances:** Richard Eisenberg, "The Money Scorecard:
How Do You Rate?" *DailyFinance*, March 30, 2013, http://www
.dailyfinance.com/2013/03/30/next-avenue-money-scorecard-how
-do-you-rate/.

154 **people who associate with more positive individuals:** James H.
Fowler and Nicholas A. Christakis, "Dynamic Spread of Happiness in a Large Social Network: Longitudinal Analysis over 20
Years in the Framingham Heart Study," *BMJ: British Medical Journal* 337, 7685 (2008): 23–27.

182 **the vast majority of people age sixty-five and over are sexually
active:** Stacy Tessler Lindau, L. Philip Schumm, Edward O. Lau-
mann, Wendy Levinson, Colm A. O'Muircheartaigh, and Linda J.
Waite, "A Study of Sexuality and Health Among Older Adults in
the United States," *New England Journal of Medicine* 357, no. 8
(2007): 762–774.

193 **forgiveness can work wonders:** F. D. Fincham, J. H. Hall, and S.
R. H. Beach, "Forgiveness in Marriage: Current Status and Future
Directions," *Family Relations* 55, no. 4 (2006): 415–427.

196 **couples having marital difficulties wait years:** "The Benefits of
     Marriage Counseling," *Dartmouth Healthy Exchange*, Spring 2010.

196 **majority of couples do not seek out counseling:** Melinda Ip-
     polito Morrill, C. J. Eubanks-Fleming, Amanda G. Harp, Julia W.
     Sollenberger, Ellen V. Darling, and James V. Córdova, "The Mar-
     riage Checkup: Increasing Access to Marital Health Care," *Family
     Process* 50, no. 4 (2011): 471–485.

222 **Sociologists have pointed out that American values:** Andrew
     Cherlin, *The Marriage-Go-Round* (New York: Vintage Books,
     2010).

226 **His teammate David Wright put it this way:** Spencer Fordin and
     Chris Iseman, "Teammates Voice Support for Slumping Ike,"
     MLB.com, May 26, 2013, http://mlb.mlb.com/news/article
     .jsp?ymd=20130526&content_id=48713396&notebook_
     id=48713510&vkey=notebook_nym&c_id=nym.

230 **Social scientists have studied the heightened sense of a limited
     time horizon:** Andrew E. Reed and Laura L. Carstensen, "The
     Theory Behind the Age-related Positivity Effect," *Frontiers in Psy-
     chology* 3 (2012): 1–9.

252 **the vast majority of single people want to get married:** Mindy
     E. Scott, Ph.D., Erin Schelar, B.A., Jennifer Manlove, Ph.D., and
     Carol Cui, B.S., "Young Adult Attitudes About Relationships and
     Marriage: Times May Have Changed, but Expectations Remain
     High," *Child Trends*, 2009-30 (July 2009), Washington, D.C.,
     http://www.childtrends.org/wp-content/uploads/2009/07/Child_
     Trends-2009_07_08_RB_YoungAdultAttitudes.pdf.

255 **a discipline, as one writer puts it, is a developmental path:**
     Peter Senge, *The Fifth Discipline* (New York: Doubleday, 2006).